LINGUISTICS FOR CLINICIANS

ONE W

LINGUISTICS FOR CLINICIANS

MARIA BLACK

and

SHULA CHIAT

Department of Human Communication Science,
University College London, UK

Hodder Arnold

A MEMBER OF THE HODDER HEADLINE GROUP

First published in Great Britain in 2003 by
Hodder Arnold, a member of the Hodder Headline Group,
338 Euston Road, London NW1 3BH

http://www.hoddereducation.com

Distributed in the United States of America by
Oxford University Press Inc.,
198 Madison Avenue, New York, NY10016

British Library Cataloguing in Publication Data
A catalogue record for this book is available from the British Library

Library of Congress Cataloging-in-Publication Data
A catalog record for this book is available from the Library of Congress

ISBN-10: 0 340 75896 1
ISBN-13: 978 0 340 75896 0

3 4 5 6 7 8 9 10

Typeset in 10/12 Sabon by Charon Tec Pvt. Ltd, Chennai, India
Printed and bound by Replika Press Pvt. Ltd., India
Illustrations by Eldad Drucks

What do you think about this book? Or any other Hodder Arnold title?
Please send your comments to www.hoddereducation.com

To Dominic Zeal

For updating and backdating

MB

Contents

Acknowledgements

Like most books, this is the product of many collaborations and experiences but our first debt of gratitude has to be to the late Rick Cromer without whom our collaboration would not have got off the ground. We still miss his enthusiasm, generosity and talent for making connections between issues and people.

We are deeply indebted to the many children and adults with language impairments who have shared their first-hand experience and expertise with us and helped us maintain our commitment to clinical linguistics. We are particularly grateful to Chris Ireland for her unique insights and wonderful way with language.

We have been privileged to start our work as clinical linguists at a time of innovation and excitement, when links across disciplines were developing and debate was especially lively. We were able to learn from some of the pioneers of aphasia therapy in the UK, in particular Sally Byng, Liz Clark, Bob and Maggie Fawcus, Eirian Jones and Judith Langley. Mary Evelyn and Jane Speake have been generous with insights and data from their work with children, extending our horizons in ways we greatly appreciate. We have benefited from the expertise and support of many clinical and academic colleagues, especially at Birkbeck College, the City University, and University College London. Some long-standing collaborations have been particularly important and fruitful for us: with Sally Byng, Jane Marshall, Tim Pring and Jo Robson.

We are indebted to the many groups of students we have taught over the years, especially those who have directly worked through the material for this book and have provided invaluable feedback and inspiring ideas for tasks.

Jo Atkinson and Bencie Woll provided valuable clarification on British Sign Language. Belinda Seeff read through the whole manuscript and gave us just the right amount of detailed criticism and encouragement. Both Belinda Seeff and Caroline Newton pulled us back from the technological brink at crucial moments. We are particularly grateful to Stevie Russell,

Sharon James and Breege Whiten in The NICeST Library for their indispensable support and expertise.

Our illustrator, Eldad Druks, not only interpreted our ideas visually but provided us with many useful suggestions and comments. Our thanks also to Christina Wipf Perry and Lesley Riddle at Arnold Publishers for their patience and assistance.

I

Introduction

1

Guide to this book

1.1 For students

This book is about some of the concepts you need to analyse language as a speech and language therapist. What do we mean by 'language'? Language is one of the many forms of communication human beings have at their disposal. It is a system for conveying and receiving meanings through sounds (oral language), characters (writing), and hand-gestures (sign language). In this sense, it is like gesture, touch, painting, drawing, photography, music, sculpture, dancing and any other form of communication you can think of, but is also quite different, with its own properties and unique ways of conveying meanings. Much of this book is about these properties and what you need to describe them – you can dip your toes in language straightaway by reading Chapter 2.

Language is a very efficient system of communication. You can test this for yourself by trying to convey to another person the exact meaning expressed by a piece of language such as:

My friend has left her purse in your room.

using only other forms of communication – for instance, gesture, drawing, or pointing to objects. To take just two examples, how would you gesture or draw *left* as opposed to *put* or *forgot*, and *has left* as opposed to just *left*?

For the beginner, however, language always presents a puzzle. It is something so simple and common that even young children can learn it without special training or education. You will have lived with at least one language for many years and feel quite at home in it. Yet, when we start thinking about it more systematically, it all becomes rather complex and abstract. It is difficult to grasp that abstraction and complexity are precisely what makes language such an efficient and flexible form of communication. So the first thing you need to get the most out of this book is a willingness to be puzzled by things you took for granted.

In trying to hold on to something more solid, people often end up confusing language with one of its physical manifestations – speech. You should resist the false comfort of this confusion and remember that, since you can have one without the other, language and speech cannot be the same thing. If a raging sore throat deprived you of speech, you would still have language. You would still understand what others said or wrote to you: you could still write and have mental conversations with yourself. But if you lost your language, many of these things would become difficult or impossible, as can happen to people after a stroke or a head injury. This is hard to imagine but you can get a sense of what losing language might be like by reading the account by Chris Ireland (see Box 1.1).

Box 1.1 The insight story

Extracted from Ireland, C. and Black, M. (1992)

I have a language problem, not a communication problem. Part of brain is dead but with a loss also a gain if work to build inner insight and strength. I think I am better communicator than before the stroke. My language is closer to my feelings.

Everyday is not a joy. Daily demands. Travelling difficult, noise and nausea. Pain permeates in my life. I can very aware of the noise. External noise interview … interferes me to listen. I can't concentrate with it. I can't screen it out.

It does take me more time to cotton what is going on. I am a bit slow to take it in but deeper perhaps. I lose something on the surface but I gain something else. But practically you need surface. My thoughts and emotions are so bigger and quicker than my language tools. I cannot compete clever with words but I'm still clever, still reflective.

In June 1988 I had a stroke. First thing in the morning I tried to get up and fell on the floor. When my mother came to me, I tried to tell her what had happened. Only strange sounds came from me. I see her mouth to move but I did not feel my right arm. I felt so frustrated, confused and anger creeped with me.

My inner thoughts were felt so very alone. My family and friends reach to me to try ways to communicate. I picked up that they felt helpless and mixtures of feelings – worry, bewildered, and anger too. My friend told me by writing down that I was saying only 'miff'. I did not monitor my language at all.

I understand more about my problems with language now. I enjoy talking perhaps even more than I did before. I have more pause and, if I don't, I have more errors. I haven't lose my excitement in me and if I get excited I make more errors. It doesn't worry me but it is embarrass to other the people at times. It depends on who they are with me. I do get fed up a few people make jokes of language to me. I irritated for

(continued)

people to take it up. It is difficult. Sometimes I want to laugh with them at my errors and sometimes I am not in the mood. And they do understand what we are going to talk about, there is enough information and communication. Why do they have to pick it up? If a person is with somebody with aphasia that person should say if they don't understand, like you would anyone else. That's respect. But people who correct you in the middle of you speaking, they make furious. They shut you up. If people knew what I was trying to say well enough to correct, why bother?

Reading is hard and less pleasure than before. So frustrating: means me cut off to learn knowledge. Belong in my private word, ... world. I can't follow poetry, understand puns and symbolism. I complain I lost poetry. My friends say I tapped on some new poetry, my own poetry. When I tried to read what I had written, I found it so hard with my raw errors. I could read 'correct' versions not too bad. Part of my brain knows the rules of reading and barks at errors. Now allow me to write more flowly, direct with errors and feel more freer. So glad I can able writing enough to communicate. Unable to write would be powerless and more lonely. Yes, mine not good grammar but alive.

On the other hand, you could lose almost all physical manifestations of language, and still have language 'in your head', as the so-called 'locked-in-syndrome' demonstrates. Sufferers of this condition can be completely unable to move or speak and yet still be able to compose phrases and sentences in their heads and convey them letter by letter by blinking at the appropriate character on a letter board (see J-D. Bauby's vivid account in *The diving bell and the butterfly*). You might find this quite surprising. So the other things you will need in working through this book are an open mind and a capacity to look at old things in new ways without letting go completely of what you know already about your own language.

What you do not need is any knowledge of 'grammar' as all the concepts and terms are defined and exemplified in detail in the book itself. We have tried to keep technical terms to a minimum and only use them when necessary to provide you with essential analytical tools. So, if you start thinking 'this is more complicated than it need be', have a little faith and eventually you will see that the complexity was necessary. You are most likely to have that reaction when tackling the parts of the book that deal with meaning – Part III, for example. Analysing meaning is not something you would have done very much in your previous education. You are used to understanding and producing complex meanings very quickly and the efficiency of language can lull you into a false sense of simplicity. To discover the complexity and subtlety of linguistic meaning can be both exciting and unsettling.

If things get too unsettling, go back to the sections entitled 'Why we need these concepts', which are a regular feature of each chapter. In those sections we have tried to explain, in a way that does not presuppose any specialist clinical knowledge, why the concepts discussed in the chapter are useful. These are only signposts, though. Do not expect a full description of language impairments, how language is represented in the brain or how we can treat different language problems. That is not what this book is about. Understanding the concepts and learning to apply them in a clinically relevant way will take time and practice – the pieces of the puzzle will not fit together straightaway.

This is not a book that you can just read through once. You cannot learn to analyse language just by reading – that is why each chapter ends with a range of exercises. You will need to read each chapter several times, do the exercises, compare what you did with the keys or models provided and return to the text again. Some of the same data pop up in different exercises. This is so that you can learn to look at data from different points of view, focusing only on what is relevant to the issue in hand. All the exercises in this book have been tried and completed by students; in fact, we have included some of our students' answers and ideas as models. The exercises show you how to put linguistic concepts to practical clinical use.

As the book is the product of over 20 years of teaching, research and clinical experience, we have tried to anticipate the most common problems and questions in the ways concepts are explained and worked through. We have also included in most chapters a section entitled 'Analytical tips', which should keep you on track. Pay particular attention to the Analytical tips in Part II where you encounter for the first time many methods of analysis and types of arguments that will occur again and again throughout the book. Although Part II deals with particular aspects of linguistic structure (what linguists call 'syntax' and the lay person 'grammar'), it is also a kind of linguistic playground, where you can explore what counts as a pattern in language, how to look for relevant evidence and how to assemble an argument from different bits of evidence. You should develop these skills before tackling other parts of the book.

After you have worked through the book chapter by chapter, you might want to go through it 'horizontally', re-reading, for instance, all the sections like 'Links to other levels', or 'Why we need these concepts'. This should consolidate your understanding of how different aspects of language are connected.

Like all books, this only deals with a small corner of a very big field. The concepts we have presented could be presented in many other ways, with quite different approaches to clinical analysis. When dealing with something as complex as language and language impairment, no one approach can possibly cover all the questions, much less provide all the answers. Nevertheless, by the time you have finished the book, you should be able to ask some of the relevant questions. In particular, you should be able to use concepts to describe data appropriately, separating the significant patterns from the chaff of irrelevant detail. You should be able to develop your analytical hunches into hypotheses that you can test systematically with tasks that are attuned to the specific needs of the children and adults you work with. Most of all, you should learn to play with language and enjoy it. As Chris Ireland says, 'Language can lurk in the back of the head and be nasty. But words, they're tools. Play my mind. You have the friends of language, you feel good' (Ireland, personal communication).

1.2 For teachers

This book gives an introduction to linguistic analysis in a clinical context. Its purpose is primarily analytical: we aim to provide a conceptual toolkit that will allow clinicians to analyse the language produced by children and adults with language impairments; will help them identify patterns of impairment, or intact functioning, in language production and comprehension; and facilitate the selection of relevant stimuli and materials for assessment tasks and therapy activities.

The focus of the book is therefore linguistic analysis for particular purposes rather than linguistic theory or theories *per se*. We draw on a range of linguistic theories and descriptions in our presentation of concepts and methods of analysis, but we do not introduce the reader to any one theoretical framework or compare different theoretical approaches. This is for several reasons.

First, our experience as linguistics teachers has taught us that practice in analysis has to come first, otherwise students will not have the means to understand and evaluate for themselves different theoretical frameworks. Learning to analyse language systematically, making precise observations and relating particular observations to more general patterns is a prerequisite for understanding, evaluating and using linguistic and psycholinguistic theories. Second, students and practising clinicians are often reluctant to use, or explore further, concepts which are not explained and justified with their particular concerns and aims in mind. Concepts and methods cannot just be introduced: they have to be worked through in detail so that readers learn to apply them to a range of data and can test their usefulness for themselves.

Third, no single theoretical framework can address the range of patterns and interconnections clinicians have to make sense of. Linguistic theories tend to concentrate on specific aspects of language, without necessarily making explicit connections to other aspects. Assessment and remediation of language impairments, on the other hand, require an understanding of different aspects of language and how these connect and interact when we use language. Our experience as clinical linguists has shown us that a 'systematic eclecticism' is essential in a clinical context.

We have concentrated on sentence syntax, semantics and phonology, and the links between them. We have little to say on the meaning of single words, except verbs and other relational terms, or on word phonology and morphology. We have been selective in this way because there are already many excellent, accessible texts on these areas.

The first part of the book introduces the reader to the components of language that are the focus of the other parts: interconnected aspects of syntax, semantics and phonology. The second part deals with basic aspects of syntactic structure and its representation. We cover standard concepts but with an explicit clinical orientation and an emphasis on analysis and argumentation. Our aim in this part is to give the reader a solid analytical foundation from which they can branch out into their own explorations of particular syntactic theories.

The third part draws on more recent theories of event structure and verb meaning – from generative lexical and semantic theories to cognitive linguistics. We cover the basic 'conceptual components' of situations but, above all, we aim to give the reader an understanding of how language allows for different 'construals' or perspectives on the same conceptual content. We believe that this aspect of language is particularly relevant to clinicians. Everyday language use is more than the transfer of information, bits of conceptual content, from one person to another. Our ability to put across our perspective on a situation, as well as our ability to understand someone else's, is equally, or perhaps more, important. We believe that this approach to meaning also provides a better stepping stone to the analysis of meaning in context – discourse and conversational analysis and their clinical applications.

In this part, we have tried to draw together a number of concepts that would otherwise not be accessible to students and clinicians. Again, all concepts are justified in relation to clinical applications and extensively illustrated with clinical examples. We have also included detailed lists of verbs of different types, which should facilitate both clinical analysis and the selection of materials for assessment and therapy tasks.

In the fourth part, we look at time and modality in language. A syntactic description of the auxiliary system in English provides the foundation for a detailed analysis of these subtle but important aspects of sentence meaning. Again, our emphasis is on the syntactic, semantic and phonological properties that come together in the expression of time and modality, and that are relevant to clinical assessment and intervention in these areas.

In the final part, we present an analysis of stress patterns in sentences. We draw together work on the relations between syntax and phonology that again would not be readily accessible to students or clinicians, and point out the importance of taking these relations into account in the analysis of problems in sentence processing.

We have tried to give the reader a wide range of examples from both children and adults with and without language disabilities. But these serve only as illustrations of the concepts and methods of analysis covered in the book. It was not our intention to provide an introduction to language impairment, psycholinguistic theories or theories of impairment. The aim throughout the book is to give a coherent analytical foundation and specific illustrations of how analysis and hypothesis testing can be carried out in the clinical context. We have tried to balance accessibility and relevance with coherence and suitable depth of analysis. We are, nevertheless, well aware of the many loose ends we have not managed to tie up.

The assessment and remediation of language impairment clearly require the linking up of different theoretical disciplines – linguistics is only one of them. While clinicians need to draw on a range of relevant disciplines, they cannot mechanically transpose and apply those disciplines' concepts and methods. Clinical practice is a specific domain of theoretical investigation, empirical analysis and therapeutic activity. It has to identify the concepts and methods – qualitative as well as quantitative – that are appropriate to its particular concerns. We see this book as a contribution to that collective endeavour.

|2|

Meaning and form in language processing

2.1 Introduction

Ask the next person you meet what they think language is. The chances are they will say 'It's how we communicate' or 'It's a means of communication'. This typical person-in-the-street notion of language focuses on one function of language: that it enables us to transmit what we have in mind to the mind of another person. A bit more reflection on language tends to elicit other, less practical functions. Language is a vehicle for acquiring information and knowledge, for thinking through ideas and problems, for expressing our cultural and individual identity, for establishing and maintaining social contact, for expressing our relationship to other people, for creative self-expression or for enjoying others' creativity, and more.

But these diverse functions of language are only the visible tip of the linguistic iceberg, most of which lies below the level of conscious awareness. At the level of conscious awareness, we remain fixated on what we use language for. We do not stop to think about what language is: what makes up the vehicle which allows us to do what we do with language, and how the nature of that vehicle affects what we do with it. This chapter introduces language as a particular means for fulfilling intrapersonal and interpersonal functions. Its focus is the nature of linguistic form, and the relation of that form to the meanings it conveys.

2.2 Why we need to distinguish language function from language form and meaning

If there was nothing more to language than its functions, any sentence that fulfils its intended function should be perfectly acceptable. With this in mind, check your reaction to the following sentences:

The thief Pete's purse stole.
Has taken all the money.
He saw minidisc player and bought.
He should haven't done that.
Pete would love to can catch the thief.

These sentences are perfectly communicative. You probably have no difficulty grasping their function and meaning – they recount a series of events,
and you know just what the events are and how they relate to each other.
Yet the sentences are not acceptable. Instinctively, you will want to 'correct'
them. You will want to change the order of words, or change words, or add
words. Yet these 'corrections' will not affect the meanings conveyed. Such
examples show that language form has a momentum of its own, which goes
beyond the functions it serves. It is possible for language to be adequate in
function and meaning, yet not in form. This point is beautifully illustrated
by the sort of utterances children sometimes produce, for example:

Why the ambulance flashed when it goed off?
She's shoe camed off.
Do mummies be ladies?
A honda bes a bicycle.

Although the form of these utterances differs from the form an adult would
use, they are communicatively 100 per cent. The children have not missed
one speck of the meaning that an adult would include. The listener has no
problem getting their meaning, and is unlikely to correct them (Brown and
Hanlon 1970; Hirsh-Pasek, Treiman and Schneiderman 1984). Yet these
forms eventually disappear from the child's language. It seems that children
go on working out the adult forms of their language even when their child
forms are getting their meaning across just fine.

   If language form, meaning and function are separable strands, we might
expect to find other mismatches between these. With this in mind, compare
your reaction to the previous ill-formed sentences with your reaction to the
following:

The phone stole the air.
The scent glistened loudly in the page.
Colourless green ideas sleep furiously.

The last is a famous example created by the influential linguist Noam
Chomsky to show that a sentence can be well-formed but nonsensical. As
you read these sentences, you probably feel happy with the order of the
words – you have no inclination to move, add, or take away any of the words.

It's the meaning that hits you. The sentences are anomalous: the meanings of the words seem to be incompatible with each other. 'Scent' is an olfactory thing that cannot have the visual properties conveyed by 'glisten' or the auditory properties conveyed by 'loudly'. 'Steal' and 'sleep' are things that animate beings do, and phones and ideas are not animate. Of course we do interpret these examples – we find our own ways of making these incompatible meanings compatible with each other. We 'make' the phone and the ideas animate and invest them with consciousness. We take the power of loudness and attribute this power to the visual impact of glistening, and so on. This is just what happens with poetry where meanings are sometimes combined in contradictory or unusual ways, as in the following lines from poems by Sylvia Plath:

> *Event*
>
> ... I hear an owl cry
> From its cold indigo.
> Intolerable vowels enter my heart.

(Couzyn 1985: 155)

> *The night dances*
>
> A smile fell in the grass.
> Irretrievable!
>
> And how will your night dances
> Lose themselves. In mathematics?
>
> Such pure leaps and spirals –
> Surely they travel
> The world forever ...

(Couzyn 1985: 158)

Notice that although the meaning of word combinations in these poems is unusual, their form is not. Their order fits in with our expectations of word order in English. It is this familiar order that enables us to create meaning relations between the words and experience their poetic effects.

As a final comparison, check out your reaction to the following examples:

He went somewhere, and got it, and then he did too.
I can make it sometimes, but I don't always, if you know what I mean.

Again, you probably feel quite happy with their form: you do not feel like adding or deleting or moving particular words. There is nothing surprising about the way the meanings of the words combine either. It is just that the meaning is not at all specific. The sentences allude to situations and participants in those situations, but indicate almost nothing about these. We therefore have very little idea of their meaning or function.

The separate strands of language that we have identified and the connections between these strands are very important when we come to think about people who have problems with language. They may get the gist behind the language they hear or read, but miss out on certain details, and those details may be crucial. When they come to talk or write, they may have very definite meaning intentions, yet be unable to convey these with recognizable or appropriate forms. Very often, communication is seriously affected. But communication is not necessarily the source of the problem.

Take 10-year-old Robert's attempts to say where his house is:

Teacher:	So there's a sign to your house?
Robert:	No. My dad's boss – house. I [mɪən] down lane. Not – not farm. Walk up.
Teacher:	So it's not actually your house?
Robert:	No. Dad's boss. House.
Teacher:	But you have got a house there as well?
Robert:	Yeah. Not on – at – farm. Down lane. Draight – turn – turn – right – draight down – roun' corner – [əʊən] bridge – roun' there – [kɪn] dog's kennel – horse – horse [nə] fields – and kennel. My house.

Robert responds to the teacher's questions appropriately. Given the appropriateness and consistency of his responses, he has clearly got the message. But putting that message into language is a problem – his words are few and are not always recognizable.

Compare the following conversation with DW, an adult who has aphasia as a result of a stroke (Wilkinson, Beeke and Maxim, in press). DW's utterances are strikingly different from Robert's, but he also demonstrates clear communicative intentions:

DW:	They don't – They don't do it.
Therapist:	Mm.
DW:	They g – got – you've got to do it. I mean I'm – I'm alright (gestures towards himself).
Therapist:	Mhm.
DW:	You know but uh – I mean she's not very well (points towards the ward). You know I mean you know (puts hands on legs) she's she – (rocks back and forth).
Therapist:	Yes.
DW:	She can't do it (moves hands on legs).

DW's gestures give some indication of what he wants to communicate, although the meanings are not filled out in his language.

PC has also had a stroke. When he tries to communicate, he often struggles for words and finds himself going off at certain linguistic tangents.

As he reaches for words to express his meaning, he gets sidetracked by a stream of other meanings which are irrelevant. These have nothing to do with his intended meaning, but they happen to share their form with the word he is actually looking for. This occurs a number of times when he is chatting about his weight problem:

> PC: I broke the weighing … so I … Well I've got the woman
>   who is on that building in London (arms spread wide),
>   do re fa so la ti do, the fish things and you know when
>   you go over the wall and this weighing thing. Now what's
>   the word?
> Therapist: Scales?
> PC: What? All of them? Are they spelt the same too? Damn
>   me, I think English is disgusting.

Here, where PC is targeting the word *scales*, he first comes up with an image of a statue representing the scales of justice on the building of the Old Bailey law courts in London, and this mushrooms into three other meanings which happen to have the same form – musical *scales*, fish *scales*, and *scaling* a steep incline, although he still has not got the form *scales*. Something similar happens when he is trying to write 'dear':

> PC: Well you see I don't know what this is … Well I do see
>   but you see the problem is I've got the animal in my mind
>   and I don't know which it is … and you see I've got the
>   one that costs a lot of money too … I don't know.
>
>   (Jones 1989)

Though PC has not been able to find the polite expression *dear*, this form has triggered the idea of an animal for which the word, *deer*, happens to sound the same.

PB, another man with aphasia, produces something rather different from DW and PC but again demonstrates a clear communicative intention (Marshall, Chiat and Pring 1997):

> PB: The garage is ringing M to say the car is bringing the
>   truck … no
> Therapist: So the garage rang M?
> PB: No M rang the garage … could it be possible … bring the
>   car a truck. No.

When the therapist checks back over what PB has actually said, he corrects this. He also shows dissatisfaction with what he has said when he punctuates his comments with 'No'.

Six-year-old Eamonn can also tell his listener when she's got the wrong message:

> E: I want batman car. Have you – have you got the – have you got the – have you got the push-button one?
> S: Is there one that's got a push-button?
> E: [av] see button one before.
> S: Huh?
> E: [av] see a button one before.
> S: You *have* seen it?
> E: No, I didn't.
> S: So what did you say? You –
> E: I didn't – see – um – (peters out).

Like PB, Eamonn seems to know just what he wants to say, but it is difficult for the listener to work out just what this is.

All these children and adults have strong communicative intentions which they are struggling to put into language. They may come up with very few words (Robert), or very general words (DW) or words that do not match their intended meaning (PC). They may also struggle to combine words appropriately for their meaning (PB, Eamonn).

Sometimes, a child or adult is able to get their basic message across quite clearly, but the form of their language is in some way limited. Their difficulty with language form still affects what they are able to express, and how they sound to the listener. It may also affect what they feel about their communication, and how clearly they hold onto their intended meaning. Twenty-two-year-old Anne illustrates the point:

> S: Do you remember what it felt like when you were little and you wanted to talk? Did you know what you wanted to say?
> A: Yeah. And you can't get it out.
> S: It's probably hard for you to imagine this, but were the words in your head?
> A: Yeah. Still sometimes happen now – but not it – not a lot now. You thinking – trying to explain something. You got [ələ] these words in your mind – and you thinking – now which one shall I choose? Go for the really long one – the one you *can't* say? Or go for the easy one – which don't explain anything [tə] all.

To get some insight into this sort of experience, think how frustrated you feel when you can't think of a word you are looking for – even if it doesn't matter a jot to your listener whether you find the exact word or not. And how, when you can't quite find the words you are looking for, you can lose sight of your meaning, or even feel 'I'm losing the thread' or 'I'm not sure what I'm talking about'.

These examples provide some illustration of the intricate relationship between form and function in language. If someone's language is unusual, odd, does not make sense to the listener, it is all too easy to assume the person is 'lazy' , 'confused', or 'can't communicate'. This is because, as we have seen, our conscious awareness of language is largely confined to its functions, so if language goes wrong, the lay person is likely to look to the functions of language as the site of the problem. The reality for the child or adult with language problems may be very different. They may have very clear and appropriate meaning intentions, but have problems in realizing these. If we are to get closer to their reality, we need to understand more about the vehicle – language – and how this enables us to express our meaning intentions.

2.3 Giving form to meaning: words

Consider the following comments made by a two-year-old girl:

It's 'party' not 'pardy' (referring to the pronunciation on an American story tape)
My thought you said 'café' ... you said 'paté'
What does 'dusty muzzle' mean?
I call them 'hands' (referring in fun to her feet)
Some people call it a 'lep' (referring to an apple)

(Examples taken from Shaw 1997)

This child already shows an implicit understanding that words involve both form and meaning. When she says it's *party* not *pardy*, she demonstrates awareness that words have a particular form. When she asks the meaning of the forms *dusty muzzle*, she demonstrates awareness that they have a meaning. She even demonstrates awareness that the connection between sound and meaning is conventional, so that a particular form is expected for a particular meaning (*party* not *pardy*), but that the conventional form-meaning connection is arbitrary, so that she can playfully re-assign forms to meanings (*hands* for 'feet') or create new forms for meanings (*lep* for 'apple').

In a small sample of comments, this child has summed up much of what a word involves. A word is nothing more and nothing less than a set of connections between form and formal properties on the one hand, and meaning on the other.

Word form

What are we getting at when we talk about the forms and formal properties of words?

The most typical form by which meaning is represented is sound-based. This is the form that a speaker articulates and a listener hears. If you look at the following picture:

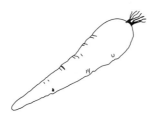

this probably leads you to a particular meaning which leads you to the form *carrot* – /ˈkærət/. This form consists of a rhythmic pattern containing two syllables /kæ/ and /rət/, with the first syllable carrying greater stress than the second, and both made up of specific segments of sound. It is distinguished from:

- forms which consist of only one syllable, for example *car* – /kɑ/ and *rat* – /ræt/
- forms which have two syllables but with stress on the second, for example *cassette* – /kəˈsɛt/, *correct* – /kəˈrɛkt/
- forms which have identical rhythm but different sound segments making up that rhythm, for example *comet* – /ˈkɒmət/, *carry* – /ˈkæri/, *carol* – /ˈkærəl/.

Each of these is a word form with a meaning. We could come up with similar forms which are not words, because they have no meaning – *kerrot* – /ˈkɛrət/ or *kallot* – /ˈkælət/, for example. These *could* be words of English, in that they fit the sound patterns of words in English. Compare forms such as [ˈxærət] or [ˈɬærət]. These are not words in English and we would not expect them to be, because they contain the sounds [x] and [ɬ] that do not occur in English, although they occur in some languages. We would be equally surprised to meet forms such as [ˈpsærət] or [ˈmbærət]. This is because they contain sequences of sounds that do not occur at the beginning of words in English, although they occur in other positions, as in *caps, capsule, number*. The sound patterns of language, illustrated by these examples, constitute the phonology of the language. The sound pattern of a word is known as its **phonological form.**

Meanings can also be represented by phonological forms which are visual-gestural rather than auditory-articulatory. This is the case in sign languages. Whereas word-size meanings are conveyed by a combination of sounds produced by the vocal organs in spoken language, in signed languages they are conveyed by a particular shape and orientation of the hand coupled with movement in a specific location in signing space.

Sound patterns are not the only form that spoken languages take to convey meaning. Visual patterns offer an alternative representation. The meaning you derived from the picture:

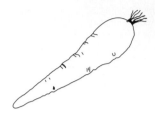

could equally be represented by written forms such as

carrot　　　　**carrot**　　　　CARROT

Written or orthographic forms are visual, produced by hand and received by eye. However, they rest on sound-based phonological forms which come first in development. When we see the visual form *carrot* we can read it aloud by invoking the corresponding phonological form, and we connect it to exactly the same meaning as the phonological form. Some sign languages also have written forms. A striking example is the sign language used in the Central American country of Nicaragua. Nicaraguan Sign Language has evolved only recently, and a written form has emerged almost simultaneously with its birth (see http://www.signwriting.org/).

A word, then, is a connection between forms and meanings:

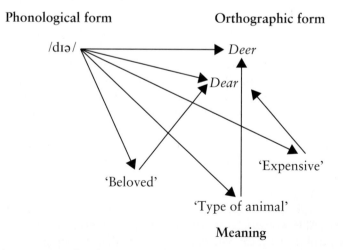

As the above example shows, words may share the same phonological form (/dɪə/) but differ in their orthographic form (*deer/dear*) and meaning (animal/expensive). Different meanings may also happen to share both phonological and orthographic forms, as with /bæŋk/ and *bank* which both encompass the meanings 'side of a waterway' and 'financial institution'.

The shaping of meaning by word form

If we think of word forms as a vehicle for conveying meanings, we might assume that meanings already exist, independently of language, and that they are just waiting for word forms to come and pick them up. According to this assumption, the forms of language simply attach to pre-given and clear-cut categories of meaning. But the picture is more complicated. Contrary to our assumption, when the forms of language pick up meanings, they package them in particular ways. So, when we come to express our meaning intentions in a language, we have to fit these to the meaning packages of the language.

Take the case of words for concrete objects. These are a good place to start, because you might think that concrete objects are pretty well-defined entities that exist independently of language, and that words simply 'stick' a label on them. Take, for instance, the word *cup*. Even without the word, we could think of a cup as a self-contained object because of its function, how we manipulate it and the various interactions we have with it. We also have words that direct our attention to particular aspects or regions of a cup – *handle*, *rim*, *bottom*, *side*, *inside* – even though we do not have words for these parts of cups in particular, for example *chandle* for the handle of a cup or *crim* for its rim. In contrast, some other areas remain in the linguistic dark and there is no word that highlights them and picks them out from their surroundings. Take that bit of the rim from which your coffee always dribbles down the side of the cup and sneaks to the bottom creating an unpleasant ring of coffee on the saucer. Or that part deep inside the cup where tea stains build up in all cups in communal kitchens. Surely, if anything has definition lines drawn in nature as well as in our minds it is that part of the cup – otherwise how could we avoid it with such precision every time we wash up! But maybe if we started talking about the *cribble* of the cup, this region would take on a sharper, better-defined existence. Think how comforting it is when you can find a word to name a feeling or problem that has been worrying you for a while. It's not just that words give expression and allow you to share it with other people. The number of words itself can make a difference: finding a single word for it allows you to mark its boundaries more sharply, to pick it out from similar feelings or problems, and makes it appear more self-contained and, perhaps, more containable and manageable. So words, especially single words, help us construct single, more clearly bounded regions in our mental or linguistic world, irrespective of whether such entities really exist with those boundaries and groupings of properties 'out there' in the world.

This effect of forms on the way our minds cut up the world is most strik-ing when we go beyond forms which relate to concrete objects. Consider the meaning represented in the following picture:

This shows two objects. But it also shows a relation between them, which can be expressed by a linguistic form. In English, that form would be 'on', as in 'putting the apple on the plate'. If we were to convey the meanings rep-resented in the following pictures:

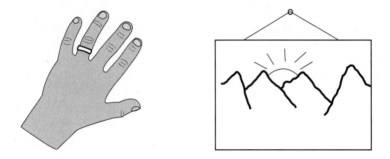

we would represent the spatial relation between the two objects with exactly the same form: 'the ring *on* the finger', 'the painting *on* the wall'. To an English speaker, the 'on-ness' in these pictures seems obvious and even inevitable. We see the relation between the objects in just the same way, and encode it with just the same form.

But this 'sameness' is neither obvious nor inevitable, as speakers of German would confirm. They would use *auf* for the apple *on* the plate, *um* for the ring *on* the finger, and *an* for the picture *on* the wall. This is because German distinguishes between contact with a horizontal surface (*auf*), a vertical surface (*an*), and a circular surface (*um*) (Bowerman 1989). To a German speaker, the differences between these scenarios are as automatic and obvious as their sameness is to the English speaker.

For signers using British Sign Language (BSL), categorization of these spatial relations would be different again. In BSL, the shape of the object located and the place where it is located are taken into account in marking the spatial relation. Take the example of the apple on the plate. After the sign for apple and the sign for plate, the spatial relation would be marked by moving a round-shaped right hand towards a horizontal left hand. For the picture on the wall, on the other hand, the spatial relation would be marked by moving a horizontal right hand towards a vertical left hand. The user of BSL must therefore register the shape of objects involved in spatial relations – not something the English or German speaker would register.

These examples show that the forms of language carve up meanings such as spatial relations in particular ways, and that different languages make cuts in different places. Consequently, the forms of language which map onto meanings also shape those meanings, causing the users of the language to pay attention to certain aspects of meaning rather than others (see Slobin 1996). Slobin points out that speakers of different languages know, in some non-linguistic sense, the differences that are picked up in other languages but not in their own – English speakers know the difference between vertical and horizontal surfaces (walls vs plates) and the shapes of objects (apples vs paintings). But English speakers do not attend to these differences when they talk about spatial relationships because English does not require them to. Those using German or BSL, on the other hand, must take some of these differences into account.

How important are such differences? After all, English and German speakers and BSL signers can all convey the spatial relationships represented in the pictures. Whoever they were addressing would end up understanding what situation was being conveyed. We might conclude that the particular details that different languages convey are insignificant. That may be true. Nevertheless, these fine-grained differences are intrinsic to linguistic representation and the way that it makes us package meaning.

This indicates how our view of things is shaped by our language. When we turn a thought into language, we structure that thought according to the distinctions that are crucial in our language. Confronted with a spatial relation in the world, we may view it from different angles and notice all manner of specific features in the scene. We cannot either contemplate or communicate all these aspects simultaneously. To get a handle on the scene and turn it into a message, we must pare it down in some way. The forms of language determine the ways in which we pare it down – whether the forms of our language group together horizontal/vertical contact (English) or separate these out (German), for example. These forms lead us to organize our view of things and their relations, and that organization may be very important in keeping a grip on our thoughts and turning them into messages (see Parts II, III and IV).

2.4 Giving form to meaning: sentences

Words are not lone beacons flashing up independent and self-contained meanings. Word forms combine with each other to create sentences. Their combination creates meanings which draw on the meanings of the individual words, but add to these.

Sentence syntax

Take the words *book, plate, fell, the, a* and *on.* If we ask you to combine these words, you are highly unlikely to come up with the combinations:

*The on fell book plate a.
*Fell plate the book a on.
*The book a plate on fell.
(An asterisk is used to indicate that an example is not well-formed: see Box 5.2)

Of the many hypothetical sequences, the only ones you are likely to contemplate are:

The/a book fell on a/the plate.
The/a plate fell on the/a book.

Both of these sound fine. This is because both conform to the patterns of English sentences. Instinctively, you know that words like *the* and *a* come before words like *book* and *plate* in English. You also know that *fell* comes after something like *the book* or *the plate*, and that it can be followed by something like *on.* The patterns of word combination in a language, illustrated by these examples, constitute the syntax of the language. The ways in which words fit into these patterns give rise to their **syntactic properties**. Part II of this book gives you an introduction to syntax and basic syntactic properties.

Sentence semantics

When words combine with each other according to the syntactic and phonological patterns of the language, they convey meaning over and above the meanings of the individual words. This is obvious if you compare two different combinations of the same words:

A book fell on the plate.
A plate fell on the book.

The individual words in these two sentences do not change their meaning. What changes is the meaning relation between these individual words. In both sentences, *fell* conveys an event and the event involves two participants which play different roles in that event: one that is undergoing the falling, and the other that is the endpoint of the falling. The difference between the two sentences is in the roles that *book* and *plate* occupy in the falling event. It is the syntactic and phonological position of these words that tells us which role they occupy. This is just one example of how the structure of a sentence contributes to its meaning, by indicating the meaning relations between the individual words. The meanings conveyed by combining words constitute sentence semantics. Parts III and IV of this book take you through the semantics of sentences.

Sentence phonology

When words come together in a sentence, the sentence also has a phonological form that goes beyond the phonology of the individual words it contains. To illustrate this aspect of sentence form, first try saying the following sequence of words when they occur singly, as in a list:

Now check out how you say the same sequence of words when they combine into a sentence:

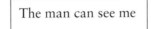

What differences do you observe in the sound patterns corresponding to the two versions of these words? How do the word forms in the second differ from the word forms in the first? What you should notice first is that when the words occur separately, in a list, they are all equally prominent. In contrast, when the words combine into a sentence, some words are more prominent than others. You might notice that the more prominent words are longer and higher in pitch:

The *man* can *see* me.

You might also notice that the less prominent words – *the*, *can* and *me* – are shorter. Notice how two words that share the same vowel when they are uttered in isolation and are equally prominent – *man* and *can* – no longer share that vowel when they occur in the sentence. This is because *man* is a word that carries stress and keeps its vowel /æ/, whereas *can* is an unstressed vowel and reduces its vowel to /ə/.

The rhythm or stress patterns of sentences in a language, illustrated by these examples, constitute the **sentence phonology** of the language. The ways in which words fit into these patterns give rise to phonological properties over and above their individual phonological form. Part V of this book deals with the phonological characteristics of sentences.

2.5 Meaning and form in language processing

We have begun to delve into the nature of form and meaning in language, and the relationship between these. Where does this take us clinically? Let's go back to our starting point in this chapter: our observation that people think of language chiefly as a means of communication, and all too readily see disorders of language only as disruptions in communication. Our discussion of forms and meanings in language opens up a different perspective on language and language disorders. Language consists of forms which organize meanings in particular ways, and this form-meaning system provides the vehicle for doing what we do with language. So, if there is a breakdown in language, the functions of language will be disrupted to a greater or lesser extent, but they are not necessarily the source of the breakdown. Problems could arise in the forms of language, or meanings, or the connections between these. Assessment of someone with a language disorder begins here. Are forms of language the main source of difficulty for this person? Or meanings? Or the connections between these? And how do they impact on each other?

The answers to these questions will not be immediately obvious. This is because we are dealing with people's processing of language, and when we observe people processing language, we observe the forms, meanings and functions of language simultaneously. To see what we are getting at here, think what is involved in an everyday sequence of communications such as the following:

Liz reads a notice that the afternoon lecture has been cancelled.
Liz has to make connections between the written forms on the noticeboard and their meaning.

Liz rings Sarah to pass on the message. Sarah's flatmate answers the phone and Liz gives her the message.
Liz has to turn the meanings she got from the written forms on the noticeboard into spoken forms, and Sarah's flatmate receives these as auditory forms.

Sarah's flatmate then relays the message to Sarah who is in the bath.
Sarah's flatmate has to turn the meanings she extracted from the auditory forms she received from Liz into spoken forms.

If we witnessed this scene, we would see Liz reading and talking, and the flatmate listening and repeating. We would not see the processing behind the scene – the connections between forms and meanings involved in the give and take of the message. Nor could we catch ourselves making these connections when we read, talk, listen or repeat. They are connections that get made unconsciously, and in a matter of split seconds (Harley 2001).

Similarly, when someone has problems in understanding or producing language, what we observe is the outcome of the connections they make between forms and meanings. To find out what they are able to do with language, and where their problems arise, we have to probe further. To probe further, we need to know about the nature of linguistic forms and meanings, and the connections between these. That is what this book is about.

Exercises

1. Which of the following activities involve language and/or speech on the part of the person carrying them out? Try to justify your decisions.

   1. Recalling your dreams. 2. Travelling somewhere. 3. Having a haircut. 4. Eating in a self-service restaurant. 5. Paying a bill in a bank. 6. Reading the newspaper. 7. Watching TV. 8. Taking children to school. 9. Cooking a meal. 10. Buying sweets in your local shop. 11.Taking a message from an answering machine.

2. When presented with single words one at a time, an adult with acquired language problems (aphasia) reads them aloud as follows:

Target	*Response*
sin	tin
sea	teas
soil	toil
loss	lot
cell	tell
coil	coil
church	church
dogs	dogs
shoe	shoe

   (i) Given these responses, would you say that:
      (a) sometimes she gets it right and sometimes she does not – it is just chance?
      (b) she has problems recognizing certain letters?
      (c) she has problems producing certain sounds?
   (ii) Given your decision in (i), do you think that, when she reads the word *sin*, she understands it as meaning 'sin' or as meaning 'tin'? Use the data to back up your conclusions (see Keys to exercises).

3. In the same task, another person with aphasia reads words aloud as follows:

Target	*Response*
knife	spoon
stool	chair
gloves	socks
boots	shoes
cap	hat
pen	pencil
guitar	violin

   Given these responses, would you say that he has problems in recognizing written words, in selecting the right meanings for the target words or accessing the appropriate phonological form? If more than one conclusion is possible, say why.

4. The following is an excerpt from a letter written by 15-year-old Lisa to her aunt, which we have reproduced just as she typed it. You will almost certainly feel there is something unusual about Lisa's writing. Referring back to the distinctions we have made between the functions, forms and meanings of language, decide which of these are not a problem for Lisa, and which may be:

Hi Aunty E!

How're you at A?

I had a nice time at home having our Christmas.

On Monday 21st December I watched a new animated series **Rex the Runt** on BBC2 in the evening at 6:25p.m. It has got a picture of 4 dogs in it that made out of plasticine. 4 of them are Rex, the light purple dog, Wendy, the white dog with her red ribbon on her head, Bad Bob, the dark brown dog with his eyepatch, his gun, and Vince the light brown dog with his teeth sticking out. He was the one who sang a classic song all the time. It was the clip story called **Holiday for Vince**, then at 7:20p.m. the other one was **Stinky Search for a Star.** And finally I watched another animated drama The Canterbury Tales at 7:30 p.m. ...

On Boxing Day, it's my birthday, and I'm 15! Then my brother Pete who had a same birthday as mine, so he's 35. My 2nd brother Samuel gave me a CD 'Spice Girls: Goodbye', and my 3rd brother Leo gave me another CD album 'Boyzone: Where we belong'. In the afternoon, I watched an animated film 'Watership Down', then after that I watched Rex who had turned into a spaghetti.

It has been taking me ages for watching Rex the Runt. It was my favourite.

That's all for now! Send me a letter soon!

II

Syntax

|3|

Syntactic categories

3.1 What are syntactic categories?

When 5-year-old Joe says

I can do all the wessues

he presents us with a sequence of sounds that we do not recognize. Yet we immediately jump to certain conclusions about that sequence of sounds. One is that *wessues* is a word. Another is that *wessues* is more like some words than others. We know, for example, that some words of English could stand in place of *wessues*, whereas others could not. You would probably agree that the following substitutions are fine:

I can do all the boxes
I can do all the jigsaws
I can do all the questions
I can do all the gestures
I can do all the songs

whereas the following substitutions are not:

*I can do all the opens
*I can do all the asks
*I can do all the sings
*I can do all the befores.

We cannot be deriving this information from *wessues* itself. Clearly, it is the context of *wessues* that provides us with clues about this unfamiliar form. As soon as we recognize 'all the …' we know that a certain type of word is required: a noun. We therefore take *wessues* to be a noun.

Having decided what type of word it is, we jump to some conclusions about its meaning. As a noun, we assume that it relates to some sort of entity – a thing or person, for instance. In line with this, it can take a plural marker -*s* which indicates more than one of that entity. But that is as far as we can go. As the substitutions above illustrate, it could refer to a concrete object (boxes, jigsaws). But it could refer to an action or event (gestures, songs). Nothing in the context revealed that Joe's target was the abstract word *levels*, and that he was referring to the levels of a computer game.

Supposing Joe had used *wessues* in a different context, for example:

That robot wessues me.

This alters our assumptions in quite predictable ways. We now take *wessues* to be a verb. As a verb, we assume that it relates to some sort of event, but again, that is as much as we can tell. It could refer to an intentional action like 'kick', an emotional state like 'hate', causation of an emotional state like 'annoy'. Again, the context has led us to deduce what sort of word *wessues* is and this gives us only a broad idea of what it might mean.

Now suppose Joe had just said:

Wessues.

Or that he had said:

Fim poller wessues bleb.

Neither of these utterances provides the 'signposts' of a familiar context. With no signposts, we have no basis for deciding what *wessues* is.

These examples illustrate an important characteristic of words: that they fall into classes according to where they occur within a sentence. These word classes are known as **syntactic categories**. Nouns and verbs are two examples of such categories.

Traditionally, syntactic categories have been defined in terms of their meaning. You may, for example, have learnt that nouns are 'names of things, people and places' or that verbs are 'doing words'. It is true that syntactic categories have certain *typical* correspondences with meaning. Nouns typically do refer to things and people, and verbs typically do refer to actions and events (see section on *Links to other levels*). However, the examples we have just worked through show that we can categorize words as nouns or verbs when we do not know their meaning, as was the case for the unfamiliar *wessues*. So, we do not need to know whether a word refers to a thing or action to identify it as a noun or verb. Our examples also showed that categorizing a word as a noun or verb tells us very little about its meaning. A noun may refer to a thing or person or place. But it may also refer to an action or event. According to the traditional definition, this should not be possible, since actions and events are the province of verbs. Following this definition, the nouns 'deed' and 'action' should be verbs. In fact, the contexts in which they occur determine that they are nouns. These examples prove that context overrides meaning in deciding the syntactic category of a word.

To confirm that you can make judgements about where words occur regardless of their meaning, see how you react to the following examples:

Which words can you fit into the blanks?

1. I was very happy to _____

    friend, fantastic, elope, disappear, afraid, go, know, idea, between, sorry, be, criticism

2. The _____ was good/terrible

    supply, demand, play, plan, porridge, appear, about, smooth, rave

3. This was/seemed very _____

    fashion, trendy, cool, wicked, groovy, rave, mean, exciting, boring, turn, high, look, buy

---

3.2 Why do we need syntactic categories?

In assessment and therapy

When we analyse language, no matter for what purpose, we are always looking for patterns, regularities that apply to sets of words that share some linguistic properties. It is precisely because someone's difficulties, or remaining abilities, can be described in relation to classes of words rather than individual words that we make hypotheses and draw conclusions about the underlying causes of their language problems.

Imagine you are working with a man who, after a stroke, has developed a language impairment. Mr A tells you about having dinner at a restaurant the evening before:

Table ... food ... waiter ... bottle ... dinner and wine ... salad ... plate ... oh dear ... down ...

On another occasion, he tries to explain what he did for his wife's birthday:

Flowers ... shop ... girl ... roses ... ribbon ... paper ... wife ... card ... off.

When he talks about a new French film he has just seen, he says:

Factory ... pupil ... actress ... theatre ... ooh [he mimes someone falling in love] ... guard ... woman ... [he gestures people talking and then splitting up].

To get a handle on Mr A's problems, you need to be able to say something about which words are easier or more difficult for him to produce. It would not be terribly useful to say that he finds words like *table, shop,* or *pupil* easier – you would simply end up repeating what the person says. Furthermore, we could not compare what Mr A says on one occasion with what he says on another, as he is bound to produce different words on different occasions. Yet, reading the three short extracts above, you can feel there is something similar about the words he produces on all three occasions. The individual words are all different from each other but there is also something that they share. Similarly, which words seem to be missing? Clearly, it would be difficult to imagine or predict the exact words Mr A might have been trying to say. All we can do, after examining several bits of conversation, is to suggest what *types* of words may or may not be easier.

Categorizing or grouping things into types on the basis of common properties is something that we do all the time in everyday life. It has many advantages: it makes acting, thinking, remembering and planning all easier. The same is true of life in the clinic. We need to be aware of different properties that allow us to group words into different linguistic types. Properties of many kinds can be taken into account in describing what is relatively easier or more difficult for someone. It could be that all the words Mr A finds easier are similar sound-wise – for instance, they might be short, one syllable words. Or they could all have similar meanings, like naming concrete objects. These, and many other, phonological and semantic properties might be relevant in some cases but they do not quite fit Mr A's pattern of production. Although the words he produces are quite varied in terms of their sound and meaning properties, all of them, except *down* and *off*, are similar in their syntactic properties. Because of how they behave in English, they can all be classed together as nouns. Conversely, we could imagine filling out Mr A's utterances by introducing words that share another set of syntactic properties – verbs.

Using syntactic category labels like nouns and verbs makes description easier in several ways: first, the labels act as a shorthand: we no longer have to list all the relevant words. Second, we are not just dealing with the specific, individual words he may or may not produce but with a more systematic and general pattern that involves classes or types of words. So we can make comparisons and predictions about the words Mr A may or may not produce in other conversations or tasks, and check whether or not our predictions are correct. For instance, we might predict that Mr A might be able to produce the noun *iron* when describing a picture like

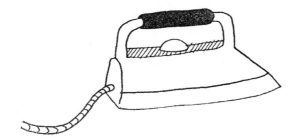

Figure 3.1. Source: Druks, J. & Masterson, J. *An Object and Action Naming Battery* (Hove, Psychology Press, 2000: 71).

more easily than the identical verb *iron* when describing a picture like

Figure 3.2. Source: Druks, J. & Masterson, J. *An Object and Action Naming Battery* (Hove, Psychology Press, 2000: 88).

So being able to refer to types of words, rather than individual words, allows us to make visible, describe and test patterns in the data we are analysing. We are therefore able to ask further questions about the patterns we have identified: what is it that makes nouns easier than verbs for Mr A? Is it something to do with his specific problems or is it something that reflects a typical pattern of relative difficulty even for people without language problems? If we could not group words into types, there would be no patterns, no predictions and, ultimately, no explanations.

Similarly, we would not know which words to select for therapy activities. In designing these activities we could only draw on the particular words

Mr A has actually produced and the particular words we guessed he was aiming at. We have to limit ourselves to the particular words. Once we can think of words in terms of types, however, we can select a wide range of words irrespective of what the person might have actually said or left out on any one occasion. Furthermore, we can check whether our therapy has had effects on other words of a similar type (e.g. other verbs) that we have not used in therapy, providing us with further evidence that the initial description of the problem was correct and that our therapy was on the right lines.

Without syntactic categories, and other ways of grouping words into types, it would be impossible to evaluate therapy. Progress can be measured only if we have some means of comparing what the person did before therapy and what they did after. Again, we have to compare like with like and that is only possible if we are comparing comprehension or production of types of words on different occasions.

Imagine, for instance, we wanted to check Mr A's progress after therapy, when he produced the following utterances to describe what he did for his wife's birthday:

Bought flowers ... girl wrap roses ribbon ... write wife card ... send.

How would we measure progress? If we just counted the total number of words, this would not show much change in the range of words he uses, as he is only producing one more word than before. Most of the words he produces on this occasion are the same as those that he produced before (*flowers, girl, roses, ribbon, wife, card*, that is, all the nouns). But crucially he is producing words like *bought, wrap, write, send*, which are all verbs. Given that these words were missing from the pre-therapy sample, we could not compare before and after – no specific words are present in the pre-therapy sample to compare with what he has produced after therapy. But we can talk about a type of word that was absent before therapy and is being produced after therapy. Clinical comparisons usually involve analysis and measurement of word types, not of individual words. Syntactic categories are one of the most important types in that they give us an initial handle on the data: by describing what someone has or has not produced in terms of syntactic type we begin to impose some order on the chaos of the data. Patterns, if there are any, begin to emerge.

If we were not able to group words into types it would be impossible to describe any patterns in language. Syntactic type is not the only way of classifying words but it is one of the most important as most patterns in language make some reference to syntactic categories. This is true whether we are talking about sound, structure or meaning-related patterns. It is also true whether we are talking about patterns in unimpaired or impaired language in adults or patterns in how children acquire language. We will give you just a couple of examples here – you should be able to spot many others scattered throughout this book.

In describing language, language acquisition and processing

When we try to say what are possible combinations of words in a language, we often use statements of the form 'Words of type X come before/after words of type Y'. For instance, we would use this kind of statement in describing the relative ordering of the two words in each of the examples below:

large book   red light   loud noise
happy memory   old friend   mere excuse.

In English, words like *book, light, noise, memory, friend* and *excuse* follow words like *large, red, loud, happy* and *mere*, and the reverse order is usually not possible:

*book large   *light red   *noise loud
*memory happy   *friend old   *excuse mere.

English only allows one order, even when it would be quite handy to have both possibilities to avoid ambiguities as in the case of *old friend*, where *old* can be interpreted as telling us something about the age of the person who is a friend, or something about the time span of the friendship. This is exactly what happens in Italian, where the position of *old* varies depending on the meaning, e.g.

vecchia amica (old friend, meaning a long-standing friend)
amica vecchia (friend old, meaning a person who is old).

What should we insert into the ordering statement instead of X and Y? Could we define types X and Y in terms of sound or meaning properties? There is no reason in principle why this could not be done. However, nobody has yet come up with a sound or meaning-based definition that would cover all the relevant words and exclude irrelevant ones. Sound-based properties are irrelevant: the words that come before do not contain particular sounds or have a number of syllables that would distinguish them from the words that come after. Meaning-based definitions may seem more promising: you could say that the word expressing a property must come before the word expressing what has the property. This would be a start but you would still have to define more precisely what counts as a property as well as what counts as having that property so that both meanings of *old friend*, and many other similar cases, would be covered by the ordering statement. The difficulties involved are considerable and have led linguists to define the types involved in this kind of ordering statement mainly in terms of syntactic categories. The use of syntactic categories, which we can define quite precisely by their distribution, simplifies ordering statements enormously. We can just say: in English, adjectives precede nouns (but see Section 3.3 below).

Even in describing phonological patterns, we often need to refer to syntactic categories. For example, in English, stress can be on the first or second syllable of a word. But, when the same phonological form can be used as a noun or as a verb, we can predict where the stress will fall simply on the basis of the syntactic category: the noun will have stress on the first syllable, while the verb will be stressed on the second, e.g.

The 'transport in this town is abysmal.
It tran'sported me to a different time.
The 'rebels fought against the palace guards.
They re'belled against injustice.

Even when reading aloud non-words, when people do not know the meaning of the phonological forms involved, they typically show a preference for placing the stress on the first syllable or second syllable of the non-word depending on their position in the sentence (see Kelly 1992; Black and Chiat forthcoming, and *Links to other levels*). You can test this for yourself by reading aloud the italicized non-words in the sentences below and noticing where you place the stress:

I despise their *baspels* completely.
They obviously *baspelled* it.

Children too seem to analyse the language, or languages, they acquire in terms of syntactic categories. Although they often 'overgeneralize' the linguistic patterns they identify and say things like *mans, gooses, childrens* (instead of *men, geese, children*) or *goed* and *bringed* (instead of *went* and *brought*), they do not mix up verb endings with noun endings, suggesting that they have implicitly understood that certain endings are only possible with certain syntactic categories. For instance, they do not seem to say things like:

*That kicked (yesterday) really hurt.

even though the noun *kick*, like its verb counterpart, refers to an action that could be carried out in the past.

Nor do children use syntactic categories randomly or interchangeably, for example, putting a verb into a noun context or vice versa. When they appear to be making such an error, they are in fact following patterns in the language. In English, we have many noun-verb pairs where the noun expresses a substance and the verb an action that involves that substance, e.g.

She put butter/oil/sugar/paint on it (N = the substance butter/oil/sugar/paint)

She buttered/oiled/sugared/painted it
(V = the action of buttering/oiling/sugaring/painting).

We also have noun-verb pairs where the noun expresses a relation or role
and the verb being or acting that role, e.g.

She mothered/nursed the abandoned child
(V = being/acting like a mother/nurse towards the abandoned child).

Notice that we need syntactic categories to describe this relationship. And
children seem to notice it. At about three or four, they come out with novel
uses of nouns as verbs that follow the kind of patterns highlighted above
(see Clark 1993), as in the following examples:

Don't milk my cornflakes! (= Don't put milk on my cornflakes!)

She is not babysitting, she's friending me
(= She is being/acting like a friend towards me).

   Syntactic categories are, therefore, an essential tool in describing all aspects
of language. Without them, what we could say about language would be
much more limited, superficial and haphazard.

3.3 Syntactic category tests: introduction

We have established that syntactic categories are defined by their **distribution**, that is, where they occur in relation to other words within a sentence.
However, as we will see in a moment, this general definition is still not quite
precise enough. It needs to be refined in order to be able to show where
classes of words can and cannot occur.
   Consider the sequence of words *door red the*. Your immediate reaction is
probably that something is wrong with this sequence, that these words
cannot occur together in this order. Now look at the following sentence:

She painted the *door red the* other day.

This sentence contains the very order of words we have just rejected. How
come we no longer baulk at this sequence of words? More than likely, you
did not even notice that the same sequence of words had occurred. The
reason is that when words come together in a sentence, some words group
together more closely than others. We automatically notice the connections
between those words, and overlook their proximity to words which do not

group together with them. Although the words *door red the* are adjacent to each other in the sentence, they are not closely connected. Each of these words is more closely related to other words within the sentence. We can illustrate the connections between words in this sentence by bracketing together those which group together:

She painted [the door] [red] [the other day].

Here, we can see that *door*, *red*, and *the* do not form a group. Each belongs to a separate grouping.

We can now account for your initial reaction to this sequence of words. When you met them outside a sentence, you automatically tried to group them together. But *door red the* cannot form a group in that order. Your response was therefore to re-arrange these words into an order which can form a group. There is only one such order: *the red door*. Instinctively, then, you want to turn *door red the* into *the red door*.

In order to show that a sequence of words forms a group, we need evidence that they act as a unit (we will come back to this in more detail in Chapter 4). One type of evidence is that they can move as a whole within a sentence without changing the meaning relations within the sentence. One possibility for moving word groups in English is known as topicalization. This moves a group of words to the beginning of a sentence to highlight it. We can apply this to the above sentence to check which words act as a unit:

Topicalization of *the other day*:	*The other day*, she painted the door red (not today).
Topicalization of *the door*:	*The door*, she painted red the other day (not the window).
Topicalization of *red*:	*Red*, she painted the door the other day (not blue).

Each of these sentences is fine if we use it in a context where we want to draw attention to the topicalized group of words. In contrast, notice what happens when we topicalize our original string *door red the*:

*Door red the, she painted the other day.

Having moved a string of words that do not form a group, we end up with an impossible sentence.

Another way of checking that words group together is to see if we can refer back to them as a whole, using what is known as a **proform**. The word *it* is a proform that refers back to certain groups of words. Which group of words could be replaced with *it* in our sentence?

She painted *it* red yesterday.

In this sentence, *it* stands in for *the door*, confirming one of the units we had identified. Try the same substitution with the words *door red the* and you end up with the impossible:

*She painted the it other day.

Suppose we create a new sentence where the words *door*, *red* and *the* are in the right order – *the red door* – to form a unit:

She painted [the red door] the other day.

Confirming that these words now form a unit, we can topicalize them:

The red door, she painted the other day (not the blue one).

We can also replace this string of words with *it*:

She painted it the other day (= the red door).

What we see is that where they group together to form a unit, *door*, *red* and *the* must occur in a particular order:

✓[the red door]   *[the door red]
                      *[door red the]
                      *[red the door]
                      *[door the red]
                      *[red door the]

Each of the impossible sequences may actually occur in a sentence, but only if the words belong to separate units. You might test this out by creating sentences which contain each of these sequences, and seeing what happens when you treat the sequence as a group by, say, topicalizing it.

We have now established why our initial definition of syntactic categories fell short. When we define syntactic categories such as nouns and verbs, we have to identify not just where they occur in relation to other words, but where they occur in relation to other words within their unit (see Chapter 4).

The category tests

The following are some of the most reliable tests you can apply to categorize words into syntactic categories (or word classes). Most words will not pass ALL the tests but as long as a word has more properties (i.e. passes more tests) typical of one category than another, that is enough. The categorization is based on relative similarity. In this sense, syntactic categorization is no different from any other type of categorization we do routinely in every day life.

The names of syntactic categories are usually abbreviated using the following standard symbols: N = Noun; V = Verb; A = Adjective; P = Preposition; Adv = Adverb; Det = Determiner; Aux = Auxiliary. Nouns, verbs, adjectives, prepositions and adverbs also form corresponding phrases that are abbreviated as NP, VP, AP, PP, AdvP. So, the first symbol tells you the syntactic category involved and the letter P that follows it stands for phrase (see Chapter 4).

NOUNS

(a) Can be preceded by Det, e.g. the murder, a flight, that smoothness, the Bob I know, the Rome of my youth.
(b) Can be preceded by As, e.g. the horrific murder, continuous flight, incredible smoothness.
(c) Can combine with P, e.g. about murders, in flight, beside smoothness, with Bob, in Rome.
(d) Can combine with VP to make a complete sentence, e.g. Murders [frighten people]; the motion [stopped]; Bob [runs]; Rome [is wonderful].
(e) Can be pluralized, e.g. murders, flights, men, children, feet.
(f) Can be substituted by a pronoun, e.g. *s/he, him/her, it, they/them*. Pronouns, as the name indicates, are a subcategory of nouns that can be used to refer back or substitute for a noun or a whole noun phrase (see also Chapter 4).
(g) Can be an appropriate answer to *What/Who*-questions.
(h) Can take 's to indicate possession and certain other relations, e.g. Bob's hat, yesterday's paper, the prisoner's escape, Bill's murder.
(i) Can complete the phrase 'They have no _____'.
(j) Can be slotted into Cleft constructions 'It is/was [___] that ...'.

VERBS

(a) Can be preceded by modal verbs such as *can, will, shall, must, may*, and the auxiliary verb *do*, e.g. He can have another bath; They may seem unbearable; He will be late; They shall swim the Channel.
(b) Their form can change to indicate temporal contrasts, e.g. past tense: kill/killed; talk/talked; sing/sang; take/took; are/were; have/had.
(c) Can be modified with *very much* (as opposed to *very* by itself), e.g. He very much enjoyed the play; *He very enjoyed the play.
(d) Can combine with NP, e.g. seems NP[a fool]; eats NP[cakes]; love NP[their children]. Note the contrast with the noun *love*: *the love NP[their children].

(e) Can be substituted by or be linked to the verb proform *do,* e.g. You arrived late, did you? Bob runs and so does Jill.

AUXILIARY VERBS

(a) Can precede the main verb – see examples under (a) of VERBS above.
(b) Can change their form to indicate temporal contrasts, e.g. The ghost has/had disappeared; The kittens are/were sleeping; He can/could swim.
(c) Can occur before the NP in questions, rather than after it as in statements, e.g.

Question: *Has* the ghost disappeared?
Statement: The ghost *has* disappeared.
Question: *Were* the kittens sleeping? *Can* he swim?
Statement: The kittens *were* sleeping. He *can* swim.

(d) Can have *n't* attached to them to indicate negation, e.g. The ghost hasn't disappeared; The kittens weren't sleeping; He can't swim.
(e) Can act as a proform substituting for or linking back to a main verb (see (e) under VERBS) in 'short' responses to questions, e.g.

Q: Has the doctor left?
A: She has.
Q: Are you enjoying this chapter?
A: I am.
Q: Does this work?
A: It does.

They also occur in 'tags' which echo and emphasize a sentence, e.g. I'm having a go, I am; and in references to a previously mentioned verb, e.g. Jack was running and Jill was too.

ADJECTIVES

(a) Can occur between Det and N in NP, e.g. the ___ book; a ___ murder; this ___ job.
Adjectives are the category that most commonly occurs in this position, but nouns (e.g. the banana sandwich) or prepositions (e.g. the down escalator) do too; so do not conclude something is an adjective just on the basis of this test.
(b) Can combine with verbs like *be, seem, appear, look, sound, feel,* e.g. He seems clever/*cleverly.
(c) Can be modified by *very,* e.g. very clever, very kind, very depressing. NB: contrast with verbs, which are modified by *very much*!
(d) Can be stacked in a series, e.g. the big white house; their irritating vacant expression.
(e) Can have *-ly* added to form a corresponding adverb, e.g. kind + ly, real + ly, infuriating + ly.

(f) Can have *un-* added to indicate negation, e.g. unhappy, unkind, unreal, unrewarding, unworthy.

PREPOSITIONS

(a) Can combine with a following NP (try it especially with pronouns *him/them*), e.g. on the floor; at breakfast; for him; after them.
(b) Can combine with another PP, e.g. from under; up in the roof.
(c) Can be substituted by *there/here/then* and be an appropriate answer to *Where/When* Questions (for locative and temporal prepositions only).
(d) Can be intensified by *right* in the sense of 'completely' or *straight* in the sense of 'directly', e.g. right at the top; straight into the wall.
(e) Can be slotted into the Cleft construction, 'It is/was [_____] that ...'.
(f) Prepositions are a large but closed class so you can also consult the list provided in Box 3.1.

ADVERBS

(a) Can modify V, A, and P but not N, e.g.

> V: I totally *disagree*;
> A: I am totally *demoralized*;
> P: I am totally *down*;
> N: I am in a *totally *crisis*/total crisis.

(b) Can complete sentences like They treat her ____; They behave ____.
(c) Never combine (by themselves) with verbs like *be, seem, appear, sound* (NB: opposite to adjectives), e.g. He seems quick/*quickly.
(d) Can be formed from adjectives by addition of *-ly*.
(e) Can answer *How* Questions (but so can adjectives and prepositions).
(f) Can be modified by *very*, like adjectives and unlike verbs.

Please note that in dictionaries and in the clinical literature there is still a tendency to treat words that express time as adverbs even though they behave more like NP or PP, e.g. *yesterday, today, now, ago*. Make sure a word is not an N, V, A, or P before you test it for Adverb properties.

DETERMINERS

(a) Only occur in NPs, usually at the beginning of the phrase.
(b) Cannot be stacked, e.g.* the a pen; *the my book; *these our tribulations.
(c) Dets NEVER occur on their own, e.g. I like *a/*the/*that (*that* is only acceptable as the noun of the same form).
(d) Dets are a very small closed class, which is always taken to comprise at least *the, a(n), this/these, that/those*. In many analyses it also includes *my, your, his/her/its, our, their*.

Box 3.1 The main prepositions of English

This list is based on the one provided in Jackendoff (1992). You should use the list in conjunction with the preposition tests in this chapter.

about	betwixt	opposite
above	beyond	out(side/ward)
across	by	over
after(ward(s))	down(stairs/ward)	past
against	forward(s)	right
along(side)	from	sideways
amid(st)	here	south
apart	in(ward)	there
around	inside	through(out)
at	into	to(ward)
away	left	together
back(ward(s))	N-ward (homeward,	under
before	shoreward, etc.)	up(stairs/ward)
behind	near(by)	upon
below	north	via
beneath	off	west
beside	on	with(in)
between	onto	

Prepositions used only non-spatially

ago	during	since
as	for	until
because (of)	like	without
despite	of	

Sentence-taking prepositions

after	before	until
although	since	while
as	unless	whilst
because		

3.4 Analytical tips

You do not have to categorize every word for patterns to emerge out of your data, be they ordinary sentences, children's approximations to the adult language or atypical utterances produced by people with language problems. While you are learning to categorize words by applying distributional tests, it is useful to categorize everything in the samples included in the exercises – you need the practice. But when you are analysing data to assess someone's language problems or evaluate their progress in therapy, you would be unlikely to miss a significant pattern – a systematic, revealing feature of the data – just because you have not managed to categorize every word. There are several reasons for this:

- You are usually looking for *general trends* which can be revealed even if some of the words are not classified – no point in wasting time deciding what you are going to call words like *uhm*, *er*, *heck*, or *blimey*. This is why we have given you category tests only for the most important and psycholinguistically relevant categories.
- There will always be words that you cannot categorize because there is not enough context to allow you to make a decision. For instance, if your client is producing only single words like /pɒtsɪt/ there is little point in worrying about its syntactic category – you simply can't tell.

    On the other hand, the person may be producing such a word in a context, as in:

    Yes, you know, it's a green glass dripping machine that you use to /pɒtsɪt/ ... you can /tʊtsɪp/ stuff and that but you don't /kɒtsɪt/ anything with it [said when naming a picture of a spoon].

    In this case, you would have enough distributional cues to say that the novel words (neologisms) this person produces are more likely to be verbs as they are, for instance, preceded by modals or the auxiliary verb *do* and combine with noun phrases.
- There will be many instances where a word can be classified in more than one way and even taking the context into account might not help you decide amongst the possibilities. Imagine the child whose language you were analysing said:

    Sarah put glass of juice/juice go over book/wet/.

    In this case, *wet* could be an adjective (e.g. My book got wet) or a verb (e.g. The juice wetted my book) or even a noun (e.g. My book got in the wet; There is a patch of wet). All you can do is take all the possibilities into account, decide which is most likely, or perhaps eliminate one of them because the child does not produce any other example of that type of category – if *wet* was the only possible adjective in all the data from this child, you might decide against treating it as an adjective.

Remember the categories are only tools for finding patterns – they are not an end in themselves. It is usual, however, for beginners to become obsessed with categorization for its own sake. If you start suffering from categorization anxiety, ask yourself whether or not categorizing that particular word would make much of a difference to your overall analysis or whether patterns would emerge more clearly if the word was categorized one way rather than another. If the answer to either question is 'no', then just ignore the problematic word.

3.5 Links to other levels

As we saw in Chapter 2, words are bundles of semantic, phonological and syntactic properties. In this chapter, we have focused on their syntactic properties. We have seen that words can be assigned to syntactic categories purely on the basis of their distribution, and that their distribution cannot be reliably determined from their meaning or form. However, although syntactic properties of words can be identified independently of their semantic and phonological properties, we find certain correspondences between properties at these different levels.

Semantics

Different syntactic categories typically correspond to different conceptual categories. It is these typical correspondences that give rise to the 'traditional' definitions of syntactic categories:

- Nouns typically relate to 'people' and 'things'. 'Things' may be concrete (tangible, visible), as exemplified by 'hat', 'chocolate', or they may be abstract (intangible, invisible), as exemplified by 'idea', 'imagination'.
- Verbs predominantly relate to actions and events.
- Adjectives predominantly relate to states and attributes.
- Prepositions predominantly relate to time, place and manner.
- Adverbs predominantly relate to manner or speaker's attitude.

When we try to interpret new words for which we have only syntactic information, we draw on these typical correspondences. You can witness yourself doing this in response to a sentence that contains nonsense words:

The flep garzed bimmily.

Your response might be that this sentence is meaningless, since most of the 'words' carry no meaning for you. But you are more likely to ascribe some sort of meaning to it. This is because the sentence contains the familiar forms *the*, *-ed* and *-ly*. These act as signposts to syntactic categories, enabling us to infer the syntactic categories of the nonsense words. Using the category tests, you should be able to explain why we infer that:

flep = noun
garzed = verb (in past tense)
bimmily = adverb.

Our knowledge of the typical correspondences between these syntactic categories and conceptual categories then leads us to assume:

flep = 'person' or 'animal' or 'thing'
garzed = 'action'
bimmily = 'manner in which the action is carried out'.

Of course, we may be wrong. *Flep*, for example, could be an event, as in 'The play ended abruptly' – the correspondences we are assuming are probable rather than certain.

Interestingly, though, our interpretation of words that go against these typical correspondences shows that we are still influenced by them. Consider what happens when we meet a noun which, contrary to the typical correspondence, conveys an action. In the following sentence:

The student gave a loud yawn

yawn acts as a noun as you can show using the category tests. The same event could be conveyed using *yawn* as a verb:

The student yawned loudly.

Again, you can use the category tests to confirm that *yawn* is now a verb. It is clear that *yawn* conveys an action whether it is used as a noun or a verb. Yet you may perceive a subtle difference between the two sentences:

The student gave a loud yawn
The student yawned loudly.

When *yawn* is used as a noun, we perceive the action as having a definite beginning and end. We probably also take it to be of short duration. In contrast, when *yawn* is used as a verb, the action is taken to spread over time. It seems that when a noun conveys an action, we treat the action as if it is a 'thing'. Things, unlike actions, have physical boundaries, and do not change over time, so we treat the action expressed by the noun as bounded and unchanging. 'The properties of the form bias us to see "things" when we are really talking about "actions"' (Black and Chiat 2000: 70).

These examples demonstrate that although syntactic categories of words are defined independently of semantic categories, each has effects on the other. Different conceptual categories are typically expressed by different syntactic categories, and the syntactic category of a word leads us to attribute certain conceptual characteristics to it.

Phonology

Similar relations of independence and interdependence are observed between the syntactic category of a word and its phonology. Clearly, we cannot deduce the syntactic category of a word from its phonology. Take a novel phonological form such as /gɪ'fɜ/. This could be a noun like *guitar*, a verb like *deter*, a preposition like *before*. Nevertheless, we find that different syntactic categories have certain typical phonological characteristics. These include their length, their stress pattern, and their phonological prominence (stress) within sentences. The following illustrate some of the correspondences observed in English:

- Nouns are typically polysyllabic, consisting of two or more syllables. Verbs, particularly those that occur with high frequency, are typically monosyllabic. These differences are illustrated by the sorts of words that children acquire very early:

    Nouns: car, bus, door, shoe, sock, mummy, doggie, horsie, baby, apple, dinner ...
    Verbs: come, go, eat, play, make, do, run, sit, help, stop, fix, open ...

- Prepositions are typically monosyllabic, and many have a reduced form where the vowel is replaced with schwa or another short vowel: on, off, down, up, to/tə/, from/frəm/, for/fə/.

    Nouns and verbs never reduce in this way. *Car* could not reduce to */kə/, *door* to */də/, or *make* to */mək/.

- Two-syllable nouns are most likely to have stress on their first syllable. Conversely, second-syllable stress is more common for verbs. This difference is most striking in words which are nouns when stressed on the first syllable and verbs when stressed on the second:

This is a heavy 'object (noun)	They always ob'ject (verb)
I love this 'record (noun)	I'll re'cord (verb) this song.

- Certain categories of words always carry some degree of stress in a sentence. These include nouns, verbs, adjectives, and adverbs. In contrast, certain categories are normally unstressed, for example determiners and auxiliaries.
- The greatest stress in a sentence normally falls on the final stressed word due to a process known as **final lengthening**. Since the final stressed word in a sentence is very often a noun, nouns often carry the greatest stress in the sentence. In contrast, verbs occur less frequently in this position, and are therefore less likely to carry the greatest stress in the sentence. Compare the stress on *yawn* as a noun and verb:

    The student gave a loud yawn (noun: sentence-final noun, greatest stress)
    The student yawned loudly (verb: not sentence-final, less stressed).

Of course, none of these phonological characteristics is absolute. A verb may be two syllables, with stress on the first, for example *follow*. It may also occur sentence-finally and carry the sentence stress:

The rest of the class will 'follow.

A noun may have stress on its second syllable, for example *po'lice*, and it may occur in a position which carries low stress:

They gave the police a 'battering.

The typical yet imperfect correspondences between syntax and phonology parallel the typical but imperfect correspondences between syntax and semantics. Again, syntactic categories of words are defined independently of phonology. But they are partially correlated with phonological properties, and the syntactic category of a word will have implications for its phonological weight within a sentence (see Chapter 14).

These links between the different linguistic properties of words will be important when we come to look at impairments in word processing. If we find that certain syntactic categories are particularly impaired, we need to explore whether semantic and/or phonological characteristics associated with these categories may be responsible for the difficulties we observe.

Exercises

1. A man with aphasia has more difficulty reading aloud verbs than nouns. Underline all the words that you think are verbs in the following sentences. Every time you make a decision, check it out with the tests for Vs you have been given in this chapter. If your decision is not backed up by the tests, make a note of the item and try to articulate your reasons for thinking it is a verb.

   1. She asked some really strange questions about my encounter with her boss.
   2. The idea of a trip cheered Sarah immensely.
   3. Everything you do interests me greatly.
   4. Everything you do is of great interest to me.
   5. Suddenly, in the middle of the film, he got up and left the cinema.
   6. I feel pretty tired at the moment.
   7. They tire very easily when we go out for a walk.

2. The same man as in Exercise 1 was asked to read aloud single words, one at a time. Which of the words in the list below would he have more trouble with – that is, which are (only) verbs? Use the tests you have been given to justify your decision. If the item can also be a noun, give examples where it is a noun. For instance, after showing that *pocket* can be a verb ('They may pocket the money'; 'She pocketed the money'; 'They pocketed that money, didn't they?'), you may also decide that it can be a noun and give some examples like:

I've got a hole in this/that/my pocket.
These trousers have no pockets.
I had the ticket in my pocket but it must have slipped out of it.

Target list: dog, chair, bottle, bacon, appear, saucepan, delight, hatred, sugar, shoe, book, telephone, bike, car, boat, hug, seem, survive, accident.

3. The same man also has problems producing verbs in conversation. Construct an imaginary conversation between this man and a friend. They are discussing a film or TV programme they have seen. Make sure the man with aphasia has at least five turns in the conversation when he speaks, without using any verbs.

4. A fashion editor with acquired language problems (aphasia) has problems producing adjectives and prepositions. Underline all the words she might not produce in the following sentences, making sure you are using the tests you have been given and consulting the list of prepositions in this chapter:

   1. The artist on my team met you near that exquisite gallery with the gorgeous cubist print.
   2. They wanted frocks in outrageously brilliant colours for that exclusive gathering at the Ritz.
   3. That little egocentric maniac stomped out of the room before the end of that excruciatingly boring show.
   4. Poor Mary sat all evening between a gossip columnist and a man with an endless supply of extremely sexist jokes.
   5. The woman at the table in the corner collects textiles from dubious sources in different parts of the country.

5. The following story is sometimes used for clinical purposes to elicit a sample of language from children (and sometimes from adults). Below you have a breakdown of the episodes that make up the story, which the children hear with or without accompanying pictures. You can treat these formulations as your 'targets'.

Dog story

   1. There was a dog who had a piece of meat.
   2. He was carrying it home in his mouth.
   3. On the way home he had to cross a bridge across a stream.
   4. As he crossed he looked down
   5. and saw his reflection in the water.
   6. He thought it was another dog with another piece of meat
   7. and he wanted to have that piece as well.
   8. So he tried to bite the reflection
   9. but as he opened his mouth his piece of meat fell out.
   10. Dropped into the water
   11. and was never seen again.

The following are two descriptions of the story by a child with acquired aphasia (adapted from Lees 1993). The first was taken six months after the onset of aphasia (when the child was 6; 6), the second twelve months after. Compare the two descriptions in terms of the syntactic categories produced by the child. Try to identify the main changes that have taken place in his language with respect to the syntactic categories produced.

6 months post onset

1. There a dog. 2. Meat in mouth. 3. Went home and … a plank. 4. His flection. 5. Thought another dog and meat. 6. Opened his mouth. 7. Meat gone.

12 months post onset

1. There was a dog with some piece of meat. 2. He went across a river. 3. Thought he saw another dog with meat in his mouth. 4. So he snapped. 5. The meat fell out from his mouth. 6. Dropped into the pond.

6. Think of at least two children's games you are familiar with that involve understanding and/or producing adjectives (e.g. 'Guess who?'). If you can't think of any, make one game up giving some specific examples of how you would play it.

7. Mark is an 8 year old with language impairment. Analyse the following data to come up with a complete list of all the syntactic categories Mark has produced. If a word can be categorized in more than one way, say so and justify the alternatives using different category tests.

 Mark told the BUS STORY (used in clinical assessment, Renfrew 1997) as follows:

The bus ran away. The man run away. The train went off. The bus went on alone.

When he was asked to tell GOLDILOCKS, after going through a picture book version, he said:

Goldilocks sitting on baby chair. Is broken, a chair (Target: a chair is broken). Is broken, a bowl. Has a bed, Goldie. She sleeps.

When he was asked to describe the first seven pictures of the Renfrew Action Picture Test (RAPT) (Renfrew 1997), he produced:

1. The girl cuddles the teddy	(appropriate as a target)
2. Wears the shoe, the girl	(typical target: the mother puts the shoes on the girl)
3. Doggie hurt	(typical target: a dog tied to a pole)
4. The man jumping over	(typical target: a man riding a horse over a fence)
5. The cat pounces on them	(typical target: the cat caught the mice)

6. Are broken, glasses   (typical target: the girl broke her glasses)
7. The letter goes off   (typical target: a boy posting a letter).

In a different picture description, Mark produced:

1. A boy getting down   (for a boy climbing down a tree)
2. Stroking the cat   (for an old man stroking a cat)
3. Has a sweet, the girl   (for a boy giving a sweet to a girl)
4. A kite flying across   (for a child flying a kite).

8. You want to do some therapy with a child who does not produce adjectives. You need to compile a list of possible adjectives that would be suitable for an 8–10 year old child.

   • Syntactically, all the words must be adjectives; you can include words that belong to other categories as well (e.g. *mean*) but make sure you mark their additional categories in some way.
   • Semantically, the adjectives can express a range of meanings of your choice but you should try and include adjectives that express physical size (e.g. *tall*, *big*), shape (e.g. *square*), colour (e.g. *red*), perceptual properties (e.g. *loud*, *rough*, *dark*, *smelly*) and emotional state (e.g. *happy, sad*).

   You should end up with a final list of at least 30 items that could be used in different therapy tasks.

9. A man with aphasia omits prepositions in speaking and repeating. The problem is particularly pronounced with monosyllabic prepositions (e.g. with *in* as opposed to *inside*). Make up a short conversation to show what his output would be like.

|4|

Hierarchical structure

4.1 Introduction

Consider the following sentence, read aloud by a radio announcer who, having read it, quickly apologized and read it again with a different intonation contour and a pause in a different position:

The council received many complaints about the smell from the residents.

Read the sentence aloud and imagine the two ways of reading it. How is it possible for a string of words, none of which are in themselves ambiguous, to give rise to a sentence that can have more than one meaning?

Similarly, consider the two possible meanings of each sentence below:

Adela saw the spy with the binoculars
Mary told the man that she liked the joke.

These examples, and many others like them, show that the meaning of sentences, their syntactic structure and pronunciation depend not only on the words that make them up, but require us to think in terms of different *groups of words*.

Words have more complex relationships than just preceding or following one another, either in time or on the page. Some words are more closely bound together than others, forming units of meaning, structure and phonology. Consider the second ambiguous sentence above. Although *with the binoculars* follows *the spy* in time and space, it does not necessarily form a structural and meaning unit with it. On one reading, it does: it tells us something about the spy, that he or she had the binoculars. On the other reading, however, *the spy* and *the binoculars* no longer form a meaningful unit, though they still follow one another. On this interpretation, the binoculars are the means by which Adela has seen the spy. So, the meaning we attribute to the sentence depends on whether or not we group together the sequence [*the spy with the binoculars*]. Similarly, the meaning we assign to the third example above, depends on whether we group together [*the man that she liked*] or [*that she liked the joke*].

These groupings of words are called **constituents** or **phrases**. The assumption that language is organized into constituents or phrases is a central assumption of linguistic theory (for our purposes, we will use constituent and phrase interchangeably to refer to groups of words). Another way of putting the same thing is to say that sentences are **hierarchically structured**. When we talk about the hierarchical structure of sentences, we are not implying that some words in the sentence are more important or powerful than others. We are simply saying that sentences consist of layered structures of constituents which are themselves made up of constituents. For example, [*the spy with the binoculars*] forms a constituent, and this contains a constituent [*with the binoculars*], which in turn contains a constituent [*the binoculars*]. The hierarchical relations within this string of words become particularly clear if we use a tree structure to represent them:

The spy   with the binoculars

All our examples so far illustrate hierarchical relations in syntax, that is, in the way words combine into sentences. But language is hierarchically organized at all levels. We can illustrate the same point in phonology. Individual sounds, for instance, do not just follow one another in time; they group together into larger units, syllables, which in turn combine with other syllables to make up word forms. Word forms in turn group together to form larger rhythmic units. As we will see, combinations of meaning also show hierarchical structure (see *Links to other levels*).

Let's now consider the assumption that sentences are hierarchically structured in more detail. How do we go about justifying this assumption? As in most theoretical disciplines, we justify an assumption or a concept by arguing that, without it, we would not be able to describe or explain some significant aspect or pattern in what we are studying – we have already seen this form of justification for syntactic categories, in Chapter 3, Section 3.2.

4.2 Why do we need constituents?

There are several linguistic phenomena that we could not describe or explain without the assumption that words are grouped into constituents or phrases. As we have just seen, it would be impossible to explain **structural ambiguities** without this assumption. Without the notion of constituent, ambiguities could only arise from ambiguities of word meaning, so called lexical ambiguities. Compare:

Adela saw a bat in the corner

with:

Adela saw the spy with the binoculars.

In the first case, the sentence is ambiguous because the word *bat* has more than one meaning – either Adela has seen a nocturnal mouse-like creature or a wooden implement for striking a ball. How we group the words is irrelevant and the meaning we attribute to the sentence depends on the particular meaning we select for the word *bat* – here we are dealing with a lexical ambiguity. In the second sentence, however, we have seen that the meaning depends not on any particular word but on how we group the words. Since meaning depends on grouping, we are dealing with a structural ambiguity. If we did not assume that words can group differently into constituents, we would not have any explanation for this type of ambiguity.

Second, we could not describe many aspects of how we hear and pronounce sentences. As we have seen, the rhythm we give to a sentence and where we put pauses depends largely on how we group the words – the constituent structure we give to the sentence. We will discuss this in more detail in Section 4.7.

Third, without the notion of constituent, we could not state even the most basic patterns of a language, as we have already mentioned in Chapter 3, Section 3.3. Let's consider patterns that involve the ordering of categories with respect to one another. In English, determiners precede nouns and not the other way round; for instance, we say:

the/a/this/that student   Det precedes N

but not:

*student the/a/this/that   Det follows N.

So why is it possible to say:

The *student the* teacher liked was ill

where the second Det follows the noun *student*? Using the notion of constituent, we can argue that the ordering Det N applies only within a constituent. The noun and the determiner in this case are not within the same immediate constituent: [*the teacher liked*] forms a constituent which then groups with the preceding Det N to form another constituent [*the student* [*the teacher liked*]]. As the bracketing makes clear, there is a 'constituent boundary' separating *student* and the following *the* – a boundary that is reflected in how we pronounce the phrase and where we might put a pause. Try going against this constituent structure: say the phrase aloud with a pause after the second Det. Would it sound all right?

Most statements of what can precede or follow another type of word rely on the notion of constituent. We can apply the same reasoning to another case to check that our argument is valid in general, and is not just something peculiar to determiners and nouns. In English, we cannot have two modal verbs in a sequence, as is clear from the ungrammaticality of the following sentence:

*Applicants *must can* learn two European languages in a year.

This is not because of the meanings of these verbs, since we can paraphrase the sentence with the perfectly acceptable:

Applicants must be able to learn two European languages in a year.

Furthermore, the same meaning can be expressed in another language where modal verbs can follow one another, e.g. in Italian where the equivalent of our ungrammatical sentence is perfectly acceptable:

I candidati *devono* (must) *poter* (can) apprendere due lingue europee in un anno.

In the case of English, we are dealing with a syntactic pattern of English that, again, can only be stated if we can employ the notion of constituent: two modal verbs cannot follow one another within a constituent. The evidence is that they can follow one another if they are in different constituents:

[Applicants [who must]] can learn two European languages in a year.

Again, the pattern does not apply across constituent boundaries. We now have enough general evidence to say that without the notion of constituent, the ordering of categories in language could not be stated.

In fact, without constituents we could not describe even the most basic patterns in the language. For instance, imagine you were asked how many words you needed to turn the following sequence into a complete and grammatical sentence:

—— costs £100.

You could say that all you need is one word, a noun like *it*, *this* or *that*. But you could also have two words, such as Det and N:

The dress costs £100.

But you could have more:

The dress in the window costs £100

and still more:

The dress in the window of that shop where my friend works costs £100

and you could go on adding words until you run out of breath or space on the page. So, how much do you have to add? If you have a theory that allows for constituents the answer is straightforward. You can add any number of words you want as long they form a constituent of type noun phrase. Once you have constituents, the number of words is irrelevant, just as it is irrelevant how many students are on a course when you are filling out a timetable. As long as you can treat them as a group, a single time tabling unit, your timetable can be written using group names rather than having to list all the individual students who make up that group. Having group names, like having constituents, makes life a lot easier.

Constituents also come in handy in answering other linguistically significant questions. All languages have items that can substitute or refer back to one or more items either earlier or later in a sentence. These special items that allow you to avoid repetition and keep track of who and what you are talking about are called proforms – you are probably familiar with one type of English proform, namely pronouns.

Imagine someone asked you how many words the pronoun *it* can refer back to. You might say one word, because of sentences like:

This costs £100 but I am still going to buy it

where the pronoun *it* refers back to the single word *this* and whatever *this* refers to when the sentence is uttered or written. But it could be any number of words:

The dress costs £100 but I am still going to buy it (2 words)
The dress in the window costs £100 but I am still going to buy it
(5 words)
The dress in the window of that shop where my friend works costs
£100 but I am still going to buy it (12 words).

Again, you could keep going without arriving at a satisfactory number. If you can answer in terms of constituents, on the other hand, you can just say: any number of words as long as they form a constituent of type noun phrase. The same reasoning can be applied to all proforms, as we will see in Section 4.3.

Similarly, someone could ask how many words make a reasonable linguistic fragment, something that is not a complete sentence but is still acceptable, for instance, in reply to a question like:

Q: What did you buy?
A: That, The dress, The dress in the window

but not:

A: *The, The dress in the, The dress in the window of.

You guessed it: the number of words is irrelevant! What is important is whether the words form a constituent. Without the notion of constituent, answering basic linguistic questions such as these would become extremely complicated, or even impossible.

Having clarified why we need the concept of constituent in linguistic theory, we are now ready to consider why we need it in the clinic.

In every job or profession you need a range of conceptual and practical tools that are appropriate to the type of problems you will have to understand and resolve. Some of these tools are not in themselves a solution to the problem but allow you to get a handle on the problem and gain more insight into it. When we start looking at a client's language, a key question is what kinds of meanings the client can express and understand in language. Our first impressions will be based on what the client says. Take the child whose telling of the 'Dog story' was presented in Exercise 4 in Chapter 3, and is reproduced below:

There a dog. Meat in mouth. Went home and … a plank. His flection.
Thought another dog and meat. Opened his mouth. Meat gone.

With no linguistics background, you will pick up some characteristics of the child's language. You might notice that the child's sentences are very short (3–5 words), and that some words are missing, but that the order of words in each sentence is acceptable. Such person-in-the-street observations are perfectly accurate, but they don't take us much further in understanding what the child's problem is. If you have worked through the previous chapter and have become familiar with syntactic categories, you might think of looking at the syntactic categories the child uses, and come up with a list that includes nouns (6), verbs (4), prepositions (1), determiners (3), conjunctions (1). But such a list would still reveal little about what the child can and cannot get across. It would just as easily allow for utterances such as 'The meat in' or 'There a dog in' or 'Thought another and', which probably strike you as implausible, and which you would indeed be unlikely to observe. This is not surprising. Because sentences are not just linear strings of syntactic categories, it is not enough to think about someone's language just in terms of the words they use and the word order. If we limit ourselves to looking at linear sequences of words, we will not capture the patterns in the child's language.

Because sentences are hierarchically structured, we need to look at the way the child's words are organized into constituents. Are words combined in the appropriate order to form constituents? Are constituents combined in the appropriate order to form larger constituents? We might note, for example, that the child is combining words into constituents in the correct order, as in [*a dog*], [*went home*], [*his mouth*], and that there is some layering of constituents, for example [*opened* [*his mouth*]]. On the other hand, the layering of constituents is limited, for example [*his flection*] occurs as an isolated constituent when we would expect it to be part of a larger constituent structure. What the child does not do is combine random fragments of constituents, which would give rise to the correctly ordered but implausible examples above. This very general description of the patterns in the child's constituent structure will be the starting point for a more detailed analysis, to identify which parts of the constituent structure are vulnerable. Through such detailed analysis, patterns of impairment may emerge.

Imagine, for instance, that you were looking at the utterances produced by someone with an acquired language impairment, who often omits prepositions that express spatial relations. This person may say:

Nurse roll *up* my sleeve. Today walk the stairs [Target: up the stairs] first time. Doctor came *in* this morning. Put tube my arm [Target: in my arm].

Before you can ask why he makes these omissions, you need to ask some *What* and *Where* questions to see whether omissions are systematic or random. Is there anything special about the prepositions he omits? Is the context of the omissions significant?

It is unlikely that it is the particular sounds involved that make a difference – sound-wise the prepositions he omits are the same as those he produces. It is also unlikely that those that he omits are less meaningful or important from the point of view of communication: when he produces *up* and *in*, they express direction and location just as much as the *up* and *in* he omits. There would also not be much difference in terms of ease or difficulty in filling in the omissions – a listener would be just as likely to guess the preposition in all cases. There is also little difference in terms of the categories that precede or follow the prepositions he produces in comparison to those that he omits. In three cases, the preposition is preceded by a verb: in two cases it is produced and in one omitted. In all cases, the preposition is followed by a determiner: in two cases, it is produced and in the other two omitted. Without the relevant analytical tools, you might conclude that there is no pattern to his omissions. But if you can look at the data through the magnifying glass of the relevant concepts, you will see patterns appear. What you might notice, for instance, is that the prepositions he omits would always form a phrase with the Det and N after them ([*up the stairs*], [*in my arm*] are prepositional phrases) while those that are produced never do (*[*up my sleeve*] and [*in this morning*] are not constituents). The difference in constituent structure has implications for the rhythm of the whole phrase, with effects on the pronunciation of the prepositions (see *Links to other levels*). So, using the concept of constituent structure to analyse these omissions makes you see things that you would not notice otherwise. Once you have noticed and described as precisely as possible any patterns, it becomes easier to ask about the causes of the omissions.

As we progress through this book and explore patterns of production and comprehension in increasing depth, you will see that the notions of constituent and hierarchical structure underpin all further analysis. You will come to appreciate that they are notions we cannot do without.

4.3 Constituency tests: general

How do you decide whether a sequence of words forms a phrase or not? Given that a constituent is a group of words that are tightly bound together, any sequence that forms a constituent should behave like a unit. How would a linguistic unit typically behave? If the sequence you are testing is a constituent, you should be able to answer positively the majority of the following questions:

1. Can the string of elements move as a unit to a different position in the sentence? (**Movement test**)
2. Can the whole string be substituted by a single proform? (**Proform test**)
3. Can the string be an appropriate answer to a *Wh*-question – a question beginning with *what/who/where/when/why/how*? (**Elliptical answer test**).
4. Can the string be coordinated with another phrase (of the same type)? (**Coordination test**).

Some of these questions should sound relatively familiar to you as they are connected to the evidence for the existence of constituents we discussed in Section 4.2.

Let's see how we go about answering these questions, using them as constituency tests that allow us to decide whether or not a sequence of words behaves like a linguistic unit – a constituent or phrase.

1. **Movement test**: consider the string of elements in italic in the sentence:

I bought *a blue book* yesterday.

I can move that string to other positions in the sentence and keep all three elements together, e.g.

That blue book was bought (by me) yesterday
It was *that blue book* that I bought yesterday
That blue book was what I bought yesterday.

This shows that these three elements are not just one after the other by accident because of English linear word order: they are bound together by relations that hold no matter where they might occur in the sentence.

Could *yesterday* be part of the same phrase? Move the string and see what the results would be:

***That blue book yesterday* was bought (by me)
**It was *that blue book yesterday* that I bought
***That blue book yesterday* was what I bought.

Similarly, compare the two strings in italic in the sentences:

John ran *up the hill*
John rang *up his friend*.

Does the string P Det N form a phrase in both cases or not? Let's move each string in turn:

Up the hill ran John
**Up his friend rang John
It was *up the hill* that John ran
**It was *up his friend* that John rang.

In the first case, the P Det N form a tightly-knit unit, but in the second case they do not. The two strings look identical but they are not – and indeed they do not sound identical when you say them as you can check out for yourselves, paying attention to your pauses and stress pattern in each case.

2. **Proform test**: can the string be substituted for or referred back to by a single proform of the appropriate type? We have seen that in natural languages there are words that can stand in for groups of words. These words, so called proforms, can substitute for or refer back to a sequence of words as long as all the items in that sequence form a phrase – the length of the string does not matter. We can now reverse this property of language and use the possibility of proform substitution as a test of constituency.

Let's take again the strings [*a blue book*] and [*up the hill*] which we saw were phrases by the first constituency test – the movement test.

Consider how the proforms *it* and *there* work in the following sentences:

I bought *that blue book* yesterday but *it* [= that blue book] is a present
for Jill
John ran *up the hill* but I didn't go *there* [= up the hill].

Without reference to some words earlier in the sentence, the proforms would
be pretty meaningless. We know how to interpret them because we know
which combinations of words they can be linked to. We know intuitively
that *it* can be linked to [*that blue book*] but not [*that blue book yesterday*],
while *there* can be linked to [*up the hill*] and not [*up the hill but*]. Our intuitions tell us to look for a string of words that is a single unit of structure
and meaning – a phrase. We can build on these intuitions and use them as a
test for constituency, proceeding as follows:

   (a) If the string you are testing is a phrase, there should be a proform that
you can substitute for the whole sequence. If the sequence is not a phrase,
you will not find a suitable proform to substitute for the whole string (proforms for different types of phrases are listed in Section 4.4).

   (b) Take the sentence you are analysing and substitute a proform for the
test string, e.g.

I bought *it* yesterday

which is fine. The proform *it* clearly substitutes for only the words that form
a phrase – *yesterday* is not included and if we removed it altogether:

I bought it

its meaning would be completely lost. Indeed, we could substitute a different
proform for *yesterday*:

I bought that blue book *then*
I bought   it   *then*.

So there are different substitution possibilities for [*that blue book*] and
[*yesterday*], confirming that we are not dealing with a single phrase.
Let's try the same reasoning with

John ran *up the hill*.

Can we find a single proform to substitute for the whole sequence? As
we have just seen, *there* could replace the whole sequence without loss of
meaning:

John ran there.

Let's apply the same test to the italicized sequence below:

Sarah *plays jazz*.

If we wanted to refer back to this sequence, we could substitute the proform *does so*:

Sarah does so (= plays jazz).

Or we could add another bit to the sentence with the relevant proform:

Sarah plays jazz and Tom does so too [= plays jazz]
Sarah plays jazz and so does Tom [= plays jazz].

Either way, it is clear that the proform substitutes for the combination of verb and noun together, not for each element separately. If it only substituted for the verb, it should be possible to say

*Sarah plays jazz and so does Tom classical music

while if it only substituted for the noun, it should be possible to say

*Sarah plays jazz and so does Tom sing.

But neither of these possibilities is well formed, confirming that the proform substitutes for both elements, and that, therefore, these elements form a phrase.

You might have noticed that, in applying this test to different sequences of words, we have changed the proform. This is because we cannot use the same proform for all types of constituents. As we will see in the next section, particular proforms must be selected to apply the test appropriately.

3. **Elliptical answer test**: can the string of words be an appropriate answer to a *Wh*-question? When we respond to a *Wh*-question, we don't usually use a whole sentence: we use an elliptical answer which gives just the information requested. But only strings of words that form constituents can be an appropriate elliptical answer. So we can use this property as a test to find out whether a string of words forms a constituent or not. To apply this test you proceed as follows:

Make up a *Wh*-question that could ask for information contained in the string of words you are testing – for instance a question about what you bought yesterday if you are testing the string *that blue book*:

Q: What did you buy yesterday?
A: That blue book (*That blue, *Blue book, *That blue book yesterday).

The fact that *yesterday* is part of the question rather than part of the answer also tells you *that blue book yesterday* is not likely to be a constituent: if it were, all the words would be in either the question or the answer.

Let's apply this test to some of the other sequences we have run through the other tests:

> Q: Where did John run?
> A: Up the hill (*Up the).

> Q: What does Sarah do?
> A: Play jazz.

Again, note that with this kind of question, we could not keep the noun in the question and only answer with the verb:

> Q: *What does Sarah do jazz?
> A: *Play.

Similarly, we could ask

> Q: How is Sarah?

and reply

> A: Extremely tired

but not ask

> Q: *How is Sarah extremely?

and answer

> A: *Tired

or　Q: *How is Sarah tired?
> A: *Extremely.

As in the case of proforms, we have selected particular types of *Wh*-questions for different types of strings. The *Wh*-questions you can choose are listed in the next section.

4. *And*-**coordination test**: as we have seen, only strings that are phrases (of the same type) can occur on either side of *and*. We can now use this property as a test to decide whether the string you are analysing is a constituent. You proceed as follows:

(a) Take a sentence with the string (or use the sentence given), e.g.

I bought *that blue book*.

(b) Add *and* plus another similar string:

I bought [that blue book] and [this red pen].

The result is fine, therefore [*that blue book*] must be a constituent. If, on the other hand, we tried the test on

I bought *that blue book yesterday*

we would get

*I bought *that blue book yesterday* and [this red pen].

Let's try the same test on the other strings we have played with:

John ran [up the hill] and [up the mountain]
*John rang *up his friend* and *up his mother.*

This test too confirms that strings of words that appear identical can behave quite differently under specific constituency tests.

Now that we have considered the logic of the tests in general, we are in a position to discuss their application to particular types of constituents.

4.4 Types of constituents

As we have exemplified constituency tests, we have talked about adapting these to different types of constituents. What do we mean by 'type of constituent', and how do we know what type a constituent is?

Using the head

The particular ways in which constituents behave go hand in hand with what they contain. As we have seen, there is no upper limit on the number of words a constituent may contain, but there is a lower limit: they must contain at least one word. That one word is known as the head of the constituent. It acts as a pivot or anchoring point around which the constituent is organized, determining its syntactic and semantic characteristics:

1. The syntactic category of the head determines the category of the phrase. For example, if the one obligatory word in a constituent is an adjective, the constituent will be an Adjective Phrase. In the following sentence:

She felt [totally exhausted]

totally exhausted is a constituent. It can be moved as a whole:

Totally exhausted, she felt.

We can refer back to it with the proform *it*:

She felt [totally exhausted] and she looked [it].

Within this constituent, *exhausted* is the obligatory element in the constituent:

She was [exhausted]

but

*She was [totally].

Exhausted is therefore the head. It is an adjective, since it occurs in a phrase following one of those verbs that takes adjectives (*be*, *feel*, *appear* – see Chapter 3, Section 3.3), and it is preceded by a degree adverb (words such as *totally*, *very*, *too*). The phrase *totally exhausted* is therefore headed by an adjective and is an AP. So the distribution of the whole phrase can be predicted from the distribution of its head. For example, if you know where adjectives can occur you will also know the possible positions of APs. You can test this out for yourself by going back to the list of distributional properties for individual syntactic categories in Chapter 3.

2. The conceptual category expressed by the head determines the conceptual category of the constituent. Using the same example, 'totally exhausted', like its head 'exhausted', refers to a state. It does not refer to degree of state, as does its non-head, 'totally' (see *Links to other levels*). So one way to find the head is to think: what does the phrase refer to as a whole? Then find the word in the phrase that expresses that meaning, and that word will be the head. For instance, if you are wondering about which is the head in

My daughter's boots

ask yourself: does the phrase as whole refer to a female human being who is in a particular relation to the speaker or to a type of object? If you are wondering about the head in

Played jazz

think: does the phrase as a whole refer to an activity or to a type of music?

3. The head determines features of the whole phrase or of other phrases linked to it. For instance, in English, the head noun will determine the number

(singular or plural) of determiners that combine with it in the NP, e.g. we say

These/those books

and

This/that book

rather than

*This/that books

or

*These/those book.

We would also say

These books *are* heavy

or

This book *is* heavy

rather than

*These books *is* heavy

or

*This book *are* heavy.

Here, the head of the NP determines the form of the verb. Similarly, the head will determine the gender of other phrases linked to it such as pronouns or determiners, e.g.

My daughter's *son* is dark-haired and *his/*her* eyes are green
My son's *daughter* is dark-haired and **his/her* eyes are green.

Of the syntactic categories introduced in the previous chapter, five can serve as the head of a constituent: a noun heads a Noun Phrase (NP), a verb heads a Verb Phrase (VP), an adjective heads an Adjective Phrase (AP), a preposition heads a Prepositional Phrase (PP), and an adverb heads an Adverb Phrase (AdvP).

Using constituency tests

In applying constituency tests you often have to select the most appropriate forms of the test for the string you are testing. Before you start the testing process, therefore, you are guessing the possible syntactic type of that string. Every time you start testing, you have to ask yourself: if this sequence of words was a phrase, what type of a phrase would it be? It might be a relative probability judgement rather than a firm conviction – more a hunch based on your intuitions as a speaker of the language than something you could prove; nevertheless, it may be enough to get the testing process started. If you have no intuitions about it, then:

- ask yourself what the most probable head of the phrase might be, and decide the type of the phrase on the basis of the syntactic category of the head (see *Using the head* above)
- ask yourself if the string begins with something characteristic of some phrase type. For instance, if it starts with Det, it could only be an NP; if it starts with P it would most likely be a PP; if it starts with Adv it could be VP, PP, AP or AdvP but not NP (see Section 4.5).

Once you have narrowed down the possible phrase types, you can take phrase type into account in the testing. If the test string passes the tests, you will not only know that the string is indeed a phrase but the testing process will have also provided you with further evidence to support your initial guess.

1. **Movement test**: different phrasal types have different possibilities for movement. So, if you are moving a string of words to check if it is a phrase, you will need to use a movement test that is compatible with the type of phrase. Below are the main constructions you can use to test 'movement' possibilities.

For NPs:

(i) Passive: this 'swaps' NPs on either side of a verb, and so allows you to see which words belong to the NP, e.g.

Fred bought *that blue book yesterday* (active)
*[That blue book yesterday] was bought by Fred (passive).

Clearly the whole string does not move, so it is not a phrase. But [*that blue book*] does move in this way:

[That blue book] was bought by Fred yesterday

showing that it is a phrase.

(ii) Cleft: this is a fixed construction that allows us to focus on one part of the sentence, as long as that part forms a constituent; it always takes the form:

It is/was [test string] that ...
It was [that blue book] that I bought yesterday
*It was [that blue book yesterday] that I bought.

(iii) Pseudo-Cleft: another fixed construction that allows you to emphasize one bit of the sentence:

What ... was [test string]
What I bought yesterday was [that blue book]
*What I bought was [that blue book yesterday].

(iv) Topicalization: allows us to focus on the phrase by placing it at the beginning of the sentence, usually for contrastive purposes, e.g.

[That blue book], I bought yesterday (not this one!)
*[That blue book yesterday], I bought.

For PPs:

(i) Cleft: this construction works for strings that are PPs too, i.e.

It is/was [NP or PP] that ...

Compare:

Madge left her purse *in the bank* today
It was [in the bank] that Madge left her purse
*It was [in the bank today] that Madge left her purse.

(ii) Preposing: most prepositional phrases can be placed at the beginning of the sentence *without contrastive emphasis*, e.g.

Madge met Bill in the street *on Sunday.*
[On Sunday] Madge met Bill in the street.

However, some PPs prepose more easily than others, as we will discuss in Chapter 9, e.g.

?[In the street] Madge met Bill on Sunday.

Again, your best bet is to try more than one construction when testing.

(iii) Topicalization:

[In the street], Madge met Bill (not in the cinema!).

For VPs:
The position of VPs if fairly fixed, so movement is not a good way of testing for these.

For APs:
Preposing: you can put the possible AP string at the beginning and then adjust the rest of the sentence for meaning, e.g.

She is *extremely clever*
[Extremely clever] she might be, but she is very immature
*[Clever] she might be extremely, but she is very immature.

For AdvPs:
Preposing: this variation is also possible for AdvPs, with some limitations related to meaning (see Chapter 9), e.g.

He did it on purpose, *quite obviously*
[Quite obviously], he did it on purpose
*[Quite], he did it on purpose, obviously.

2. **Proform test**: this test is especially sensitive to the type of phrase. You should select:

For NPs:
Pronouns like *he/him; she/her; it; they/them*, making sure that the pronoun you select is compatible with the probable head of the phrase in animacy (*s/he* as opposed to *it*), gender (*he* vs *she*), and number (*s/he/it* for singular heads, *they/them* for plural ones), e.g.

My eldest daughter's son is 8 next week but *he/*she/*it* seems much younger
My eldest daughter's sons are 8 next week but *they/*he* seem much younger.

For VPs:
Proverbs like *do/does/did so* or *so do/does/did*, e.g.

Madge *left her purse in the bank* and *so did* Sarah
Madge *did so* too!

For PPs:
This proform substitution is particularly sensitive to meaning. The substitution only works if the PP expresses time or spatial relations. The relevant proforms are *here/there* for spatial prepositions, and *then* for temporal ones, e.g.

Madge put the books *on the shelf*
Madge put the books *there/here*

Madge met Bill in the street *on Sunday*
Madge met Bill in the street *then*.

For APs:
The only proform you can use to substitute or refer back to a string that forms an AP is *it*, which must follow a verb that can take an AP (*feel, appear, seem, sound* ...), e.g.

Madge was *extremely angry*
But she didn't sound *it*!
*But she didn't sound extremely *it*!

For AdvP: The possible substitutions are more limited and complex; you will be better off avoiding this test for AdvPs.

3. **Elliptical answer test:** in applying this test, you will need to formulate particular *Wh*-questions for particular types of potential phrases:

For NPs:
What/Who?

> Q: What did you buy yesterday?
> A: That blue book (*That blue book yesterday).

> Q: Who are you picking up from school?
> A: My eldest daughter's son (*My eldest daughter's, *Daughter's son).

For VPs:
What does/did ... do?

> Q: What did Madge do?
> A: Left her purse in the bank.

For PPs:
Where/When/Why?

> Q: Where did Madge leave her purse?
> A: In the bank (*In, *The bank).

> Q: When did Madge meet Bill in the street?
> A: On Sunday.

> Q: Why did Madge leave her purse in the bank?
> A: By accident, For no good reason, Because of her absent-mindedness.

For APs and AdvPs:
How?

> Q: How did Madge sound?
> A: Extremely angry (AP)

> Q: How did Madge react?
> A: Extremely angrily (AdvP).

4. *And*-**Coordination test:** as we have seen, this test is based on the fact that only phrases can occur on either side of *and*. But they must also be

phrases of the same type, so when you apply the test, you need to choose the right kind of phrase to slot in on either side of *and*. For instance:

For NPs:

I bought [that blue book] and [this lovely dress]
*I bought [that blue book yesterday] and [this lovely dress].

For VPs:

I [love concerts] and [detest parties]

Note that in

I love [concerts] and [parties]

it is two NPs, rather than two VPs, that are coordinated. So be especially careful with VPs where it is easy to confuse coordination of phrases inside the VP with coordination of whole VPs.

For PPs:

Madge met Bill [on Sunday] and [after work].

Again, be careful to distinguish this from coordination of the NPs inside the PP, e.g.

Madge met Bill [on [Sunday and Monday]].

For APs:

Madge is [extremely angry] and [quite fed up].

For AdvPs:

Madge reacted [extremely angrily] and [rather impulsively].

4.5 Types of constituents and their internal structure

All phrases have common characteristics with respect to their internal structure – what can occur inside them. We have already established that the constituent will contain at least a **head**. In addition, the internal structure of a constituent will include:

(a) Any constituents that the head requires, because of its meaning and/or syntactic properties. These constituents combine with the head and are closely linked to it both semantically and syntactically. They are usually called **arguments** or **complements** of the head and are often obligatory – we will discuss them in detail in Chapter 9.

(b) Any optional constituents that are not required by the head. These are usually called **modifiers** which will be discussed in more detail in Chapter 9.

Different types of phrases will contain particular types of complements and adjuncts. We have set out some examples below, to give you an idea of the main patterns. These lists, however, do not cover all the possibilities; more detailed descriptions can be found in the references listed in *Further reading*.

INTERNAL STRUCTURE OF THE NOUN PHRASE (NP)

An NP will contain at least a head noun, e.g.

Mary loves $_{NP}[_N[jazz]]$.

In addition it may contain:

(a) Complement phrases that combine with the head noun, depending on the properties of the head, e.g.

PPs: $_{NP}[the murder _{PP}[of that personality]]$
$_{NP}[his desire _{PP}[for fame]]$
$_{NP}[her trip _{PP}[to Genoa]]$
$_{NP}[their talk _{PP}[with Ken]]$.

(b) Adjuncts. These can be:

APs: $_{NP}[_{AP}[really cool] clothes]$
$_{NP}[_{AP}[very loud] music]$
NPs: $_{NP}[_{NP}[avocado] sandwiches]$
$_{NP}[_{NP}[my daughter's] son]$
$_{NP}[_{NP}[two hour] journey]$

which usually precede the head noun in English. Following the head, you can get adjuncts that are:

PPs: $_{NP}[my cousin _{PP}[in Australia]]$
$_{NP}[sandwiches _{PP}[with avocado]]$
NPs: $_{NP}[that lecture _{NP}[yesterday]]$
$_{NP}[my trip _{NP}[last week]]$.

As we have seen, nouns may also be preceded by:

Determiners: $_{NP}[the books]$
$_{NP}[those blue books]$

Quantifiers: these include numerals (*one, two, forty-two, three hundred* ...) and items such as *many, several, all, every, some*.

INTERNAL STRUCTURE OF THE VERB PHRASE (VP)

A VP will contain at least a head verb, e.g.

Mary $_{VP}$[$_V$[sneezed]]
It $_{VP}$[$_V$[rained]]
Ivan $_{VP}$[$_V$[runs]].

The verb heading the VP has such important consequences for VP structure that we are devoting an entire chapter to this (see Chapter 6). The VP may contain:

(a) A range of complement phrases such as:

NPs: $_{VP}$[bought $_{NP}$[a blue book]]
            $_{VP}$[loves $_{NP}$[jazz]]
            $_{VP}$[posted $_{NP}$[the letter]]
            $_{VP}$[is $_{NP}$[an engineer]]
            $_{VP}$[seems $_{NP}$[a good student]].
PPs: $_{VP}$[went $_{PP}$[to the club]]
            $_{VP}$[talks $_{PP}$[about his feelings]]
            $_{VP}$[argued $_{PP}$[with Tom]]
            $_{VP}$[walked $_{PP}$[across the fields]].
APs: $_{VP}$[is $_{AP}$[rather foolish]]
            $_{VP}$[seems $_{AP}$[fond of his children]]
            $_{VP}$[look $_{AP}$[extremely exhausted]].
AdvPs: $_{VP}$[behaved $_{AdvP}$[badly]]
            $_{VP}$[dresses $_{AdvP}$[very elegantly]].

(b) A range of adjunct phrases such as:

NPs: $_{VP}$[arrived $_{NP}$[last night]]
            $_{VP}$[ran $_{NP}$[two miles]]
            $_{VP}$[left $_{NP}$[yesterday]].
PPs: $_{VP}$[arrived $_{PP}$[at night]]
            $_{VP}$[left $_{PP}$[in the morning]]
            $_{VP}$[ran $_{PP}$[for several hours]]
            $_{VP}$[danced $_{PP}$[in the park]]
            $_{VP}$[spoke $_{PP}$[with deep emotion]].
AdvP: $_{VP}$[$_{AdvP}$[quickly] left]
            $_{VP}$[arrived $_{AdvP}$[hurriedly]]
            $_{VP}$[spoke $_{AdvP}$[well]].

INTERNAL STRUCTURE OF THE ADJECTIVE PHRASE(AP)

An AP will contain at least a head adjective, e.g.

He seemed $_{AP}$[$_A$[happy]]
They are $_{AP}$[$_A$[tired]]

She looks AP[A[bored]]
We are AP[A[tall]].

It may contain:

(a) Complement PPs:

AP[fond PP[of his children]]
AP[angry PP[with Mary]]
AP[afraid PP[of spiders]]
AP[anxious PP[about the exam]].

(b) A range of adjunct phrases such as:

NPs: AP[NP[two inches] thick]
            AP[NP[six hours] long].

AdvPs, especially degree adverbs like *very, quite, rather, incredibly unusually*:

He seemed AP[AdvP[incredibly] happy]
They looked AP[AdvP[really] fit].

INTERNAL STRUCTURE OF THE PREPOSITIONAL PHRASE (PP)

A PP will contain at least a head preposition, e.g.

He walked PP[P[out]]
He fell PP[P[down]]
She looked PP[P[up]]
They ran PP[P[across]].

It may contain:

(a) Complement phrases such as:

NPs: He fell PP[down NP[the stairs]]
            They ran PP[across NP[the road]]
            They met PP[before NP[dinner]].
PPs: He crawled PP[from PP[under the bed]]
            It jumped PP[out PP[of the cupboard]]
            She placed it PP[away PP[from the light]].

(b) Adjunct phrases such as:

NPs: PP[NP[two miles] down the road]
            PP[NP[six hours] after the meeting].
AdvPs: PP[AdvP[completely] out of his mind]
            PP[AdvP[right] down].

INTERNAL STRUCTURE OF THE ADVERB PHRASE (ADVP)

An AdvP will contain at least a head adverb, e.g.

He walked $_{AdvP}[_{Adv}[$fast$]]$.

It may contain:

(a) Complement PPs, though this is more rare than in the case of other phrase types:

$_{AdvP}[$fortunately $_{PP}[$for our hero$]]$
$_{AdvP}[$unusually $_{PP}[$for Sarah$]]$.

(b) Adjunct phrases, especially other AdvPs expressing degree:

He walked $_{AdvP}[_{AdvP}[$very$]$ fast$]$.

As you have worked through the internal structure of the different phrase types, you might have noticed that, irrespective of the phrase type, the head of a phrase always precedes any complement phrase. This is a characteristic of many languages like English, while in many other languages complement phrases come before the head. Instead of saying, for instance,

[likes [jazz]]
[down [the road]]

you would be saying the equivalent of

[[jazz] likes]
[[the road] down].

Whereas complement phrases are quite restricted in their order with respect to the head, adjuncts are freer to occur before or after the head (see Chapter 9, Section 9.3).

4.6 Analytical tips

Checking your hunches

We have seen that the process of identifying the type of phrase you are dealing with starts with a hunch. But hunches are sometimes fuzzy and sometimes wrong. For example, when people begin linguistics, they often find it difficult to decide whether a string of words like

My wonderful cousin in Australia

is an NP or an AP – that is, they are uncertain as to whether the head is *wonderful* or *cousin*. Knowing that the string begins with the Det *my* should be enough to decide: only NPs begin with Det, therefore the string must be an NP. Alternatively, or in addition, you could reason like this:

- Movement test possibilities:
  If it is an NP, it should fit in a Cleft. If it passes the test, it is likely to be NP.
    Check the test:

  It was [my wonderful cousin in Australia] that sent me the present.

  The result is good, therefore the string is not only a single phrase but is also likely to be an NP.
- Proform substitution possibilities:
  If it is an NP, it should be substitutable by *he* or *she*, not *it* because *cousin* refers to an animate being, a person. If it were an AP, we should be able to substitute the proform *it*, since *it* is the proform for APs.
    Check the substitution possibilities:

  She/He sent me the present
  *It sent me the present.

  Only *she/he* are possible substitutes, so the string must be an NP.
- Elliptical answer possibilities:
  If the whole string is an NP rather than an AP, then it should work as an elliptical answer to a *What/Who* question.
    Check the test:

    Q: Who sent me a present?
    A: My wonderful cousin in Australia.

  Note that you might be able to formulate a *How* question that you could answer with just the AP *wonderful* but you are unlikely to find a *How* question that can be answered with the whole string [my wonderful cousin in Australia].

This example shows how your initial hunches can – and should – be checked out against the evidence.

How much evidence?

But how much evidence do we need? Do we need to try every test for a particular phrasal type? And does the constituent need to pass every test to qualify? The answer to these questions is that constituent categories are not absolutely uniform, and the use of tests is not an all-or-nothing affair:

- Some tests are widely applicable and highly reliable. For example, we can refer back to (almost) any NP or VP using a proform, so this is a powerful test for these phrasal categories.

- Some tests apply to a constituent only in certain positions. For example, the passive only affects NPs before and after the verb, so can only be used where the string we are testing is in one of these positions:

[The fan] approached [the filmstar]

can be passivized by 'swapping round' the two constituents:

[The filmstar] was approached [by the fan]

proving that they are NPs.
- Some tests apply only in certain semantic contexts. For example, the passive does not apply with *be*-type verbs, e.g.

[Alice] became [an engineer]
*[An engineer] was become [by Alice].

So passive cannot be used to identify NPs in these contexts. In fact NPs following this category of verbs do not comfortably pass other NP tests:

Cleft: It's an engineer that Alice became   (not too good)
Pseudocleft: What Alice became is an engineer   (better)
Pronoun substitution: Alice became it   (not acceptable)
                     Alice became one   (much better).

What definitely marks this constituent out as an NP is its internal structure: it begins with a determiner *a* and has a noun *engineer* as its head. Since this internal structure is not compatible with any other phrasal type, we must be dealing with an NP – but it is atypical in that it fails many of the NP tests.

What these examples illustrate is that the categorization of a phrase is only as strong as the evidence we find for it. At the minimum

- the head of the phrase must match the phrasal type;
- the phrase must not pass tests that apply to other phrasal types.

In most cases, though, phrases will pass many if not all tests for their type, and the evidence will leave us in no doubt.

4.7 Links to other levels

Semantics

Just like the lexical categories on which they are based, constituents are defined by their syntactic properties, but these syntactic properties show some correspondence with semantic properties.

1. Words that act as a unit syntactically also act as a unit semantically: they refer to a conceptual category as a whole. Consider the following example:

She ate the cherry on the cake.

Here, *the cherry on the cake* forms a constituent. You might check this using the movement and proform tests:

Cleft:	It's the cherry on the cake that she ate
	*It's the cherry that she ate on the cake.
Proform:	She ate it
	*She ate it on the cake.

As a constituent, *the cherry on the cake* refers to a conceptual category as a whole: a 'thing'. Compare the sentence:

She put the cherry on the cake.

This contains the same sequence of words. But in this case, they cannot be moved or replaced as a group:

| Topicalization: | *The cherry on the cake, she put |
| Proform: | *She put it. |

Instead, they make up two separate constituents:

She put [the cherry] [on the cake]

which can be moved and replaced independently of the other:

Topicalization:	The cherry, she put on the cake
	On the cake, she put the cherry
Proform:	She put it there.

As two separate constituents, each refers to a separate conceptual category: *the cherry* on its own refers to a 'thing', while *on the cake* refers to a 'place'.

2. The head of the constituent determines the type of conceptual category it conveys. Recall that nouns typically represent things and people, but that they can also represent places and events (see Chapter 3, Section 3.5). Whatever

the conceptual category it conveys, a noun will pass this on to the NP it heads. This is illustrated in the following three sentences which contain structurally identical NPs differing only in their head noun:

		head noun ↓			constituent refers to ↓
I hated	_{NP}[that awful	mirror	in the lift]	→	thing
I hated	_{NP}[that awful	feeling	in the lift]	→	state
I hated	_{NP}[that awful	accident	in the lift]	→	event.

As you can see, the meaning of the head noun determines what the NP refers to.

So, if you are not sure which word is the head of a constituent, one way to check this out is to identify what the constituent as a whole refers to, and find the word which carries this meaning.

3. What about the other elements in the phrase apart from the head? Semantically, these serve to modify the head: they give more information about it. Take our example:

She ate [the cherry on the cake].

We have seen that the constituent as a whole refers to a 'thing'. This is because its head, *cherry*, refers to a 'thing'. The PP *on the cake*, which is part of the constituent, contributes to our identification of that thing. It tells us *which* cherry she ate. In later chapters, we will be exploring the different types of modification conveyed by constituent structure.

4. The hierarchical structure of the sentence at the syntactic level is mirrored by the semantic level. Our interpretation of *She ate the cherry on the cake* bears witness to this. Syntactically, the constituent *cherry on the cake* contains a further constituent:

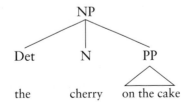

The embedded PP *on the cake* conveys a conceptual category in its own right. It refers to a 'location'. So, corresponding to the syntactic structure, we have a 'location' which is embedded in a 'thing' (see (3) above). The higher constituent, and the 'thing' to which it refers, is embedded within a still larger constituent.

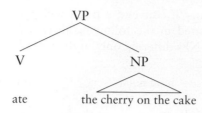

VP

V   NP

ate   the cherry on the cake

Semantically, we now have a 'thing' embedded within an 'event'.

Phonology

The hierarchical structure of the sentence has phonological correlates as well. When we looked at syntactic categories, we saw that the final stressed word in the sentence carries the greatest stress. But this is not the whole story. We do not make a simple two-way distinction between the last stressed word and all others within the sentence. Sentences have a complex rhythmic pattern, and this reflects their syntactic organization. Within each constituent, certain syntactic categories carry stress (see Chapter 14, Section 14.3), but the final one of these carries the main stress. So, if *the cherry on the cake* is a constituent, *cherry* and *cake* both receive lexical (word) stress, but only *cake* carries constituent stress. We can represent this stress pattern using a cross to mark each level of stress:

```
Constituent stress:                        ×
Lexical stress:         ×       ×          ×
             She ate [the cherry on the cake]
```

As the final stressed category in the sentence, *cake* also carries the sentence stress. You might check this out by saying this sentence aloud. You should find that *cake* is the most prominent word in the sentence.

Now compare the sentence where *the cherry* and *on the cake* are separate constituents. Here, both *cherry* and *cake* receive constituent stress:

```
Constituent stress:              ×         ×
Lexical stress:         ×        ×         ×
             She put [the cherry] [on the cake]
```

In addition, *cake* carries the sentence stress:

```
Sentence stress                            ×
Constituent stress:              ×         ×
Lexical stress:         ×        ×         ×
             She put [the cherry] [on the cake]
```

Again, you can check this against your intuitions. You should find that *cherry* is more stressed than in the contrasting sentence.

Thus, the units we identified on syntactic grounds find an echo in the rhythmic organization of the sentence.

Exercises

1. Decide whether the sequences of words in bold form a phrase (constituent) or not. Use the constituency tests you were given and your intuitions about meaning.

    1. **My friend in Granada** invited me over.
    2. **Suddenly it** started to rain.
    3. I'm **very fond of Sally**.
    4. I took **off my hat**.
    5. I went **up the stairs**.
    6. She bought **it yesterday** in that shop.
    7. They built **the house in a hurry**.
    8. They own **a house with a large garden**.
    9. She cut **the cloth with the scissors**.
    10. She cut **the cloth with the stripes**.
    11. He fell **off the bike**.
    12. He wrote **off the bike**.

2. The following sentences were produced by a child with language impairment. Decide whether the sequences of words in bold form a phrase (constituent) or not. Use the constituency tests you were given and your intuitions about the intended target and its meaning.

    1. **David be** school. 2. I love **my friend**. 3. **You know** Martha? 4. Mimi eat **upstairs dinner time**. 5. **Big boys** like coffee. 6. We got **Ribena today**. 7. He **our class** Monday. 8. Frida bring **him home**.

3. Imagine you are assessing a child with specific language impairment. You are told that she tends to omit determiners after a preposition if the P, Det and N form a phrase. If the Det only follows the P but is not part of the same PP, she produces the determiner, e.g. she would say:

    The boy sat on chair   but   *The boy rang up his friend.*

    Give five examples where she would produce the determiner and 5 where she would not. Justify your choice of examples with appropriate constituency tests.

4. For each of the underlined sequences in the sentences below, identify the syntactic type of the phrase and the head and give arguments for your decisions.

1. I want <u>a long holiday</u>.
2. That man can walk <u>on a tightrope</u>.
3. I <u>admire her novels</u>.
4. He sniggered <u>rather obviously</u>.
5. I have not seen <u>my friend from college</u> in a while.
6. Tom was eating <u>an extraordinarily thick sandwich</u>.

|5|

Representing structure

5.1 Brackets, trees and other devices

So far, we have mainly used brackets to show the constituent structure of phrases. For instance, to show the different constituent structure of sentences like

(a) She cut _{NP}[the cloth _{PP}[with the stripes]]
(b) She cut _{NP}[the cloth] _{PP}[with the scissors]

we have bracketed together *the cloth* and the PP in (a), and kept *the cloth* separate from the PP in (b). In (a), the PP is part of the larger NP, which is indicated by having one set of square brackets contained within another set. In (b), however, the NP only contains *the cloth* and the PP has its own separate set of brackets. The brackets mark out the hierarchical structure in the sense that everything within a pair of square brackets is part of a constituent. The label at the foot of the first left bracket tells you the type of constituent. Glance through the previous chapter again, especially Section 4.5, and you will see many examples of this use of brackets.

Because we were mostly interested in marking out the main constituent boundaries, we did not show all the structural details, i.e.

(a) [the cloth [with [the stripes]]]
(b) [the cloth] [with [the scissors]].

In both cases, the PP contains an NP. We could have also spelt out the syntactic category of the words in the brackets like this:

(a) [Det N [P [Det N]]]
(b) [Det N] [P [Det N]].

Now the similarities and differences between the two sequences are brought out even more starkly: it is purely a difference in constituent structure indicated by the position of a right bracket to close off the NP. In (a), it comes at the end of the whole sequence, while in (b) it comes after the first N. Everything else is exactly the same.

Using labelled brackets is one way of representing structure. Another way of presenting exactly the same information is by means of **tree diagrams** – something very similar to family trees. In this format, being part of a constituent is symbolized by being a branch attached to a particular label (a node) in the tree, e.g.

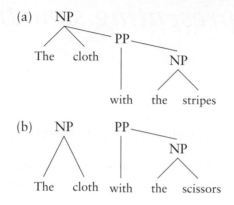

In (a) all the words in the sequence are attached to branches that either link up directly to the top NP (*the, cloth*) or link to the NP via other branches (*the* and *stripes* via NP; that NP and *with* via the PP which is the third branch of the top NP).

In (b), on the other hand, nothing joins together the NP and PP: there is no 'parent' node from which both originate. We could also show the syntactic category of the words by adding another layer to the tree:

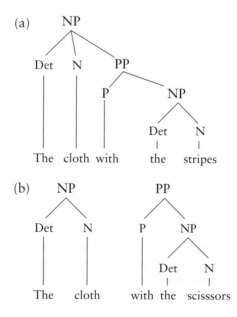

Again, the tree diagrams allow us to represent explicitly similarities and differences between the two sequences. But what about the verb *cut* and the verb phrase that goes with it? We can either add another pair of labelled brackets around the whole string:

(a) VP[V NP[Det N PP[P [Det N]]]]
(b) VP[V NP[Det N] PP[P [Det N]]]

or add a new 'parent' node higher up the tree:

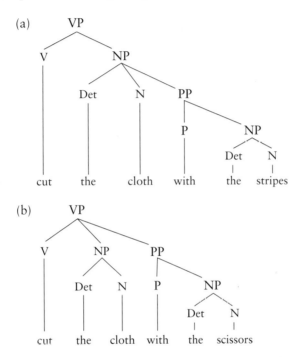

Note how only two branches originate from the VP in (a), whereas there are three branches coming out of the VP in (b). This precisely captures the difference in number of constituents within the two verb phrases, reflecting appropriately the differences in meaning. [*With the stripes*] tells you something about the cloth, while [*with the scissors*] tells you which instrument was employed in cutting.

Both methods for representing structure allow us to indicate linear order as well. The left-to-right order of symbols in the brackets or in the trees mirrors the order of spoken or written elements in a language. For instance, since in English we say *the cloth* rather than *cloth the*, we show the structure of an NP as:

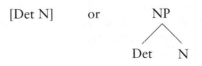

rather than:

*[N Det]   or   *NP

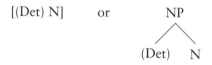

N   Det

Another device often used in representing linguistic structure is round brackets to indicate that the word or phrase in brackets is optional – it may occur but does not have to be there. So, the fact that many NPs in English are well-formed without a Det is reflected in representations of the structure of NPs in English such as:

[(Det) N]   or   NP

(Det)   N

Curly brackets are used in both types of diagrams to indicate mutually exclusive alternatives. For instance, the following diagrams:

[V {NP}]   or   VP
   {PP}

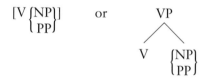

V   {NP}
           {PP}

would be interpreted to mean that a particular VP contains either an NP or PP after the verb – only one of those alternatives is possible at that point in the structure but not both.

As we have seen above, when representing structure we can choose the amount of detail we put in. It all depends on what we are focusing on and why we are analysing a sentence. For instance, if we were discussing the phrases that combine with the verb in the verb phrases

(a) cut the cloth with the stripes
(b) cut the cloth with the scissors

we might represent them as simply:

(a) [V NP]   (b) [V NP PP]

without bothering to show what each NP or PP is made up of – we would just ignore their internal structure. Similarly, linguists often use a triangle in a tree to indicate that all the words along the base of the triangle are part of a particular phrase but the internal structure of the phrase is irrelevant at that point in the analysis, e.g.

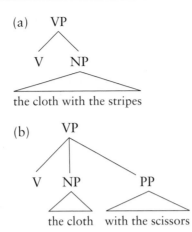

(a) VP

V   NP

the cloth with the stripes

(b) VP

V   NP   PP

the cloth   with the scissors

Many more representational devices and conventions, as well as discussion of the formal systems used in representing language, can be found in *Further reading*. For a summary of notational devices, see Box 5.2 at the end of this chapter.

5.2 Why do we need diagrams?

There are two main reasons for using diagrams in clinical practice: to reveal significant patterns in the data as clearly as possible, and to facilitate the construction of assessment and therapy materials. Let's consider each of these reasons in turn.

As we have already shown, the data you collect from clients must undergo a process of analysis that allows you to move from the specific (e.g. individual words and combinations of words) to the general (e.g. combinations of syntactic categories representing types of words and phrases). In order to reveal and keep track of significant patterns in the data, you will need different ways of displaying the linguistic data you have analysed – for other kinds of data you may use graphs, pie charts, histograms or tables.

For example, many aspects of the utterances produced by Mark, the child described in Exercise 7, Chapter 3, could be summarized by means of a single statement using labelled brackets or tree diagrams. You could say that most of his verb phrases have the structure:

$$_{VP}[V\left(\left\{\begin{matrix}PP\\NP\end{matrix}\right\}\right)]$$

VP

V $\left(\left\{\begin{matrix}PP\\NP\end{matrix}\right\}\right)$

This makes it clear that, although he talks quite a bit, the structure of what he says is very limited, especially in comparison with the kind of structures you might expect from an 8-year-old doing similar tasks. A typical 8-year-old would produce verb phrases that contain not only a greater range of phrases but also a greater number of phrases in combination with a verb. Summarizing and displaying the data you have analysed in this way allows you to pinpoint some of Mark's abilities and weaknesses, as well as making comparisons with other children much easier and more specific.

Imagine you wanted to investigate Mark's problems further. You might want to check whether he can repeat verb phrases with a more complex syntactic structure, even though he does not produce them spontaneously. You could use another set of diagrams to specify the structure of the stimuli you may use in your repetition task. For instance, you may decide that the verb phrases in the stimulus sentences should all be:

$$_{VP}[V\ NP\ PP]; \quad _{VP}[V\ AP\ PP]; \quad _{VP}[V\ PP\ PP]; \quad _{VP}[V\ AdvP\ PP]$$

so that you would be assessing his ability to repeat verb phrases containing two rather than only one phrase after the verb, as well as a greater variety of phrases (APs and AdvPs as well as NPs and PPs). Using category symbols and diagrams like this has several advantages. First, it helps you see clearly what linguistic variables you are manipulating, what other variations you might want to employ and what possibilities you are leaving out. You are therefore more likely to select your test sentences appropriately and accurately. This, in turn, will improve the overall design of your task and make analysis of the results quicker and easier. Finally, it will be much easier to come back to those materials later, when you might want to adapt them for therapy purposes: you will not have to reconstruct your thinking out of vague memories and imprecise notes – the structural features of the test sentences will remain clearly spelt out in the diagrams.

Would plain old English words not do just as well? In some cases they might, especially when people are very experienced and can describe the patterns they are interested in very precisely. But it is very easy to make errors when you are thinking up stimuli for a task as you are usually trying to juggle different factors – you may be trying to select your sentences in terms of both structure and meaning. The more checks and balances you build into the process, the less likely you are to find yourself with a task that does not test what you wanted to test, or that has uninterpretable results (see also *Analytical tips*).

5.3 Defining structural relations

Some structural relations between phrases can be defined more easily in terms of relations between labelled nodes in a tree diagram. One such relation, which is particularly important in linguistic descriptions, is that of **domination**. We can define it as follows:

Domination: a node X dominates another node Y if and only if there is a downward path (a branch) from X to Y and not vice versa.

If we apply this definition to the (a) tree we have discussed above

(a)
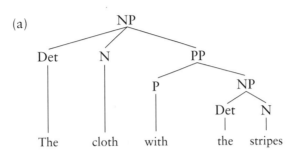

we can say that the top NP dominates not only Det, N, and PP but also all the other nodes 'below' it that are connected to it by a branch or sequence of branches, e.g. the noun *stripes*, as there is a downward path from the top NP to PP to the NP branching off PP to the N *stripes*.

Having defined domination, we can now define the constituent or phrase more precisely:

Phrase or Constituent: a string of items (one or more items) dominated by the same node. The dominating node dominates that string and nothing else.

Consider the tree diagram (a) above: all the elements in the string *the cloth with the stripes* are dominated by the top NP and therefore meet the definition of constituent. The top NP does not dominate anything else beside *the cloth with the stripes*.

The definition we have arrived at picks out precisely the sequences that behave as units on the basis of constituency tests: not only the whole sequence *the cloth with the stripes* but also *the stripes* and *with the stripes*. Compare the (a) tree diagram and (b):

(b)
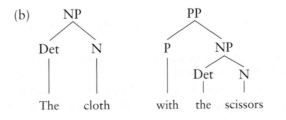

Here the sequence *the cloth with the scissors*, which can be shown not to behave as a unit in terms of constituency tests, does not meet the definition of constituent either since there is no single node that dominates both the top NP and the top PP. What if we took the VP into account, so that the tree was:

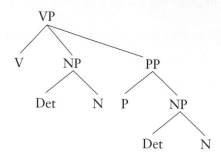

Then, you might want to say, there is a single 'parent' node that dominates both NP and PP since there is a branch from VP to NP and from VP to PP. This is why we have a second part to our definition: the VP does dominate both NP and PP but not exclusively since it also dominates V. So, only the three elements V, NP and PP together are represented as a single constituent – not just NP and PP by themselves.

As we will see in the next chapter, we often need to describe relationships or interactions between nodes 'at the same level' of structure. To do this, it is useful to define a subtype of domination, **immediate domination**:

Immediate domination: a node X immediately dominates a node Y if X dominates Y and there is no intervening node between them.

Applying this definition to the VP tree above, we can say that VP immediately dominates V, NP and PP as it dominates each of them and there is no other node intervening between VP and each of the three nodes. On the other hand, VP dominates but does not immediately dominate Det and N because the node NP intervenes between VP and these two nodes. In other words, immediate domination is like a child–parent relationship, while domination can go back several generations of grandparents. Many important linguistic relations hold between nodes that have the same parent node, and linguists often refer to these as sister nodes.

5.4 The general structure of phrases

So we now have a **set of tests** we can apply to decide whether a sequence of words forms a constituent and to justify our analysis; a **method of representing** constituency structure and relations between elements of the structure and a **definition** of the concept of constituent or phrase. Bringing together what we have seen so far, we can also represent more generally the minimal structure of all phrases as:

$$_{XP}[... \ X \ ...] \qquad \text{or} \qquad \begin{matrix} XP \\ | \\ X \end{matrix}$$

where X can be any one of the categories N, V, A, P or Adv.

These diagrams represent explicitly what we said in Section 4.4 of the previous chapter: all phrases must have at least a head of the same type as the phrase. If the syntactic category of the head is N, the type of the phrase will be NP; if the head is V, the phrase is VP, and so on for the other categories A, P, and Adv. Our syntactic descriptions, therefore, make use of two main types of syntactic categories: those of the individual words that head the phrase (**lexical syntactic categories** such as N, V, A, P, Adv) and those that indicate the type of the phrase (**phrasal syntactic categories** such as NP, VP, AP, PP, AdvP).

All the phrases we discussed above conform to this template. For instance, the noun phrase *the cloth with the stripes* has an obligatory head N (*cloth*) and could be stripped down to this minimal structure, e.g.

All the other elements in it are optional: not only can you have just the head *cloth* as in 'This is made of [cloth]', but you could have just Det N as in 'I cut [the cloth]', or just the head and the PP as in 'I bought [cloth with stripes]'.

Can we say anything more about the structure of phrases that applies to all phrases irrespective of their type? If you look back at Section 4.5 of the previous chapter, you will see that, apart from the head, each phrase could contain:

(a) **arguments or complements of the head** – phrases of different types that are most closely related to the head, both syntactically and semantically.
(b) **specifiers and modifiers** – items or phrases that precede or follow the head and its complements, and add information about these.

So if we abstract away from the particular types of complements, modifiers and specifiers that occur in particular types of phrases, we could represent the overall structure of all phrases as:

_{XP}[(Specifiers) Head (Complements) (Modifiers)]

or

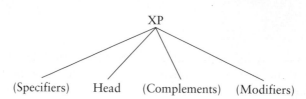

This constitutes a general schema or template that tells us what we can expect in a phrase. It is a hypothesis about the general structure of phrases in all languages, though languages select particular types and numbers of specifiers, modifiers and complements. Each language works from the same phrasal 'recipe' but varies the ingredients and their quantities. The relative order of these elements will also vary depending on the language. For instance, as we have already seen in Chapter 4, Section 4.5, in English a modifier AP comes before the head N it modifies, while in Italian it can occur before or after the head, e.g.

English: [[old] friends]   *[friends [old]]
Italian: [[vecchi] amici]   [amici [vecchi]].

Most of the diagrams you will see and work with do not actually include labels like Specifier, Modifier, Head or Complement. These labels do not usually figure in bracketed or tree diagrams when you are analysing and representing the syntactic structure of particular phrases. For instance, if you were analysing syntactically *the cloth with the stripes*, you would usually draw a tree like (a) above, i.e.

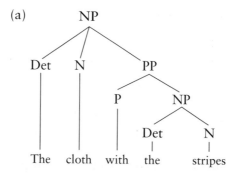

without any other labelling.

Labels like Specifier, Modifier, Head or Complement are more like 'placeholders' that remind us of what, in general, can or must occur in a phrase.

They also act as a bridge between syntactic structure and meaning in two main ways: first, they express the fact that phrases of different syntactic types can contribute to the meaning of the whole phrase in similar ways. For instance, prepositional phrases and adverb phrases can both function as modifiers expressing the manner in which an action is carried out, e.g.

Deborah left ₚₚ[in a hurry]/_AdvP_[hurriedly]
         ₚₚ[without a word]/_AdvP_[silently].

Conversely, phrases of the same syntactic type, or even the very same phrase, can contribute very differently to the meaning of a larger phrase depending on whether they are interpreted as complements or modifiers of the head, as an unfortunate sign in a London chemist's window shows:

We dispense [with accuracy].

Here, the PP *with accuracy* could be interpreted as what the chemist is doing without (i.e. as a complement of the verb that heads the verb phrase) or as a manner in which they dispense medicines (i.e. as a modifier), with quite different practical implications for potential clients!

Second, these labels pick out aspects of meaning that have wide-ranging syntactic consequences, as we will see in Chapter 9 (see also Box 5.1).

Box 5.1 How hierarchical is hierarchical structure?

The careful reader might be wondering about the constituency structure of the phrasal template we have discussed. All the elements of a phrase were represented as being equally related – all sisters of the same parent node XP.

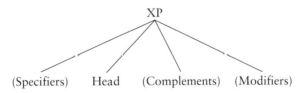

(Specifiers)   Head   (Complements)   (Modifiers)

Yet we talked about the complements being more closely related to the head both syntactically and semantically. Shouldn't this greater closeness be represented explicitly in the structural representation? And what about our hints that being a modifier as opposed to a complement has syntactic consequences – why are we not representing those consequences?

You would be entirely right in wondering! Our template left something out: some of the sisters should have been represented as closer to
(continued)

the head than others. To be consistent with what we have said, we should have at least represented the hierarchical structure as:

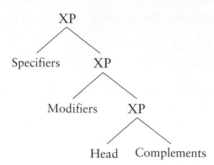

with additional 'layers' of structure marking out 'intermediate' sub-constituents of the same syntactic type as the head and the phrase as a whole. This is indeed what most linguistic theories assume – it is often referred to as X-bar syntax (see *Further reading*). Let's draw out the implications of what we have said so far to clarify the need for a more layered phrasal structure.

We have seen that the same syntactic type of phrase can be a complement or a modifier, e.g. the italic phrases below are both NPs:

Bill drinks ~NP~[*Australian wine*]
Bill drinks ~NP~[*every night*].

With the 'flat' structures we have been assuming, we have little choice but to attach them both as sisters of the V in the VP. Indeed both are included in the meaning of a VP-proform like *do so*, as the patterns of grammatical and ungrammatical sentences below show:

Bill drinks ~NP~[*Australian wine*] and so does Tom
*Bill drinks ~NP~[*Australian wine*] and so does Tom ~NP~[*German beer*]
Bill drinks ~NP~[*every night*] and so does Tom.

Note, however, that

Bill drinks ~NP~[*every night*] and Tom does so ~NP~[*every morning*]

is possible, creating a paradox: a modifier phrase like the NP [*every night*] can be shown to both occur in the VP and be outside it. The same problem arises in relation to most modifier phrases in VPs, no matter what their meaning might be, e.g.

(continued)

John changed his shirt [*at work*] and Bill did so [*at the gym*]
Paula collects the children from school [*on Thursdays*] and Tom does
so [*on Mondays*].

The more 'layered' structure allows us to resolve the paradox rather
elegantly since phrases that are modifiers can now be attached at a different level of structure but still within the same syntactic type of constituent, e.g.

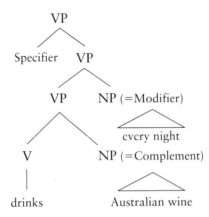

This type of structure neatly captures the closer relations between a
head and its complements (e.g. the verb *drinks* and the NP *Australian
wine*) which are sisters and share a common parent node – the lowest
VP node. The relation between the modifier NP *every night* and the verb,
on the other hand, is more indirect, since the modifier NP is the sister
of the whole VP [*drinks Australian wine*] rather than just the verb *drinks*.
This is exactly what we would want from a semantic point of view: the
modifier NP tells us about the frequency of the action of drinking
Australian wine, not just of drinking. It is the whole VP that is modified by the NP. Thus the syntax mirrors more accurately the meaning –
an obvious advantage of X-bar syntax.

This type of 'layered' phrase structure is the logical outcome of the
arguments we have used in Chapter 4 to justify hierarchical structure in
the first place. Just think about the movement argument: we saw that
phrases in different constituents are more independent of each other –
they don't have to move together. If both NPs were in the same VP constituent, we would expect them to behave similarly and be equally
dependent on the verb. But they are not, as the modifier NP can move
away from the verb more easily than the complement NP, e.g.

Every night Bill drinks Australian wine

(continued)

is just as acceptable as:

Bill drinks Australian wine every night

but

*Australian wine Bill drinks every night

said with neutral intonation (without a comma after *wine*) is probably out or at least much worse than the other two sentences. The proform argument too, as we have just seen, leads us to similar conclusions. And so does the argument based on structural ambiguities: without this 'layered' structure we would not be able to represent the two meanings of the chemist's sign:

We dispense with accuracy.

We could not capture the two interpretations with the 'flatter' structure because there would be only one VP and therefore one possible attachment of the PP within it, irrespective of the meaning. With X-bar syntax, however, each meaning is mirrored in the different attachments of the PP. For the reading where the chemist is doing away with accuracy, the PP will be attached to the lowest VP as sister of the V – its complement:

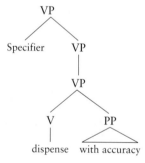

while the reading where the chemist is dispensing accurately can be represented as:

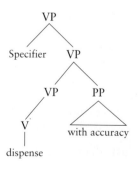

(continued)

We will assume X-bar syntax throughout this book – the arguments for it are strong. Furthermore, as we will show, the distinction between modifiers and complements is of psycholinguistic and clinical importance (see Chapter 9). But we will keep this syntactic assumption in the background and continue to use 'flatter' trees to make representation as simple as possible. We do not want unwieldy trees to block your view of linguistics.

5.5 Analytical tips

When we learn a particular skill, we inevitably go through a phase where the mechanics of the skill seem more important than what we are learning the skill for. This always happens when people start to analyse syntactic structure and represent it with structural diagrams – they literally can't see the wood for the trees. So here are some things you should keep in mind:

- Draw diagrams only for those aspects of the data, or task stimuli, you are interested in. For instance, if you are making up sentences for a therapy task and you just want them to contain verb phrases with a verb and a noun phrase, you might not care how the noun phrases themselves are structured. So you might use as your structural pattern something like [V NP] without worrying about the contents of the NP, or controlling only for the number of words occurring in the NP rather than the types of categories within it.
- Spend more time on the evidence for an analysis than on the representation. Make sure you can first justify your analysis with appropriate syntactic tests (e.g. category and/or constituency tests) before you draw any diagrams. The diagrams are simply a convenient way of displaying, or summarizing, the results of your analysis – don't let your analysis be guided by your sense of what 'looks better' in a tree.
- Use whatever method of representation is most appropriate and convenient for what you are doing. For instance, if the constituency structure of a phrase is very complex in that it involves several phrases, which in turn contain other phrases, you might find tree diagrams easier to draw and interpret than bracketed diagrams. On the other hand, if the hierarchical structure is simpler but the number of phrases is larger, bracketing would probably be better.
- Don't try to represent everything in one go. Sometimes it is easier to analyse and represent the structures a person can produce and then those they omit or have difficulties with. For instance, when you are looking at the data in terms of what the person *can* produce, you might want to represent the fact that someone produces NPs in VPs even though they omit

required prepositions, with a consequent loss of the prepositional phrases, e.g.

put my cup that box as $_{VP}[V \ _{NP}[Det \ N] \ _{NP}[Det \ N]]$.

On the other hand, if the main focus of your analysis is what the person is *omitting* or *producing incorrectly*, then you might want to represent the probable target with the omissions or errors marked in, e.g.

$_{VP}[V \ _{NP}[Det \ N] \ _{PP}[*P \ _{NP}[Det \ N]]]$.

You can decide which method suits your purposes better at any one time – just make sure you use the method consistently and you are clear about what you are doing.

- If you are using diagrams to guide the selection of stimuli for an assessment or therapy task, make sure that, at the end, you check all the stimuli again against the pattern you have used.

    For instance, it is very common for beginners to start out with a structural pattern such as:

$_{VP}[V \ NP \ PP]$

and end up with sentences like:

She [bought a bag with a shoulder strap]

where there is indeed a PP but following the head N inside the NP, rather than as a separate PP following the whole NP – i.e. at the relevant level of analysis the verb phrase has the structure $_{VP}[V \ NP]$. In this case, the types of categories involved are correct but the constituency structure is not.

- Pay particular attention to the main constituents and their relations. If you do not know the syntactic category of some words, don't let that get in the way of your overall analysis. For instance, if you can't decide what category the word *several* is in

Gina bought several bags with shoulder straps

just apply the constituency tests to see whether it forms a constituent with *bags with shoulder straps* or not; then draw the tree accordingly, leaving out the syntactic category label for *several*.

- Try to bring out general patterns by drawing together into a single diagram, or a small set of diagrams, the syntactic analysis of individual utterances. For instance, if a child produces nouns phrases with:

[Det N]; [AP N]; [N PP]

you could reduce these three patterns to one general pattern such as:

$_{NP}[(Det) \ (AP) \ N \ (PP)]$

using some of the representational devices we have discussed. But if there is no evidence in the data that the child can produce the whole sequence, e.g.

the large bag with a shoulder strap

keep the different patterns separate or only combine those you have evidence for. Otherwise, you would attribute too much structural complexity to the child's utterances.

5.6 Links to other levels

In this chapter, we have focused on the representation of syntactic information. It is important to remember that the representation is not to be confused with the information represented. When students find phrase structure trees cropping up all over their linguistics notes and textbooks, and start using trees in sentence analysis, they often assume that syntax means trees, or even more extremely, that linguistics means trees. Neither of these assumptions is correct. Trees – as well as bracketing – are simply a means of depicting hierarchical relations. If you looked at a tree before starting linguistics, you would probably assume that it represented a family structure. This is because the family tree is the most familiar use of this form, in this case to represent hierarchical relations in kinship.

Trees and bracketing are useful for representing hierarchical relations at other levels of language apart from syntax. In phonology, for example, trees or bracketing can be used to show how syllables are organized into words. This is illustrated by the bracketing of syllables for the word *crocodile*:

[[krɒ] kə] [daɪl]

Here, /krɒ/ and /kə/ group together to form a phonological constituent known as a foot. This foot /krɒkə/ groups together with /daɪl/, another foot, to form the word.

Taking this even further, trees or bracketing can be used to represent the internal structure of each syllable. The syllable consists of at least a vowel, and this combines with any following consonants, known as the coda, to form a rime:

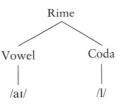

Any consonants preceding the vowel form the onset, and this combines with the rime to form the syllable:

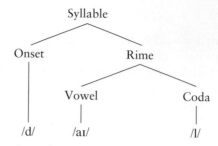

See Gussenhoven and Jacobs (1998) for more on the representation of hierarchical structure in lexical phonology.

Our final example involves the internal structure of words. Trees and bracketing can be used to represent the way words can combine with smaller meaning units like suffixes to create new words. For example, the suffix *-al* can be added to a noun to produce an adjective:

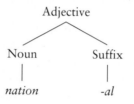

to which *-ize* can be added to form a verb:

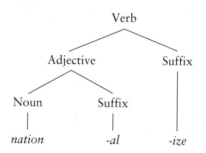

to which *-ation* can be added to form a different noun:

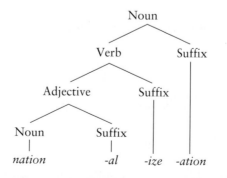

The same morphological organization could be conveyed by bracketing:

_N[_V[_A[_N[nation] al] ize] ation].

Box 5.2 Summary of main notational devices in syntax and semantics

*   The item is not well-formed.
??   The item is of borderline grammaticality or acceptability.
[ ]   Marks phrase boundaries: everything within the brackets is part of the constituent.
( )   Marks optionality of the item(s) within brackets.
{ }   Marks mutually exclusive alternatives: either one or the other but not both.

Exercises

1. For each of the following phrases, identify its phrasal type and its head; then draw a tree diagram or use brackets to show its structure. Make sure you can justify your decisions by reference to the relevant linguistic tests.

   1. A wonderful trip. 2. bores me to death. 3. absurdly jealous. 4. completely over the top. 5. in a jam. 6. an incredible traffic jam. 7. quickly left the room. 8. quite disgracefully. 9. on a bumpy road. 10. across the fields. 11. with great joy. 12. especially annoying. 13. is very grumpy. 14. that very grumpy clerk.

2. The utterances below were produced by a child with language impairment – you have already worked on them in Exercise 2, Chapter 4. Identify all the NPs he has produced and then say which of those NPs might have been intended as a different phrase, e.g. a PP. Choose your own way of representing what the child has omitted.

   Make sure you compare your analysis with that you worked out for the exercise in Chapter 4, checking that they are compatible.

   1. David be school. 2. Mimi eat upstairs dinner time. 3. Big boys like coffee. 4. We got Ribena today. 5. Frida bring him home.

3. Imagine you want to construct a reading task for a man with aphasia who can read adjectives in APs within VPs but not when the AP is within NP. In other words, he can read the A in [V AP] but not in [(Det) AP N]. Make up 12 sentences to check out this pattern of reading impairment. Apart from the structure of the sentences, what other factors would you take into account to make the contrasting sentences as comparable as possible?

When you are satisfied with your stimuli sentences, give them to a friend to read aloud to check that there are no unforeseen problems with your task – there often are, so it's good to pilot tasks.

4. The following commands are part of a task to test the comprehension skills of people with head injuries who have severe language impairments. This task was developed by Emma Gale and Claire Bennington at the Royal Hospital for Neuro-disability. The person being tested hears each command and then has to carry it out using an array of objects in front of them. Look through the commands and work out the structure the therapists were using in making up the commands. Use bracketed diagrams rather than trees and come up with a single structure for all the commands.

   1. Drop the comb.
   2. Drop the pen.
   3. Throw the toothbrush.
   4. Hide the key.
   5. Push the tin.
   6. Throw the spoon.
   7. Slide the key.
   8. Toss the key.
   9. Rub the red pen.
   10. Touch the black comb.
   11. Throw the purple toothbrush.
   12. Drop the comb on the floor.
   13. Hide the toothbrush in the tin.
   14. Slide the key to me.
   15. Push the tin over the edge.

5. The following utterances were produced by a 6-year-old girl with language problems. Imagine that, on the basis of these data, you have to write a report detailing the lexical and phrasal categories the child can produce. What would your report say?

   1. Me got haircut. 2. Lily drinking that up. 3. Seen it TV. 4. Running round and round playground. 5. You give me that now quick.

6

The syntactic shape of sentences

6.1 What is a sentence?

We have talked a great deal about sentences being made up of constituents. But we have hardly talked about the sentence itself, and what we mean by this. In everyday language, the term 'sentence' is often taken to refer to an utterance, or to something that conveys a whole idea. These rather loose notions hint at the phonological unity and semantic unity that characterize sentences (see *Links to other levels*). But in linguistics, the term 'sentence' is defined very precisely in syntactic terms.

A sentence is a syntactic unit consisting of a Noun Phrase and a Verb Phrase:

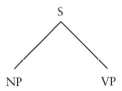

You can deduce from this that the least a sentence will contain is a noun heading the NP, and a verb heading the VP:

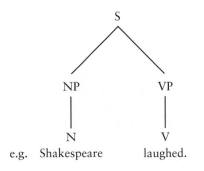

And the most? As we established early on, there is no limit to the length of a sentence. So we could equally have:

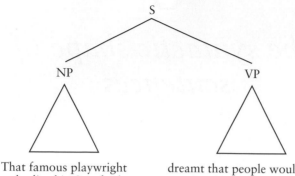

| That famous playwright who lived in Stratford | dreamt that people would go on reading his plays for centuries. |

To confirm that both these sentences consist of NP and VP you can use the proform test for each of these constituents. Try adding *Yes, he did* after each sentence and checking out what each proform refers back to:

Shakespeare laughed
Yes, he did
he = Shakespeare
did = laughed.

That famous playwright who lived in Stratford dreamt that people would go on reading his plays for centuries
Yes, he did
he = that famous playwright who lived in Stratford
did = dreamt that people would go on reading his plays for centuries.

So, when you are analysing a sentence, however long and complex it may appear, you can be sure it contains an NP and a VP, and if you can find these two constituents, you'll be off to a good start.

But knowing this much about sentences enables us to make further generalizations. We know that each constituent must contain at least a head, and will do well to search for each head. But we also know that the head determines what complements must or may occur in the constituent. Applying this to the VP, we know that its head verb will determine much of its structure. For example, if the verb is *laughed*, this may be the whole VP, as in the example above. But if the verb is *grabbed* –

Shakespeare grabbed …?

Instinctively, you will feel that this is not enough, and that the sentence is incomplete. This is because the verb *grab* demands something more, as in:

Shakespeare grabbed his pen.

To confirm that you can make judgements about the structures verbs demand, see what you can do with the following examples:

Which verbs can you fit into the blanks?

1. The child may _____ the flowers
    throw, fall, drop, move, squash, bloom, grow, look, see, bring, give, put, keep.
2. That cat will _____
    throw, fall, move, escape, grow, faint, kill, frighten, worry, sleep, disturb.
3. Our friends will _____
    amuse, laugh, celebrate, congratulate, help, rescue, find, win, own, belong.
4. You should _____ me a ticket
    give, send, bring, receive, accept, put, keep, sell, buy, pay, save.

Which of the above verbs can be used in more than one frame?

These examples illustrate the pivotal role of the verb in sentence structure.

6.2 Why do we need to focus on verbs?

Imagine someone said to you

I this to Tom/ but then Bill him/quite suddenly last week/he never Tom/

Would you be able to work out what they are talking about? As long as their intonation allowed you to chunk various words together, you would at least have some idea of what formed an utterance – something we have marked by '/'. But how would you relate the words and phrases within each utterance? In this case it would be practically impossible or at least extremely difficult, even if you knew something about the context of the conversation. What is the source of the difficulty? After all, each utterance contains perfectly grammatical and understandable words and phrases.

If you were feeling particularly perverse, you could even do some neat constituency analysis on each utterance. Yet we simply do not know how to fit the phrases together meaningfully, unless we slot in one crucial kind of word – a verb. See what difference this makes:

I sent this to Tom/but then Bill sacked him/quite suddenly last week/
he never liked Tom/

This is clearly an extreme case where the meanings of the phrases around the verb do not give you any cues as to what their relations could be. Usually, though not always, the meaning of the phrases limits the ways they could be related. Consider, for instance, this bit of conversation between a man with aphasia and his therapist (Lawson 2001):

Yes ... just a minute ... er Australia ... Australia and back again and ... er now ... eight years ago ... working working working working ... and now ... partner ... partner now. Money money ...

Although there is only one verb in the whole conversational turn, it is relatively easier to imagine how the phrases might be related because of their meaning – that *Australia* and *back again* are likely to be the end points of some trip taken eight years ago. The verb *work* also triggers some possible connections for the remaining phrases – that he has either acquired a partner or has become one, and that he has made money. If we then consider this fragment in the light of the therapist's question:

SLT: What does your son do now?

our detective work becomes even easier. Even so, it is detective work rather than just listening and understanding what someone is explicitly saying – and all because most of the verbs are missing. This shows not only that verbs are crucial in communication but also that some words are more difficult to guess than others. This relative difference has been confirmed in experiments. For instance, Gleitman and Gillette (1995) asked people to watch a silent video of mothers playing with their infants. When a beep sounded, they had to guess a target word the mother had used. When the target word was a noun, people guessed correctly 50 per cent of the time at first and then improved as they went on. When the target was a verb, on the other hand, they only guessed correctly 15 per cent of the time (see also Black and Chiat 2000). So, without verbs the whole process of communication becomes much more laborious and guess-ridden.

This would be reason enough to pay attention to verbs clinically, as problems with production and/or comprehension of verbs are fairly common for both adults and children with language problems (see Chiat 2000, and

Black and Chiat 2000). But, for many of these children and adults, not being able to produce the verb also means not producing much of the rest of the sentence. Without verbs as anchoring points, their utterances crumble into an unstructured heap of words. Consider, for instance, how the man with aphasia we mentioned above describes the domestic scene pictured in *The assessment of aphasia and related disorders* (Goodglass and Kaplan 1983):

Cookies and ... chair. A girl and boy ... washing ... flowers ... garden and shrubs and ... cupboard ... and in here ... sock ... stop ... mess ... plates

(adapted from Lawson 2001). He seems to be simply listing things and people. A listener would not even know which phrases are part of the same event, let alone how the participants in each event interact and which verb was intended. Absence of verbs seems to mean absence of basic sentence structure. Conversely, as verbs begin to reappear with recovery and treatment, so does sentence structure (see *Further reading*). A similar connection between verbs and sentence structure can be observed in language development.

When children first start talking, they don't generally produce full sentences. Their verb vocabulary is limited, and they are likely to use complements without verbs and verbs without complements. With development, the range of verbs grows, and increasingly, children combine verbs with their appropriate complements. To illustrate these developments, here are some examples from a detailed record that Tomasello (1992) kept of his daughter's verb use:

16–18 months	*18–20 months*	*20–22 months*	*22–24 months*
Go Maria go	Go	Go seven-eleven ...	Go to the new playground Go by there Go to store I go outside ...
	Put it in Put it in there Put on Mommy's shirt	Put Grover on there Putting spoons in there Put on me Put hat on these feet	Put my shoes back on Put my toothbrush down Put it in the drink Put the 9 by the letter M
Woops Fall down Fall down man Ball fall down	Bottle fall down Fall down garbage Popsicle fall down	Box fall down Maria falling out car	Not fall down playground I fell down

(continued)

16–18 months	18–20 months	20–22 months	22–24 months
	Drop it Drop it ice Drop the checkbook Woops – Dropped it	Popsicle drop it Daddy dropped paper	You dropped that toy I dropped the keys
Stay	Stay here rug Stay here		You stay right there
Get it Block get it Bottle get it Get it hat Flowers get it	Get it Pokey Get it birds Cup get it Get the pencil Get it puppet	Get the flowers Get it spoon Mommy get sauce Daddy get it bottle Get me up there Get raisins to me	Get that paper for me Get it by myself I get it Get me up here Get this away on my guitar
Back	Back salt Back these	Star back here Come back Have that back Put my shoes back on	Put it back Roll it back for me Put my spoon back in my cup
	Off Light off Off TV		Turn it off Turn the light off

Taken from Tomasello (1992)

Over this period, children tend to stick to the verb frames they have heard. A little later, they start using verbs more creatively, using them in ways that an adult wouldn't, for example:

Age of child	Verbs used in novel verb frames
2; 8	Daddy go me round
2; 9	You go it in
3; 10	Go me to the bathroom before you go to bed
4; 3	Why didn't you want to go your head under?
2; 2	Tommie fall Stevie truck down
2; 3	Kendall fall that toy
2; 9	I'm just gonna fall this on her
2; 6	Mommy, can you stay this open?
3; 2	I'm staying it in the water
3; 7	I want to stay this rubber band on

Taken from Bowerman (1982)

To understand better what these children and adults are, or are not, doing with verbs and sentence structure, we need to delve into verbs and how sentences are woven round them.

6.3 Verb subcategories

Although the structure of the VP varies according to the verb, the variation turns out to be quite constrained. All verbs occur in one of a small set of verb frames. Some verbs are very restricted, tolerating only one frame. Others are more versatile, accepting two or more. In such cases, the meaning of the verb is subtly affected by the frame in which it occurs. We will pick up this point when we focus on verb semantics, in Chapter 8.

Verbs occurring in a particular frame form a verb subcategory, and are said to **subcategorize** the complements they take. Below, we introduce and exemplify the basic verb frames in English. As you work through these, see if you can think of other verbs that can slot into each frame:

Verbs taking no complements

$$_{VP}[V\ \varnothing] \quad \text{or} \quad \begin{array}{c} VP \\ | \\ V \end{array}$$

They $_{VP}$[slept]
They $_{VP}$[sneezed]
They $_{VP}$[exploded]
They $_{VP}$[escaped]
They $_{VP}$[hesitated]
They $_{VP}$[broke]
They $_{VP}$[melted].

When verbs occur in this structure they are said to be **intransitive**.

Verbs taking an NP complement

$$_{VP}[V\ NP] \quad \text{or}$$

They $_{VP}$[built $_{NP}$[that nest]]
They $_{VP}$[bought $_{NP}$[a red nose]]
They $_{VP}$[found $_{NP}$[the button]]
They $_{VP}$[irritate $_{NP}$[us]]
They $_{VP}$[broke $_{NP}$[the glass]]
They $_{VP}$[melted $_{NP}$[the ice]].

This verb frame is the one that allows the passive construction which we used to identify NPs:

Active	*Passive*
NP[They] built NP[that nest]	NP[That nest] was built by NP[them]
NP[They] bought NP[a red nose]	NP[A red nose] was bought by NP[them]
NP[They] found NP[the button]	NP[The button] was found by NP[them]
NP[They] irritated NP[us]	NP[We] were irritated by NP[them]
NP[They] broke NP[the glass]	NP[The glass] was broken by NP[them]
NP[They] melted NP[the ice]	NP[The ice] was melted by NP[them].

When verbs occur in these structures, they are said to be **transitive**. Note that some verbs are optionally transitive: they allow an NP complement but do not demand one:

They ate (a meal)
They wrote (an article)
They helped (us).

Notice how the presence of the NP complement affects the nature of the event. Where the verb has no complement, as in 'They ate', it conveys an activity that is consistent over time. When the complement is added, as in 'They ate the apple', the verb conveys an accomplishment, with the activity of eating resulting in the apple being consumed. If we replace *eat* with a verb that demands an NP complement – for example *devour* – we find that it necessarily refers to an accomplishment:

They devoured
They devoured the apple.

Devour implies that the complement NP is fully consumed.

Verbs taking a PP complement

VP[V PP]   or   VP

The taxi VP[arrived PP[at the station]]
The student VP[leant PP[on the desk]]
They VP[stared PP[at the photo]].

In some cases, the verb not only determines the occurrence of the PP, but also selects the preposition that heads the PP. This is true of the last example, where *stare* selects *at*. Other examples are:

She decided on the red dress (where *decide* dictates *on*)
My aunt believes in ghosts (where *believe* dictates *in*)
We thought of a brilliant idea (where *think* dictates *of*).

People often express doubts about the analysis of these verb structures. They point out that *at* in *stare at* is meaningless, and want to treat it as 'part of the verb'. You might think of evidence that it is not part of the verb. For example, notice where the past tense *-ed* goes: on *stare*. If *at* were syntactically part of the verb, we would expect *-ed* to follow it, giving

*They stare at-ed the photo.

Notice also that, although *at* is 'meaningless', it cannot be omitted:

*They stared the photo.

Similar points arise with examples where the verb is followed by a PP containing just a preposition:

Cinderella ᵥₚ[ran ₚₚ[away]]
Some apples ᵥₚ[fell ₚₚ[out]]
The leaves ᵥₚ[dropped ₚₚ[off]]
The baby ᵥₚ[dropped ₚₚ[off]]
The student ᵥₚ[switched ₚₚ[off]].

A common reaction is that *run away, fall out, drop off* and *give up* are verbs. If you look at where the past tense occurs in the above examples, you can see that this is wrong. The past tense goes on *run* rather than *away* (*ran away* not *run awayed*). The feeling that the preposition is part of the verb has its roots in the semantics of these forms. In some cases, the verb and preposition have separate but closely tied meanings, with the verb referring to a movement and the preposition to the path of that movement (*run away, fall out*). In other cases, the verb and preposition are even more closely linked: they only have a meaning as a whole and may be described as idiomatic (*switch off*). The two examples with *drop off* show that some verb + preposition combinations can be more or less idiomatic: in the first, *drop off* refers to a downward movement (*drop*) away from something (*off*); in the case of 'The baby dropped off', on the other hand, *drop off* has a meaning as a whole which is not the sum of its parts *drop* and *off*. The close semantic relation of the preposition to the verb leads us to 'feel' as if they are a single item although they are syntactically separate.

Verbs taking NP and PP complements

_{VP}[V NP PP]   or   VP

                                    V   NP   PP

The prototypical verb in this subcategory is *put*:

She _{VP}[put _{NP}[the books] _{PP}[on the shelf]]
She _{VP}[put _{NP}[the books] _{PP}[away]].

But other verbs may occur in this frame:

She _{VP}[chucked _{NP}[the rubbish] _{PP}[into the bin]]
She _{VP}[pushed _{NP}[the car] _{PP}[across the road]]
She _{VP}[threw _{NP}[it] _{PP}[out]]
She _{VP}[tore _{NP}[them] _{PP}[off]].

Again, where the PP contains just a preposition as with *throw out* and *tear off*, it is sometimes felt to be 'part of the verb'. The feeling is particularly strong with combinations like *give up, write off, turn on, track down*:

She _{VP}[gave _{PP}[up]] _{NP}[the course]]
She _{VP}[wrote _{NP}[it] _{PP}[off]]
That music _{VP}[turned _{NP}[them] _{PP}[on]]
They _{VP}[tracked _{NP}[me] _{PP}[down]].

Again, this is because the verb and PP have an idiomatic meaning as a whole. Syntactically, the PP is separate and distinct from the verb.
    Further evidence for the separateness of these PPs comes from their syntactic behaviour. Notice that they can occur in two places. They can precede or follow the NP complement of the verb:

She gave *up* the course
She gave the course *up*

She wrote *off* the car
She wrote the car *off*.

If the NP complement is a pronoun, however, they must follow it:

She gave it up
*She gave up it

She wrote it off
*She wrote off it.

Verbs taking two NP complements

_{VP}[V NP NP]   or   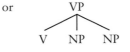

The prototypical verb in this subcategory is *give*:

She _{VP}[gave _{NP}[her friend] _{NP}[the flowers]].

But many other verbs allow it:

She _{VP}[sent _{NP}[the teacher] _{NP}[a letter]]
She _{VP}[made _{NP}[me] _{NP}[a cake]].

A distinguishing feature of these verbs is that most occur equally comfortably in the NP–PP frame. In this case, the order of the two NP complements changes. The first NP complement now occurs second, in a PP which is headed either by *to* or *for*:

NP–NP frame: She _{VP}[gave _{NP}[*her friend*] _{NP}[the flowers]]
NP–PP frame: She _{VP}[gave _{NP}[the flowers] _{PP}[*to her friend*]].

NP–NP frame: She _{VP}[sent _{NP}[*the teacher*] _{NP}[a letter]]
NP–PP frame: She _{VP}[sent _{NP}[a letter] _{PP}[*to the teacher*]].

NP–NP frame: She _{VP}[made _{NP}[*me*] _{NP}[a cake]]
NP–PP frame: She _{VP}[made _{NP}[a cake] _{PP}[*for me*]].

Verbs taking two NP complements are known as **ditransitive**. *Give* is a verb which demands both complements:

She gave her friend a present
*She gave her friend
*She gave a present.

But most verbs in this subcategory are optionally ditransitive, allowing one or other of the NPs to be omitted:

She showed me (the photo)
She told me (the news)
She threw (me) the ball
She sent (me) a present.

Be-*type verbs*

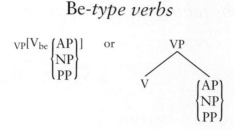

$$_{VP}[V_{be} \begin{Bmatrix} AP \\ NP \\ PP \end{Bmatrix}] \quad \text{or}$$

Be-type verbs form a relatively small subcategory of verbs that take an AP complement. The prototypical *be*-type verb is, of course, *be*:

They $_{VP}$[are $_{AP}$[extraordinary]]
That $_{VP}$[looks $_{AP}$[dead cool]]
They $_{VP}$[seemed $_{AP}$[pleased with their present]]
She $_{VP}$[is $_{AP}$[fond of her cousin]].

You might recognize these verbs because you have met them before – we included a list of them in our tests for adjectives (Chapter 3, Section 3.3).
   Be-type verbs may also take an NP complement:

She $_{VP}$[is $_{NP}$[an engineer]]
That $_{VP}$[seems $_{NP}$[a brilliant idea]].

The NP behaves very like the AP complement; indeed AP and NP complements can sometimes be used to express almost identical meanings:

The president $_{VP}$[is $_{AP}$[foolish]]
The president $_{VP}$[is $_{NP}$[a fool]].

Note that this NP complement is different from the NP complement occurring with transitive verbs (see *Verbs taking an NP complement* above). It cannot be moved by the passive:

*A fool was been by the president
*A brilliant idea is seemed by that.

Finally, *be*-type verbs may take a PP complement:

She $_{VP}$[is $_{PP}$[in the bath]]
They $_{VP}$[are $_{PP}$[out of their minds]]
They $_{VP}$[seem $_{PP}$[down in the dumps]].

Verbs taking complex complements

The subcategories presented above all give rise to simple sentences – even if they do not strike you as such! What this means is that they contain only one verb. Some verbs take **complex complements** which themselves contain a verb, resulting in **complex sentences**. Consider the following examples:

She ᵥₚ[enjoys ₂[reading novels with happy endings]]
She ᵥₚ[expects ₂[to win the lottery]].

What is the question-marked constituent in these sentences? Notice that it contains a verb, and that verb takes its usual complements. It seems that we have a VP. We can confirm that this is so using the *do so* proform test, which works:

She enjoys *doing so* = *reading novels with happy endings*
She expects to *do so* = *win the lottery*.

Here, then, we have a verb which takes a **VP complement**. Compare the following examples:

She ᵥₚ[believes ₂[(that) the sun will come out]]
She ᵥₚ[knows ₂[(that) the earth is round]].

Here, the question-marked constituent is more than a VP. You might recognize that it contains an NP followed by a VP – which suggests that it is a sentence. Confirming this hunch, we find that the constituent following *that* contains a group of words that can stand alone as a sentence:

ₛ[The sun will come out]
ₛ[The earth is round].

Confirming that each string of words forms a constituent within the larger sentence, we can replace the whole string with the proform *it*:

She believes *it* = *that the sun will come out*
She knows *it* = *that the earth is round*

and it can stand as an answer to the *Wh*-word *what*:

What does she believe?   *That the sun will come out*
What does she know?   *That the earth is round*.

We have not described the details of these VP and S complements and the subcategories of verbs which take them. Our purpose here is just to alert you to a further and more complex range of verb complements. For more extensive description and fuller analysis of these verb subcategories, see *Further reading*.

Last word on subcategorization

This chapter has concentrated on the subcategorization of verbs based on the complements they take. Other head categories also determine complements, and fall into subcategories according to the complements they take. If you would like to explore subcategorization further, look at Box 6.1.

By now you may be wondering why we have devoted so much attention to verb subcategories and worked through these in such detail. This brings us back to the key point: that verbs play a pivotal role in the sentence. Once you have cracked the verb frames in this chapter, you have cracked the structure of sentences in English. You will be able to take the most unfamiliar of sentences and see that it actually fits one of these familiar verb frames. You will be able to take a sample of sentences and identify patterns across the sample by looking at the range of verb frames that occur in it. And you will be able to construct sentences 'to order', targeting selected verb subcategories and finding verbs and verb frames to represent these. This ability to recognize and create syntactic patterns in sentences is one of the basic tools we need to analyse the strengths and weaknesses in a person's sentence processing. To make use of this tool, we must go beyond the syntactic shape of sentences, and think about how this links to their semantic and phonological shape.

Box 6.1 Subcategories of syntactic categories

Prepositions
- Prepositions taking no complements:
  PP[upstairs]
  PP[inside]
  PP[then]
  These are **intransitive**.
- Prepositions taking NP complements:
  PP[at NP[the house]]
  PP[to NP[the house]]
  PP[from NP[the house]]
  These prepositions are obligatorily **transitive**. Some prepositions are optionally transitive:
  PP[up] —— PP[up NP[the mountain]]
  PP[off] —— PP[off NP[the roof]]
- Prepositions taking PP complements:
  PP[down PP[to the sea]]
  PP[out PP[of the house]]
- Prepositions taking NP and PP complements:
  PP[across NP[the road]PP[from the pub]]

  (continued)

Adjectives
- Adjectives taking no complements:
  AP[tall]
  AP[purple]
  AP[wet]
- Adjectives taking one or two PP complements:
  AP[close PP[to the house]]
  AP[keen PP[on the idea]]
  AP[grateful PP[to you] PP[for your help]]
  AP[dependent PP[on her job] PP[for an income]]
  In rare cases, the PP complement is obligatory:
  She is PP[fond NP[of that city]] ——— *She is PP[fond]

Nouns
- While nouns most typically do not take complements, some do. Their complements are PPs:
  NP[the idea PP[of a holiday]]
  NP[his debt PP[to his friend]]
  NP[their passion PP[for linguistics]]
- Nouns derived from verbs take the same number of complements as their parent verb, but these always occur in PPs:
  He VP[loves/hates Paris] ——— NP[his love/hatred PP[of/for Paris]]
  He VP[owns this house] ——— NP[his ownership PP[of this house]]
  You VP[agree with my view] ——— NP[your agreement PP[with my view]]
  He VP[depends on us for ideas] ——— NP[his dependence PP[on us] PP[for ideas]]

6.4 Links to other levels

At the outset of this chapter, we suggested that everyday notions of a sentence as 'an utterance' that 'conveys a whole idea' are based on its typical phonological and semantic characteristics, rather than its strict syntactic definition. What did we mean by this?

Phonology

A sentence will often be uttered 'in one breath', with no pauses in the middle, but pauses at each end. It will also have an intonation contour and stress pattern as a whole. You can check this by reading out the examples in this chapter. You will probably find that each comes out in a single flow – with no pauses, and with a melodic and rhythmic pattern as a whole. We began to explore the rhythmic patterns of sentences in previous chapters. We saw that the greatest stress falls on the final stressed word in a sentence. The stress of other words will depend on their position in the constituent structure: any word that ends a constituent will carry greater stress than other words in that constituent. Now we have looked at the syntactic shape of the sentence in more detail, we can be more specific about its relation to the phonological shape of the sentence, and the effects of stress on particular syntactic categories in the sentence.

A sentence could end in one of a number of syntactic categories which will then carry the sentence stress, e.g.

Kate 'left (verb)
Kate felt 'sad (adjective)
Kate ran 'off (preposition)
Kate loves 'trees (noun).

Notice that, as soon as the verb takes a complement, as it typically will, it no longer occurs at the end of the sentence, and the complement which follows the verb attracts the sentence stress – as in all but the first example above. Furthermore, when the verb takes a complement, that complement is part of the VP, so the verb does not even occur at the end of the phrase. Consequently, it does not carry constituent stress either. This weakens the verb further, making it less stressed than, say, the nouns that end NPs. You can check this out using the above examples: you should find the verb is less stressed than any noun, adjective or preposition that ends a constituent. Thus, the stress pattern of the sentence to some extent reflects its syntax, and will need to be taken into account in identifying the source of problems with sentence structure.

Semantics

The sentence structures we have exemplified in this chapter allow us to talk about an infinite range of meanings. The way they do this is to some extent predictable. Each sentence conveys a situation. It is the verb in the sentence that largely determines the particular situation it conveys. If we change the verb in a sentence, we change the situation:

The child stroked the horse
The child watched the horse
The child pushed the horse
The child liked the horse
The child annoyed the horse.

The complements of the verb, on the other hand, convey **participants** in the situation. So, changing the complement of the verb does not alter the situation, but it does alter who or what is involved:

The woman liked the horse
The woman liked the TV programme
The woman liked chocolate
The woman liked that painting by Picasso
The woman liked the idea of a long holiday in Spain.

All of these sentences convey a 'liking' situation, but what is liked varies.

Notice how this works with complex sentences (see Section 6.4), where the verb takes a whole VP or sentence as a complement:

The woman liked VP[writing letters to the newspaper].

This sentence still portrays a 'liking' situation. But now one of the participants in the liking situation is itself a situation (a 'writing' situation) with its own participants ('letters' and 'the newspaper'). Similarly, in the sentence:

Everyone knows S[that Shakespeare wrote plays]

the 'knowing' situation, in the main sentence, has a participant which is a 'writing' situation with its own participants 'Shakepeare' and 'plays'.

In the next chapter, we go further into the situations that sentences convey and how they do this.

Exercises

1. Divide each utterance below into NP and VP, ignoring the internal structure of these phrases, e.g.

   1. NP[He] VP[opened several letters to his boss].
   2. I obviously misunderstood her point.
   3. My uncle in Paris sent me some money.
   4. Tania nearly missed her plane.
   5. Her lecture on syntax bored those poor students to death.
   6. A terrifying storm swept the man into the sea.
   7. You clearly learn very fast.

   Make sure you can justify your decisions by reference to the constituency tests (see Chapter 4).

2. For each of the following utterances, produced by a child with language impairment, identify the VP and then use both brackets and trees to represent its internal structure. Make sure that:

   (a) the two methods of representation show the same structure for each VP;
   (b) your analysis for this exercise is compatible with those you have carried out in previous exercises (see Exercise 2, Chapter 3; Exercise 3, Chapter 4).

   1. David be school. 2. Mimi eat upstairs dinner time. 3. Big boys like coffee. 4. We got Ribena today. 5. Frida bring him home.

3. Draw detailed trees showing the structure of each of the following utterances, which were produced by a 6-year-old girl with language problems – you already dealt with them in Exercise 5, Chapter 5. After drawing the trees, check back that your trees are compatible with the report you wrote for Exercise 5.

   1. Me got haircut. 2. Lily drinking that up. 3. Seen it TV. 4. Running round and round playground. 5. You give me that now quick.

4. A task often used in assessing comprehension of verbs is sentence completion. The person whose language is being assessed hears and/or sees a simple sentence from which the verb has been removed. They have to complete the sentence by providing a verb that is syntactically and semantically appropriate. The person has to generate a suitable verb, or they are given a small set of verbs to choose from.

   Imagine you have to construct such a task for a woman with aphasia. You need to make up 12 simple sentences such as:

   Children _____ games

   and select three verb options for each sentence. How do you select the verb options? Your selection depends on a number of factors – e.g. the aspects of comprehension you are assessing and what you know about the person's problems. In this case, we would like you to select the three verbs according to the following criteria:

   • Target: a verb that can fit into that syntactic frame and is compatible with the meaning of the phrases around it, e.g. *enjoy*.
   • First distractor: a verb that could fit into the syntactic frame but is not semantically appropriate, e.g. *shock*. Note that it would be ideal if this distractor was also not too far in meaning from the target – for instance, we have used *shock* which, like *enjoy*, expresses a mental state or process.

- Second distractor: a verb that does not fit into the syntactic frame and is not appropriate semantically, e.g. *laugh*.

(See Marshall, Pring and Chiat 1998 for a sentence completion test offering a similar range of distractors.)

Once you have completed your test, pilot it on a friend to make sure that a person without language problems can do it.

III

Syntax – semantic links: situations

|7|

Shaping situations: making them dynamic or static

7.1 Introduction

One of the many things language allows us to do quickly and effectively is to shift and guide the attention of our listeners or readers to particular aspects of the world. Compare, for instance, pointing and using a word or phrase. Imagine you have a cup in front of you. You want to indicate something in relation to that object and, using gesture, you point to it. In most cases, you would succeed in directing your listener's attention to a place and an object occupying that space. But how would your listener know whether you want to say something about the cup as a whole, or about its handle, or its shape, material, colour or function? The gesture works as a way of shifting and guiding attention but only in a limited way. Language allows much greater precision: by choosing particular words, or combinations of words, you can make clear whether you are talking about the whole object (the/a/this cup); or some part of the object (its handle, the rim, its sides), its shape or size (the roundness, its width), material or colour (bone china, purple) or function (a container). Even when we try to communicate about objects or events in our immediate environment, there is always too much going on. We need some way of directing our listeners to notice specific aspects of situations and disregard others. The more complex the object or situation, the more we need to zoom in on what is important to us and our listener, while blurring the rest. Imagine the situation where a child has just broken a rather precious cup and must tell his mother (see Figure 7.1).

Any of the following utterances would be truthful descriptions:

Mum, the cup is broken
Mum, the cup broke
Mum, the cup has been broken ... (by me)
Mum, I broke the cup.

Figure 7.1

With the first utterance, using the verb *be* and the adjective *broken*, the child would simply tell us about the state of the cup without saying anything about the process that brought it about or who caused it. With the second utterance, using the verb *break* in one of its possible frames (see Chapter 6), the child would convey that the cup has undergone a process of change – as if by magic, it went from being whole to breaking without any apparent cause. With the third, the child begins to acknowledge that there was a caused process resulting in the broken state. If he omits *by me*, he would give the impression that the cause was not known, while, if *by me* is added, he would at least admit to his role in the situation, albeit it a fairly minor, back-grounded one. It is only with the final utterance that the child comes clean and presents the situation as an event where he did something that caused the cup to break. Whatever our motives, we are all capable of such linguistic manipulations, even if we are not explicitly aware of them.

So language is never a simple copy or reflection of how the world is – more often than not, it reflects how speakers want the world to appear to their listeners. In saying something about the world, we inevitably communicate a great deal about ourselves and our view of the world. To understand this crucial role of language, we have to concentrate on how language itself portrays things, people and situations, while disregarding to some extent how 'the real world' might actually be.

Consider a sentence like:

Sam was at the station

which tells us that a particular individual, Sam, is at a certain place. The sentence focuses on Sam's state, his being in a place and does not tell us anything about how he might have got there or where he was before being at the station. Yet, in reality, he must have gone from another place to the station – there must have been a process that got him there. By uttering this sentence, however, we are both telling our listener where Sam is and directing their attention to this state as opposed to anything else about Sam or his movements. If we had used

Sam arrived at the station

we would have foregrounded the process that led up to Sam's being at the station, as well as saying something about where he was as a result of that process. Language gives us a choice to represent a situation simply as a state, a process or activity, or an action that may result in a state. In this chapter, we will consider the general distinction between static situations (states) and dynamic situations that involve some kind of change (events).

7.2 What makes events and states different

Temporal properties

Consider the following sentences:

John stole £50   (event)
The book cost £50   (state)

and imagine videoing situations that correspond to them (see Figures 7.2 and 7.3).

If we froze the film of John stealing £50 at different points, we would have a sequence of quite different shots: in one, John may be looking around suspiciously, then forcing open a locked drawer; in the next, he may be taking money out of the drawer and counting it, and finally pocketing the £50 and tiptoeing out of the room. Each frame would be quite different from the other and depict segments, or sub-events, of the total situation. Stealing £50 implies the execution of a series of different sub-processes at different points in time resulting in the stealing of the money. Events are built up of different stages that together make up the particular action or lead up to a particular result.

What would a video of the book costing £50 look like? Probably more like one of those videos you find in trendy art galleries – one frame much the same as another, showing the book in the same state of having a certain price. In the real world, the book will have come to acquire its price through a series of events, but the 'linguistic picture' does not show this. In contrast to, for instance,

John priced/sold the book at £50 (event)

Figure 7.2

Figure 7.3

it simply says that the book is in a state, which remains the same over a certain period of time. States are like snapshots of the world at a given moment and are not made up of different sub-states – they are temporally uniform or homogeneous. They stretch or last over time, without change.

So, a crucial difference between events and states in language is to do with their temporal characteristics: events are more dynamic and involve temporal change, while states do not unfold over time and are more temporally stable. Because of these temporal characteristics, verbs expressing events and states occur in different time-related constructions. Event verbs can occur in the progressive, where an *-ing* suffix is added to the verb, which is then combined with the auxiliary verb *be*, e.g.

John is arriving soon
My bag was breaking
That child is breaking my cup
John was stealing £50.

State verbs, on the other hand, do not occur in the progressive, e.g.

*John is being at the station/tall
*The book is costing £50
*I am knowing Swahili.

The semantic effect of putting a verb in the **progressive** is to extend the situation in time, implying that it is ongoing and has not yet reached its end state or result, if it has one. If we put in the progressive a verb expressing an event, the semantic effect is a stretching out in time of its sub-events, making their unfolding in time, rather than their beginning or end, more prominent. When not in the progressive, event verbs are like rubber band that you hold at each end, making you aware of its beginning and end. Turning them into the progressive is like stretching the rubber band so that its middle part increases in length and takes up more of your attention (see also Chapter 12, Section 12.4). But you can't stretch any further a rubber band that is already fully stretched. Verbs that express states are already extended in time and, because they do not have different sub-states that distinguish their beginning, middle or end, it would not make sense to stretch them further by applying the progressive – the sentence would snap in your hand!

State verbs can sometimes occur in the progressive but only if they can be interpreted in a non-stative way (see also *Degrees of execution and control* below). Stretching them in time, for instance, makes sense if the verb expresses the kind of state that can increase or decrease gradually over time. For instance, adding phrases like *more and more* makes some state verbs more acceptable in the progressive, e.g.

??I'm liking linguistics
I'm liking linguistics more and more.

Because states, unlike events, are not made up of distinct segments, it is relatively more difficult to pick out their beginnings and ends – their time boundaries – and therefore treat them as conceptual and semantic units. When we can't quite see where something begins or ends, it is harder to treat it as something separate that can be counted or compared to other units of the same type. In this sense, states are a bit like mass nouns, whereas events are more similar to count nouns – think how much more natural it is to talk about one, two or three bread rolls as opposed to one, two or three flours. The relatively unbounded nature of states makes them less appropriate to use in constructions that require something 'unit-like' to focus on and emphasize. One of these constructions is the Pseudo-cleft, a close relative of the Cleft construction we have already seen (see Chapter 4, Section 4.4). Like the Cleft, the Pseudo-cleft is a construction with slots (*What* NP *did be* VP) that require particular syntactic and semantic 'fillers'. VPs that express unit-like situations fit better into the final VP slots than those that do not, so VPs that express events tend to fit better than VPs that express states, e.g.

What John did was $_{VP}$[steal £50]	(event VP)
??What the book did was $_{VP}$[cost £50]	(state VP)
What George did was $_{VP}$[smash the cup]	(event VP)
??What George did was $_{VP}$[be furious]	(state VP).

The temporal characteristics of states, therefore, make state verbs and verb phrases semantically and syntactically incompatible with two constructions (Progressive and Pseudo-cleft) that are possible for event verbs and verb phrases. The Pseudo-cleft is also sensitive to features of execution, control and intention we discuss in the next section.

Degrees of execution and control

Let's compare again the two sentences we started with:

John stole £50
The book cost £50.

Stealing is something that John does, an action he carries out and is under his control. The verb *cost*, on the other hand, expresses a property the book has or has acquired. **Events** typically involve activities or actions that are executed – something is done. **States,** on the other hand, are properties attributed to someone – you are *in* a state but do not do it or carry it out. As nothing is done in a state, states are awkward in constructions that focus on what has been done. That is another reason why states do not fit into the Pseudo-cleft, which is precisely that sort of construction, e.g.

What NP[John] did was VP[*steal £50*]   (event VP)
??What NP[the book] did was VP[*cost £50*]   (state VP)
What NP[Margo] did was VP[*buy* another house]   (event VP)
??What NP[Margo] did was VP[*own* another house]   (state VP)
What NP[Gabriel] did was VP[*learn* the local language] (event VP)
??What NP[Gabriel] did was VP[*know* the local words]   (state VP).

Since in a state nothing is done, verbs that express states cannot be modified with phrases that say something about how the action or activity was executed, e.g.

??John *carefully* knows Swahili/weighs too much
??The book *carefully* cost £50

or with modifiers expressing **control** or **intention**, e.g.

??John *deliberately* knows Swahili/weighs too much
??The book *deliberately* cost £50.

With events, on the other hand, such modifiers are possible as there is something that can be done carefully or deliberately, e.g.

John *carefully* stole the money/removed his fingerprints
John *carefully* learnt the local language
John *deliberately* stole the money/put on weight.

Because of the lack of something that can be carried out intentionally or controlled, states are also incompatible with commands and instructions. For instance, they cannot occur in the imperative, a construction we can use to issue a direct command:

??Cost/weigh 50 pounds!
??Know linguistics!
??Own another house!
??Receive the prize!

Events, however, are fine in the imperative, e.g.

Steal £50!
Put on some weight!
Learn linguistics!
Buy another house!
Accept the prize!

Events are more active and whoever carries them out is presented as more in control – another reason why events but not states are compatible with the progressive (*be* + V*ing*) which, by plunging the listener 'in the middle of the action', heightens the impression of activity and control. Consider, for instance, the different interpretations of a typical state verb, such as main verb *be*, in the progressive when we combine it with an adjective that can have both an active and a stative interpretation:

You are silly/polite/clever
You are being silly/polite/clever.

The first sentence is a comment on your character while the second, in the progressive, is a comment on your behaviour – it is equivalent to saying that you are acting in a silly, polite or clever way. If the state verb is combined with an adjective that does not allow both interpretations, then the result is odd – its stative properties simply clash with the semantic properties of the progressive as no alternative interpretation is possible, e.g.

*You are being tall/blue-eyed.

States never express an action and therefore never express something that may or may not be controlled and voluntary. Events, on the other hand, always express a dynamic process or action which may be controlled or voluntary in varying degrees. Consider the verbs *sneeze* and *cough*. Both express a dynamic situation and can occur in the progressive and Pseudo-cleft:

He was *sneezing/coughing* throughout the concert
What NP[he] did was VP[*sneeze/cough* throughout the concert].

Compare them with a state verb like *be*:

*/? He was *being* irritable throughout the concert
*What NP[he] did was VP[*be* irritable throughout the concert].

Nevertheless, the verbs *sneeze* and *cough* show subtle variations in degree of control and intention, as their different behaviours in combination with *carefully/deliberately* suggests:

He carefully sneezed into his handkerchief
??He carefully sneezed so as not to spread his germs around
?He sneezed carefully so as not to spread his germs around
?He deliberately sneezed to attract my attention
He carefully coughed into his handkerchief
??He carefully coughed so as not to spread his germs around
? He coughed carefully so as not to spread his germs around
He coughed deliberately to attract my attention.

Although there are not many ways of sneezing and coughing and usually we cannot control these actions, we can at least initiate the action of coughing voluntarily, unlike that of sneezing. We do as the doctor says when she tells us 'Cough!' but would not know how to respond to the imperative 'Sneeze!'.
    Note how picky language is: even when very similar situations are involved, the specifically linguistic properties of verbs can make all the difference. You might request

Listen carefully to this advice! (imperative + modifier)

but not

Hear carefully this advice!

Or you might explain to someone why you are cross with them by saying

What you did was VP[*listen* to my private conversation]!

but not

*What you did was VP[*hear* my private conversation]!

The verbs *listen* and *hear* express the same type of perception, yet *listen* presents it as an intentional act, while *hear* makes it appear more like a state. This is why you should not rely exclusively on your intuitions about actual situations but test linguistic meaning with the tests we have discussed (see also Box 7.1).

7.3 Why we need the distinction

All natural languages appear to mark the distinction between events and states. Without this distinction, therefore, we would not be able to describe an important aspect of natural languages (see Frawley 1992). For instance, languages as different as English, Italian and Chickasaw, an Amerindian language, all distinguish between events and states, though they use different means to do so. As we have seen in Section 7.2, in English we can use the same verb *be* for both events and states but have to signal the event interpretation by putting the verb in the progressive – we add *-ing* to it and an auxiliary verb:

I *am* good   (state, characteristic of the speaker)
I am *being* good   (event, behaviour of the speaker).

The progressive form signals that the verb *be* should not be interpreted in its usual stative meaning. In Italian, we use two completely different verbs to mark the distinction: *essere* for the state of being and *stare* for the event interpretation:

Sono buona   (state, characteristic of the speaker)
Am good

Sto buona   (event, behaviour of the speaker).
Am good

In Chickasaw, on the other hand, it is the word for 'good' (*chokma*) that carries a special marker to signal the state or event interpretation:

Sa-chokma   (I am good, state)
Chokma-*li*   (I'm being good, event).

The distinction between events and states appears to be a powerful influence in the way we see the world. Even very young children seem to observe this distinction. Early on, they talk about both. They use verbs like 'play', 'put', 'go', 'get', 'eat' for actions, and verbs like 'got', 'have', 'want', 'like' and 'know' for possessive, emotional and mental states. Children also use the progressive *-ing* at an early stage: it is typically the first 'word ending' to be used reliably. As we have seen, *-ing* is naturally compatible with events but not with states. So what do children do with it? Roger Brown, in his detailed study of children's early word combinations (Brown 1973), noticed that the children's use of *-ing* was strikingly appropriate. They attached it to events (processes, in Brown's discussion), but not to states. In talk about actions, children typically produce utterances like

Go [ə] bed *and* Going [ə] bed
Eat lunch *and* Eating lunch.

In talk about states, on the other hand, they are likely to say things like

Want lunch
I like that

but never

*Wanting lunch
*I'm liking that.

They do not overgeneralize *-ing* and try it on state verbs. This cannot be because they are totally averse to overgeneralization. Researchers have observed overgeneralization of other word endings. For example, we hear children adding the plural *-s* to nouns that do not pluralize, coming up with novel forms like *moneys* and *sugars*. It seems that the distinction between nouns that do and do not pluralize is not as obvious to them as the distinction between verbs that do and do not take *-ing*.

Given the importance of this distinction, we need to take it into account when we are working with someone who has difficulties understanding or conveying situations in language. All too often clinical work centres on a limited range of events, most typically actions. The reason becomes obvious when you stop to think about the materials and methods that support clinical work. How do we typically go about testing comprehension or eliciting production? With pictures. Precisely because language is a sticking point, we rely on the visual modality to represent meaning. The problem is that some meanings are more amenable to visual representation than others. Just try picturing the following:

book, hammer, star, circle, shop, story, pain, idea
eat, push, throw, laugh, take, be tall, be hot, be funny, cost, like, know.

Obviously, concrete objects like 'book' and visually-based meanings like 'circle' are more picturable than abstract objects like 'idea' and non-visual meanings like 'pain'. Perhaps less obviously, events tend to be more picturable than states – you can visualize 'eat' and 'push' more easily than 'cost' and 'know'. It may be easy to picture events that cause pain (e.g. hurting someone) or actions that suggest pain (e.g. someone crying) but it is harder to represent visually the state of pain itself. Consequently, assessment and therapy techniques relying on pictures are more likely to tap into events than states. If you run through some familiar picture selection and picture description tests, you'll see the point. It is not surprising that we have an *action* picture test (Renfrew 1997), but not a *state* picture test. If we want a more comprehensive view of situations in language – including unpicturable as well as picturable ones – we need to extend and supplement our clinical methods (see Exercise 2).

Even in testing language comprehension, we might have to take into account the event/state distinction. For instance, Black, Nickels and Byng (1991) found that adult English speakers were more accurate in matching event sentences to pictures than matching mental state sentences to pictures, even when the sentences were identical in all other respects. That is, people were significantly better and quicker at selecting a picture like

Figure 7.4 Source: Byng, S. & Black, M. *Reversible Sentence Comprehension Test* in Marshall, Black and Byng (Oxon, Winslow Press Ltd., 1999).

after hearing the sentence *The queen **splashes** the nun* (event), than in selecting a picture like

Figure 7.5 Source: Byng, S. & Black, M. *Reversible Sentence Comprehension Test* in Marshall, Black and Byng (Oxon, Winslow Press Ltd., 1999).

after hearing the sentence *The queen **sees** the nun* (state).

Perhaps the most pressing reason for thinking about how different types of situations are represented in language is that language gives us a uniquely precise and effective way of expressing our *internal states* – moods, sensations, feelings, thoughts and opinions. Through the use of pictures, body language, gesture, music and many other forms of communication, we can express some of these feelings and share them with others. But imagine you want to tell a friend that something has disappointed, rather than upset, saddened, depressed, disturbed, surprised, discouraged, enraged, disgusted or irritated you. How easy would it be to express this range of feelings without language? How would you keep mental track of what you felt long enough to analyse it, understand it, and gain some perspective on it? How long would it take you to dispel someone's incorrect impression of how you felt? This is what many of our conversations with others or with ourselves are about, especially in times of change, uncertainty or trouble. Yet this is precisely what many people who have become aphasic after a stroke or head injury can no longer do. People with aphasia, even those who have recovered enough to get by on a practical level, often complain that they no longer have access to 'real conversation'. To understand deeply what it is that they are missing, we have to grasp language in all its complexity.

7.4 The event/state continuum

Although the event/state distinction is both clear and necessary, it should not be seen as an absolute classification where items fall either on one side of the divide or the other. It is something more shaded and gradual, forming a continuum from items that have all the characteristics of events (i.e. pass all the tests we have discussed) to items that have none of them (i.e. fail all the tests). Like most classifications we use in dealing with the world as well as in language, some items may not have all the properties of a category but are still closer to that category than any other – a three-legged chair is still a chair. Or they may have such split properties that they genuinely fall in-between: a chair with an extremely low back might be considered as either a stool or a chair (see Figure 7.6 below for some examples of verbs on the continuum).

Events   States

steal	learn	rain	receive	please	believe	know	own	like	be
buy	think	sneeze					cost	seem	

Figure 7.6 The event/state continuum.

Consider, for instance, the verb *rain*. It clearly involves a dynamic process where something is happening and its unfolding in time can be stretched out – hence its compatibility with the progressive:

It was/is raining.

It is also not impossible in the Pseudo-cleft, especially if we choose the context appropriately, e.g.

We had to give up the idea of going on a picnic yesterday. (?)*What it did all day was* vp[*rain non-stop*].

But it expresses a process rather than an action executed and controlled by someone or something, so it is odd with *carefully/deliberately* and in the Imperative:

??It carefully/deliberately rained all day
??Rain, you silly weather!

If we imagine some force of nature or divine being responsible for the process, then it becomes easier to attribute it control and intention, so that modification with *deliberately* becomes more acceptable, e.g.

I'm not hopeful about going on a picnic. You know what English weather is like, it will *deliberately rain* to spoil our fun.

Box 7.1 Summary of tests

1. *Progressive*
   Events, but not states, can occur in the progressive, the construction Aux *be* + V*ing*:

   John is *buying* that book
   *John is *liking* that book.

2. *Pseudo-cleft*
   Events, but not states, can occur in the Pseudo-cleft, the construction
   What NP *do be* VP:

   What John did was *buy* that book
   ??What John did was *like* that book.

3. *Modification with* carefully/deliberately
   Events, but not states, can be modified with one or both of these
   adverbs:

   John carefully/deliberately *bought* that book
   ??John carefully/deliberately *liked* that book.

4. *Imperative*
   Events, but not states, can occur in the Imperative:

   Buy that book, John!
   Like that book, John!

For state verbs, or verbs nearer to the state end of the continuum, it is impossible, or much harder, to create a context involving control or intention, e.g.

??Like that present so you won't upset your aunt!
??Fred deliberately knew the answer just to show Peter up.

7.5 Analytical tips

- When the verb you are testing fails a test, examine the failure carefully (or even deliberately!) to try and pin down the aspect of meaning responsible for it. This will help you decide whether you are dealing with something more like an event or more like a state. For instance, a verb like *sneeze* passes the tests that are related to the temporal properties of events (see Section 7.2):

John was sneezing   (Progressive)
What John did was sneeze   (Pseudo-cleft)

but not those that are sensitive to the features of control and intention:

??Sneeze!
??John carefully/deliberately sneezed.

If you test the verb mechanically without trying to understand what is going on, you would not know what to conclude – *sneeze* passes two of the tests and fails the other two. But if you notice that all the failures are to do with control and intention, you can conclude that you are dealing with an event, an action, though one that we cannot control voluntarily. Remember that it is possible for events to have varying degrees of control and intention – consider, e.g.

John tripped and fell
The avalanche/the rescue team rolled down the mountain
The floods/the army destroyed many villages.

All of these verbs, and many more like them, clearly express dynamic situations involving sub-events that unfold in time. None of them, however, requires control or intention to bring out change.

- Try testing the verb with different types of NPs before it. If you carried out the tests with an NP that refers to an inanimate thing, try substituting it with an NP that refers to a human being and compare the results. For instance, if you started with

??*The boulder* deliberately rolled down the mountain

try

The soldier deliberately rolled down the mountain

so that you can check whether the sentence is odd because of the meaning of the verb, which is what you are testing, or because of an irrelevant incompatibility between the NP and *deliberately* – inanimate things don't have intentions.

- *Be*-type verbs (see Chapter 6, Section 6.3) and *have* are typically states but they can become events in combination with particular APs and NPs after them, as we have mentioned in Section 7.3 above. For instance, compare:

  She was sick vs She was being sick
  She was having a bath/a baby/a drink
  ??She was having a headache/a new car/a broken leg.

- Remember that some verbs can have more than one meaning, so that they may express an event under one interpretation and a state in another, e.g. *stand* and *sit* can be interpreted as an event (a controlled action that usually involves a change of position) or a state, with the meaning of 'being situated', e.g.

  Bill stood up in the middle of the speech
  Bill stood in the middle of the square.

- If the verb has a related, semantically equivalent noun, you can use an additional test that is easier to apply to nouns. Only nouns that express events can combine with and precede verbs or verb phrases like *happen*, *occur* and *take place*. For instance,

  Sarah's *promotion* occurred a few days ago
  Mary's *lecture* took place yesterday
  The *murder* happened last week
  *Sarah's *love* occurred a few days ago
  *Mary's *happiness* took place yesterday
  *The baby's *illness* happened last week.

- Remember that adjectives, in combination with the main verb *be*, express a state, while corresponding verbs express the related event, e.g.

  The door was open   (adjective, state)
  The door opened   (verb, event)
  The soup was cool   (adjective, state)
  The soup cooled   (verb, event).

- Most of all, remember to use the tests to check your intuitions. An error beginners often make is to think about the real world situation rather than the meaning of the verb. For instance, they focus on the fact that crying is often a sign of emotional upset and conclude that the verb *cry* expresses a psychological state. Yet it clearly expresses an event linguistically, e.g.

She was crying
She was crying deliberately to annoy me
What she did was cry all day
Cry! It will make you feel better.

Exercises

1. Identify the main verb in each of the sentences below. Decide whether it expresses an event or a state. Make sure you have evidence for your decisions by applying the tests and giving the relevant examples to back up your conclusions.

    1. That bottle contains poison.
    2. Bill poured the medicine down the sink.
    3. Tommy resembles his dad to an incredible extent.
    4. The meeting lasted all morning.
    5. He watched the television every night.
    6. The arrangement suited her perfectly.
    7. This letter relates to your client's case.
    8. This soup lacks salt.
    9. Your scheme really appeals to me.
    10. Sue possesses a fine sense of humour.
    11. The outcome depends on your efforts.
    12. The water froze in the intense cold.
    13. Sally froze the blackberries.

2. The following utterances were produced by a typically developing child. For each sentence, decide whether the main verb (or the most likely intended main verb) expresses an event or a state. Make sure you give arguments with examples to back up your conclusions. If more than one interpretation is possible, say why.

    1. Daddy like book. 2. Bus go there. 3. Car make noise. 4. Me show mummy. 5. Drink up! 6. Me keep it. 7. Want egg. 8. Put hat on. 9.That ball really big.

3. The following utterances were produced by two children with language impairment – you have analysed these syntactically in previous exercises.

Analyse each utterance semantically following the instructions in Exercise 2 above.

Child A: 1. David be school. 2. Mimi eat upstairs dinner time. 3. Big boys like coffee. 4. We got Ribena today. 5. Frida bring him home.

Child B: 1. Me got haircut. 2. Lily drinking that up. 3. Seen it TV. 4. Running round and round playground. 5. You give me that now quick.

4. You have collected a sample of language from a 5-year-old while he is playing a computer game. The sample includes a very limited range of verbs, all referring to actions. This is not surprising as the game affords many more opportunities to talk about actions than states. To find out whether the child is capable of expressing a wider range of situations, you decide to try an activity where you tell a story that refers to states as well as actions, and you ask the child to re-tell the story (preferably to a listener who has not heard it before). The purpose is to see whether the child's re-tell includes reference to the states, and if so, how the child refers to these.

In this exercise your task is to create a story that includes at least five states and five actions. In creating your story:

- Make sure it is engaging, by making it funny or surprising or shocking, so that the child will be motivated to listen and retell.
- Make sure the states are crucial to the story, rather than peripheral, descriptive information, so that the story cannot be conveyed without reference to these.
- Include a range of states such as location (*be* + PP, *live*), possession (*have, have got, own*), visual (*look, seem*), psychological (*want, like, know*).
- You might accompany the story with pictures or actions which can serve as prompts.

5. Imagine you are working with a woman with aphasia. She seems to have difficulties in comprehending state verbs more than event verbs in picture selection tasks. You want to check this out further and see whether it is because states are more difficult to represent pictorially.

So you want to construct a task that does not involve pictures, for instance, a synonym judgement task (see Marshall *et al.* 1999) with at least 12 target states and 12 target events.

8

Shaping situations: making the focus narrow or wide

8.1 Introduction

We have seen in the previous chapter that language can direct our attention to particular aspects of a situation and make us construe that situation in different ways – for instance, as an event or a state. In this chapter we extend and deepen our understanding of how language can function as an attention-directing device and shape our perception or construal of a situation.

Consider the sentence

My hamster is *dead*.

The adjective *dead*, in combination with the verb *be*, focuses our attention on the state of the speaker's hamster. As we have already seen in the previous chapter, the sentence does not tell us anything about what brought about the hamster's death, though in the real world there must have been some cause of the hamster's change of state from being alive to being dead. All the sentence tells us is that the hamster is in a particular state (see Figure 8.1).

If we understand the meaning of *dead*, we also know which specific state the hamster is in – it's not in the state expressed by *alive, asleep, agitated, scared* or *hungry*. The language zooms in on the state and ignores or backgrounds everything else. We could, however, widen our linguistic take on the situation and include something of the process that led up to the death, saying something like

My hamster *died*.

The verb *die*, as opposed to the adjective *dead*, allows us to present the situation as a process that has taken its course and reached its end point – the state expressed by *dead*. That the process is now included is clear from the fact that we could add a phrase that specifies the time course or manner of the process – something that can't be done when only the state is focused:

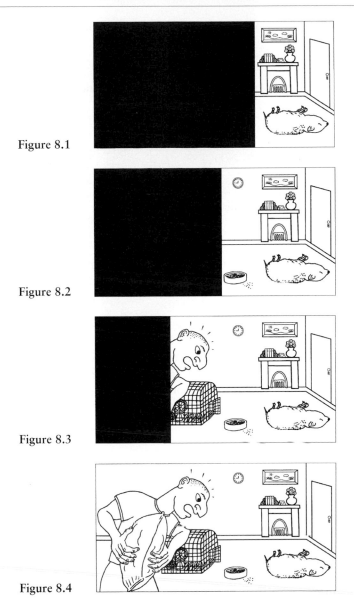

Figure 8.1

Figure 8.2

Figure 8.3

Figure 8.4

My hamster *died slowly/quickly/painfully*
*My hamster is/was *dead slowly/quickly/painfully*.

The single verb wraps up the process and its end state as a single meaning package, and it is easy to lose sight of the fact that there are two sub-situations, or two components, to what the single verb presents as a single process–state combination (see Figure 8.2). Compare it, for instance, with sentences where the two components are separated out:

My hamster *became/went dead*.

We could represent diagrammatically the two components that *dead* and *die* express as follows

ACT ⟶ PROCESS		STATE
		dead
	die	

The verb *die* leaves out of the linguistic picture the cause of death. We could, however, widen the linguistic lens even further and include what caused the process of dying, e.g.

George/an infection *killed* my hamster.

The choice of the verb *kill* allows us to bring into the picture the cause of the change of state and tie it closely into the situation as a direct trigger of the change (see Figure 8.3). Two or more words, rather than the single word *kill*, would have had a different effect, presenting the causal chain as more indirect, e.g.

George made my hamster die
George caused my hamster to die.

Both of these sentences could be preceded or followed by a phrase like

... by leaving it with a neighbour who hates pets ...

while such an addition would seem rather odd with *kill*:

?George killed my hamster by leaving it with a neighbour who hates pets.

Had we not used verbs at all, the causal chain would have been weakened even further, e.g.

Because of George, my hamster died
My hamster died *on account of George*.

Again, we could use a diagram to represent the different sub-situations included in the meaning of *kill*, as opposed to *die* or *dead*.

ACT ⟶	PROCESS	STATE
kill	die	dead

The verb *kill*, however, does not give us any information about what George did to kill the hamster. Again, we could add a phrase to specify how the death was brought about:

George killed my hamster *with poison/a blow*.

Or we could use a verb that incorporates information about the specific action that triggered the process of dying, e.g.

George *suffocated/poisoned* my hamster.

ACT ⟶	PROCESS	STATE
kill	die	dead
suffocate		

This seems to be as wide as language can get. It does not seem possible to pack into a single verb any further sub-situations, such as an action that triggers another action which, in turn, causes a process that leads to a state. We can, of course, express longer, more complex causal chains by linking two or more sentences together, e.g.

After drinking too much, George suffocated my hamster.

But, in natural languages, we do not find single verbs like *druffocate*, meaning 'suffocate after drinking too much'. The three sub-situations in our diagram above can be thought of as a kind of template or schema, which specifies both how wide we can open the semantic lens of a single word and how narrowly we can focus on different components of the total situation. On this approach we would expect to find words that encompass all three sub-situations – like the verbs *suffocate* and *kill*, or two sub-situations like *die*. But we would also expect words that express a single component, such as a single act that does not trigger any causal chain (e.g. *frown, shudder, laugh, kiss*); or a single state (e.g. *be, seem, reside, love*).

Now we can see exactly why states are homogeneous in time (see Chapter 7) while events are more likely to comprise distinct stages that unfold in time. When a word expresses a state, its meaning focuses narrowly and

States

ACT ⟶	PROCESS	STATE

exclusively on the static component of the situation – everything else is blurred out of the linguistic picture.

A word expressing an event, on the other hand, has more focusing possibilities. It can focus narrowly and exclusively on a dynamic act or process (Figures (a) and (b) below); it can widen its focus to encompass two distinct components (Figures (c) and (d) below), or widen it even further to bring together all three components into a single meaning (Figure (e) below).

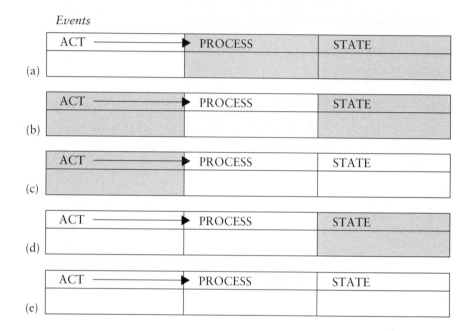

In the following sections, we will consider verbs with 'narrow focus' and the semantic structure of the situations they express.

8.2 Narrow focus verbs

States

ACT ⟶	PROCESS	STATE

Verbs that focus on the STATE component of the situational schema have already been discussed in detail in Chapter 7, where we have seen how they can be distinguished from events verbs. In this section, we will consider the semantic structure of a state and the two main types of state verbs: verbs of location and verbs of psychological state.

All that is present in a state are two participants connected by a static relationship. The verb expresses the relationship and separate phrases express the participants. These participants, however, are not equal: one is made more prominent than the other and it is its relationship to the other participant that is expressed by the whole sentence. Consider, for instance, the visual array below which represents visually a spatial arrangement of two shapes

and how we may describe it. We could make the star more prominent and express its relationship to the circle by using the most neutral of state verbs, *be*, and locate the star with respect to a particular place expressed by a prepositional phrase, e.g.

The star is above the circle.

Or we could make the circle more prominent and express its relationship to a place expressed by a different prepositional phrase, e.g.

The circle is below the star.

The visual array, the 'real' situation, remains exactly the same but we can give a subtly different linguistic picture of it – we can construe the same 'conceptual content' in different ways. These different construals of the same situation are like an instruction to our listeners or readers to direct their attention to one participant and 'see' the situation from that participant's perspective. Similarly, imagine you were thinking about a static relationship of possession that links your friend Sarah and some bike. You might present the relationship from Sarah's perspective – the possessor's – and say

Sarah owns that bike

or foreground what is possessed and present the situation from the bike's perspective:

That bike belongs to Sarah.

The basic semantic structure of a state, therefore, involves two participants on whom our attention is unequally distributed. The relationship between them can be reduced to two main types: a locative relation where the more prominent participant is located with respect to the other participant; or a psychological relationship where one participant is in a perceptual, cognitive or emotional state with respect to the other participant. We will consider these two types of state in turn.

The prototypical State-focus verb that expresses a locative relation is the verb *be*. This verb can express a variety of locative relations depending on the type and meaning of the phrases it combines with. *Be* can express location in physical space and with respect to time, a position on some scale of measurement or a property, e.g.

Location in physical space:
The cup is PP[on the table]
The bike is PP[in the shed]
The picture is PP[above the mantelpiece]
The cat is PP[under the table]
The shop is PP[across the road].

Location in time:
The meeting is PP[at two o'clock/in a few days/during the lunch break]
My job interview is NP[tomorrow/next week]
Our film is PP[after the documentary].

Location on a temperature scale:
The temperature is NP[5 degrees]
The soup is AP[hot/warm/tepid/cool/cold/frozen].

Location with respect to a physical property:
The box is AP[large/wide/round/flat/red]
Chris is AP[tall/thin/short/blonde/tanned/fit]
Stuart is NP[a giant].

Location with respect to behavioural or psychological properties:
Pat is AP[kind/polite/happy/foolish/depressed]
Pat is NP[a fool/a depressive/a bully/a sweetie/a pain]
Mary is PP[down/out of her mind].

Other *be*-type verbs also fall into this category (see also Chapter 6, Section 6.3), e.g.

The soup seems AP[hot/warm/tepid/cool/cold/frozen]
His hair looks AP[awful]/NP[a mess]

Pat seems ᴀᴘ[kind/polite/happy/foolish/depressed]
Pat looks ᴘᴘ[down/out of her mind].

Other verbs of location are verbs of possession and verbs of spatial configuration (see Box 8.1 for examples).

Box 8.1 Narrow focus verbs

STATE-focus verbs:

- *Be*-type verbs: *be, appear, seem, look, sound, feel, taste*
- Verbs of possession: *belong, have, possess, owe, own*
- Verbs of spatial configuration: *contain, extend, fit, hang, jut, kneel, lean, lie, line, nestle, occupy, perch, project, protrude, rest, sit, slope, surround, sprawl, stand, straddle, tilt, tower*
- Psych verbs that foreground the experiencer: *abhor, admire, adore, delight (in), desire, detest, dislike, dread, esteem, fancy, fear, hear, hate, know, like, loathe, love, need, perceive, prefer, prize, respect, revere, see, yearn*
- Psych verbs that foreground the stimulus or content of the state: *amaze, amuse, annoy, appal, astonish, baffle, bore, comfort, con-cern, confuse, delight, disgust, dumbfound, embarrass, fascinate, flabbergast, frustrate, horrify, interest, intrigue, irritate, matter (to), mystify, please, puzzle, remind (of), soothe, trouble, worry*

The second type of State-focus verbs are those that express perceptual, mental or emotional states – what linguists often call '**psych**' verbs (see Box 8.1 for examples). Just like locational states, psychological states involve two participants: someone who experiences the particular psychological state expressed by the verb and the content or stimulus of that state. One of the two participants is relatively more prominent or foregrounded than the other – compare, for instance:

I *like* that idea
That idea *pleases* me

I *fear* that possibility
That possibility *frightens* me.

The verbs *like* and *fear* foreground the experiencer and present the situation from the experiencer's perspective, while the verbs *please* and *frighten* give more prominence to the content or stimulus of the experiencer's state (see also Chapters 9 and 10).

When the experiencer is foregrounded, the state is presented as something that originates in the self and is directed or oriented towards something or someone. On the other hand, when the content or stimulus of the state is foregrounded, the state appears to have been triggered externally by some property of the stimulus (see Talmy 1985). As the stimulus is given more prominence, it is possible to construe the situation as not only triggered by some characteristic of the stimulus but actually caused by it – the situation becomes more like a 'wide focus' event. It is the meaning of the phrases that combine with the verb that usually tip the meaning one way or the other. Compare, for instance:

That idea really annoyed/irritated/troubled/worried me
Karen really annoyed/irritated/troubled/worried me.

In both cases, *that idea* and *Karen* are mental constructs: it is the speaker's thought or memory of Karen that stimulates the state because of some annoying, irritating, troubling or worrying characteristics. But the second sentence can also be interpreted as expressing a causative event where Karen, the actual person, has acted or behaved in a way that caused the speaker's state.
   Why do we not treat the attribution of a psychological property as a psych-verb? That is, why do we not group sentences like:

Mary is sad

with sentences that contain psych-verbs? Because there is a subtle, but significant, meaning difference. Language allows us to present psychological states from the outside, as something we infer as external observers, with varying degrees or types of evidence for our inference – hence the choice of the verb *be* when we are pretty sure of what we are saying, as opposed to *seem/appear* (visual or less firm evidence), or *sound* (auditory or indirect evidence). Or we can present it from the inside, as an internal state of the person we are talking about. Compare, for instance, the *be*-type verb *feel* and the psych verb *feel*:

Mary/the room feels cold (to me)
Mary/ ??the room feels cold
Mary feels sad/happy.

The first sentence expresses a property of Mary or of the room – they are located on a temperature scale. What is located is foregrounded and the observer or perceiver is left out of the linguistic picture or backgrounded inside a prepositional phrase (see also Chapter 10). In the second and third sentences, we are expressing Mary's own feeling, her internal experiences. It is a bit like the difference between *roof* and *ceiling* which, in a one-storey house, refer to the same upper surface viewed either from the outside (roof) or the inside (ceiling).

Narrow focus verbs: ACTs

ACT ⟶	PROCESS	STATE

The prototypical English verbs that focus on this component are verbs that express a bodily gesture or movement of part of the body. The act has a physical manifestation but does not involve any fundamental change in the identity, general characteristics or position of the actor. This type of event always involves one participant – the actor – whose body or part of body is brought into relief or foregrounded by the verb. The action, if it can be controlled at all, can only be controlled by the person engaging in it, usually because of their intrinsic properties – control cannot be handed over to an external controller. This characteristic of intrinsic control is reflected in the fact that these verbs favour the 'alone' interpretation of the PP *by* X-*self* rather than the 'without outside help' one. Compare, for example, a sentence with action verbs like *laugh*:

Mary laughed *by herself*

where the PP is more likely to be interpreted as meaning 'alone', with sentences with verbs expressing a process of change that can have an external controller:

Mary tripped by herself
The door opened by itself

where the PP is more likely to be interpreted as 'without outside help'.
Examples of these verbs are given in Box 8.2.
Given their meaning, it is not surprising that these verbs should be mainly intransitive (see Chapter 6) and not require any NP complement, though

---

Box 8.2 Narrow focus verbs

ACT-focus verbs:

- Bodily action: *blink, cough, cry, frown, grimace, laugh, leer, quiver, scowl, sleep, sneer, sneeze, shiver, shudder, tremble, weep, wink, yawn*
- Action + contact: *caress, elbow, fondle, grab, hit, hug, kiss, kick, pat, pinch, pull, punch, push, shake, slap, smack, stroke, tap, touch*

Features:

- No change in identity, characteristics or position of X that acts
- Act intrinsically controlled, no external cause
- No change in Y, unless implied by additional phrase or context

some of them can have what linguists call a 'cognate' NP – an NP having the same origin and form as the verb, e.g.

Mary yawned/sneezed/laughed/slept
*Her mother yawned/sneezed/laughed/slept Mary
Mary laughed a shrill laugh
Mary slept a deep sleep.

Some of these actions can be directed towards another participant in the situation. The action is construed as oriented to that other participant but without any effects on or changes in them, e.g.

Mary winked/laughed PP[at Sue].

Note that, in the real situation corresponding to the sentence, Sue may well be pleased, annoyed, irritated or delighted by Mary's winking or laughing. But this is not what the sentence depicts. The possible effects are something we can add given our knowledge of the world and people but the language just says that a certain action took place. Indeed, any addition of results or effects on the second participant sounds rather odd even though we can understand what the person is trying to convey, e.g.

*Mary winked/laughed at Sue into a frenzy
??Mary winked/laughed Sue into a frenzy.

Some of the verbs of bodily gesture or movement include a surface contact component: a part of the body of the actor moves and makes some kind of contact with the surface of another participant. Examples of these verbs are given in Box 8.2.

These verbs extend the idea of orientation towards another participant further. The action is not only directed towards the second participant but there is physical contact between the part of the body of the actor and the body of the second participant. The increase in contact some of these verbs imply is expressed in the structure of the sentence itself. All linguistic 'barriers' between the actor and the second participant are removed and an NP rather than a PP can appear after the verb as its complement:

Mary touched/stroked/caressed/kissed NP[the cat]
*Mary touched/stroked/caressed/kissed PP[at the cat].

Some of these verbs allow both NP and PP complements as the action they express can be construed as being either directed towards or making contact with something, e.g.

Mary *hit at the wall* (no contact implied)
Mary hit the wall (contact implied).

We can think of the basic structure of the ACT component as either an action carried out by a single participant (the actor, X, in the diagram below); an action carried out by an actor and directed towards a second participant (the Y in the diagram below)

$$X \xrightarrow{\text{ACT}} Y$$

or an action carried out by an actor with not just orientation but actual contact with or pressure on the second participant Y:

$$X \xrightarrow{\text{ACT}} Y$$

On this approach, all Act-focus verbs are similar in their semantic structure. We can think of the two diagrams above as representing the semantic skeletons on which the flesh of particular semantic differences is hung: the precise manner of the action (*stroke* vs *pat*); the part of the body involved in the action (*slap* vs *kick*); or the amount of energy or noise involved (*tremble* vs *shudder*). But none of these more specific semantic differences have much of a syntactic impact: as long as the situational skeleton is the same, the verbs behave syntactically in pretty similar ways.

Some of these verbs of contact can be interpreted as involving such pressure on the second participant Y that Y changes position or state. This interpretation is usually dependent on the addition of a phrase, usually a PP, expressing Y's resulting state, e.g.

X pushed Y pp[to the ground]
X kicked Y pp[against the wall].

It is as if the additional phrase brought into the linguistic picture another situational component – something like

ACT ⟶	PROCESS	STATE
X pushes Y		

The effect of the contact is something we can infer from the additional phrase or from the context – not from the meaning of the verbs themselves. The semantic focus of the verbs is still on the action, how it was carried out and what type of contact was involved.

Compare these cases with a verb such as *throw*, which has 'wide focus' and includes in its meaning an act that causes a process of change – see Section 8.4 below. With verbs like *throw*, we cannot add a phrase denying the effect, e.g.

*X threw Y but Y didn't budge.

though this is possible with contact verbs like *push*:

X pushed Y but Y didn't budge.

With 'narrow focus' verbs of contact, the exact process by which the second
participant changes its position or state is backgrounded: we know what
X did and where Y ended up but we are not explicitly told anything about
how Y got there, except for what we can infer from the X's action, the type
of contact and amount of pressure. With verbs like *throw*, on the other hand,
there is more specification of how the second participant moves while
changing position – for instance, ballistic motion in the case of *throw, toss,
fling* rather than the kinds of motion expressed by *drag, tug, yank* (see
Pinker 1989).

Narrow focus verbs: Processes

ACT ⟶	PROCESS	STATE

The prototypical process verbs are those that express a change of position –
what are often called **motion verbs** (see Box 8.3 for examples). Someone or
something changes from one place to another in a change of position that
involves the whole entity – it's not just the movement of a part of their
bodies. The verb meaning specifies the particular change involved (e.g. *go* as
opposed to *come* or *run*). The phrases that combine with the verb tell us who
is undergoing the process, e.g.

Mary is going

and sometimes also the direction or end point of the change:

Mary is going *up*
Mary is going *to her desk*

or where the change started from:

Mary is going *from the computer* to her desk.

The entity that undergoes the process is presented as changing of their own
accord, thanks to intrinsic properties that allow them to move or change in
the relevant ways – the change is presented as *internally caused*. Compare,

---

Box 8.3 Narrow focus verbs

PROCESS-focus verbs:

- Motion + manner: *amble, bolt, bounce, bound, charge, crawl, creep, dart, dash, drift, drop, float, fly, gallop, glide, hobble, hop, hurtle, inch, jog, jump, leap, limp, lope, lurch, march, meander, mince, move, nip, parade, plod, prance, prowl, race, ramble, roam, roll, romp, rove, run, rush, revolve, roll, rotate, slide, spin, swing, turn, twirl, twist, walk, wander, whirl, whiz, wind, zigzag*

- Emission:
  - Light: *beam, blaze, burn* (in the sense of emit heat and light, rather than be consumed by fire), *flash, flicker, gleam, glimmer, glint, glisten, glitter, glow, shimmer, shine, sparkle, twinkle*
  - Substance: *bleed, dribble, drip, drool, exude, gush, leak, ooze, pour, seep, shed, spew, spill, sprout, spurt, squirt, stream, sweat*
  - Smell: *reek, smell, stink*
  - Sound: *babble, bang, beep, bellow, blare, blast, boom, buzz, chime, chug, clack, clang, clank, clatter, clink, crackle, creak, gurgle, hiss, hoot, jangle, jingle, knell, knock, peal, pop, rattle, ring, roar, rumble, rustle, sizzle, sputter, squawk, squeak, squeal, squelch, swish, swoosh, thud, tick, toll, trill, wheeze, whistle*

Features:

- A change in the position or state of the entity undergoing the process
- Intrinsically controlled process
- External cause only introduced by additional NP

---

for instance, internally caused motion of this kind:

Mary went to the park
Mary/the rock rolled down the hill
Mary/the bottle floated across the pond
Mary/the plane flew to Paris

with 'wide focus' verbs, where *another entity* triggers the change of the entity that moves:

Sue took Mary to the park
Sue rolled the rock down the hill
Sue floated the bottle across the pond
The pilot flew the plane to Paris.

(See also Section 8.4 below.)

In this sense, Process-focus verbs are similar to the Act-focus ones in that both of them involve something self-generated, internally caused. However, the Process-focus verbs involve a change in the position or state of the entity that generates the change, while the Act-focus ones do not involve any fundamental change to the actor (see the Acts section above).

Many theorists have argued that verbs of change of position are the basic processes on which many other types of change are modelled (see Jackendoff 1983, 1987 and 1990). One of the main reasons for this claim is that, cross-linguistically, we find motion verbs used also for other changes, e.g.

Mary went/turned red (change of physical state)
The soup has gone cold (change of temperature)
Mary swings from happiness to depression (change of mental state).

We can think of sentences containing motion verbs as expressing a process directed towards an end point or actually reaching its end point. In this sense too, processes are similar to the actions we considered above, which could be oriented towards a second participant or actually make contact with that participant. The verbs *come* and *go* can express either orientation towards an end point or reaching the end point, depending on other features of the sentence, such as the **tense** or **aspect** of the verb (see Chapter 12) or the preposition that heads the PP. Compare, for instance:

Mary *went* to the park
Mary *is going* to the park

and

Mary went *into* the park
Mary went *towards* the park.

Some motion verbs such as *arrive* and *enter* focus on the process but also imply the reaching of the end point. This is clear from the fact that getting to the end point cannot be denied, e.g.

*Mary arrived at the park *but she never got there*
*Mary entered the room *without going in*.

Other motion verbs focus on the beginning point of the motion and imply that change is away from it (e.g. *depart, exit, escape, flee, leave*) while others imply a particular direction or path of the motion (e.g. *ascend, descend, cross, plunge, rise*). But the most common aspect of the process expressed by English motion verbs is the manner of the motion (e.g. *run, dash, drift, limp* – see Box 8.3 above for examples).

English seems to mind its manners much more than languages like Spanish or Italian (see Talmy 1985; Naigles and Terrazas 1998). For instance, what we might describe in English as *running out of the house*, with the verb *run* expressing motion and manner together, would be expressed in Spanish as *salir de la casa corriendo*, with the verb *salir* expressing motion and direction together while the manner of the motion is expressed separately by *corriendo* – literally, *exit the house running*.

Similarly, in English we could say

Mary limped home

while in Italian we would have to say

Maria è andata a casa zoppicando
Mary went home limping.

When a phrase expressing the direction or end point of the motion is also present, it seems to attract some of our attention so that we construe the scene primarily as moving to reach an end point, rather than just moving in a certain manner, even if the verb involves both motion and manner of motion. The end point becomes the more prominent aspect of the situation, monopolizing any modifier that would otherwise have modified the verb or the verb in combination with other complements. Consider, for instance, how the PP *for an hour* is interpreted in the two sentences below:

John ran *for an hour* (PP tells us the period of time *during which John ran*)
John ran home *for an hour* (PP tells us the period of time *during which John was at home*, not how long he was running home).

So it seems that our attention is not equally spread amongst all the aspects of a situation, or sub-situation, that a verb expresses. Prominence or fore-grounding is necessarily a relative quality: to be prominent or foregrounded something else must necessarily be less prominent or backgrounded. If a verb expresses a number of aspects – e.g. motion as well as manner of motion – which of the two aspects will be more prominent will also depend on what the verb combines with. If the verb combines with a phrase expressing direction or end point, the motion component related to it in the verb's meaning will become more prominent. If there is a phrase giving more details of how the motion took place, the focus will be on the motion as something done in a particular way – we'll construe the scene more like an act than a change in position. So the linguistic environment will bring to the fore different aspects of verb meaning – just like different environments can bring out different aspects of our personalities.

This shifting of attention or prominence is particularly clear in a language like Italian where selection of auxiliary verbs depends on whether we construe a scene as more act-like or more process-like (something linguists refer to as the unergative/unaccusative alternation, see Levin and Rappaport

Hovav 1995; Pustejovsky and Busa 1995). Where in English we would always select the auxiliary verb *have* to express the perfect aspect (see Chapters 11 and 12), e.g.

John *has* run (fast)
John *has* run (home)
*John *is* run

in Italian, we can select either the auxiliary *be* or *have* depending on whether we want to present the situation as more of a change of position or more act-like, e.g.

Giovanni *é* corso a casa
John is run home

Giovanni *ha* corso in fretta
John has run fast.

If the phrase that combines with *correre* (run) expresses an end point (e.g. *a casa*, home), the auxiliary *be* is more likely to be selected. If a manner phrase occurs instead (e.g. *in fretta*, fast), auxiliary *have* is most likely. It's not that the verb *correre* (run) totally shifts from Act to Process-focus. It is a Process-focus verb but the phrases it combines with can bring out its motion or its manner components.

Other Process-focus verbs are those where the change involves the emission of a substance (see Box 8.3 for examples). Many of these verbs incorporate into their meaning what undergoes the process – the type of light, substance, or sound that is emitted. Since the participant that undergoes the process is incorporated into the verb itself, another participant can be picked out and expressed as a separate phrase. This is usually the beginning point of the process, e.g.

The stars shimmered/twinkled/glittered
His face/hands bled/sweated
Your machine is bleeping
The curtains rustled.

The entities picked out by these phrases can generate light, substance or sound because of their intrinsic properties – they are not acting to bring forth light, substance or sound (see also Chapter 10, Section 10.3).

The manner of the emission is also specified as part of the meaning of some verbs of emission. In these cases, what is emitted and the beginning point of the emission are expressed by separate phrases, e.g.

Water was leaking *from the pipe*
The pipe was leaking *water.*

Like the Act-focus verbs we discussed in above, some Process-focus verbs can widen their focus when *an additional NP* is included in the sentence, e.g.

The ball bounced across the yard (Process-focus, internally caused, intransitive)
The child bounced the ball across the yard (widened-focus, externally caused, transitive)

The torch flashed several times (Process-focus, internally caused, intransitive)
Tim flashed the torch several times (widened-focus, externally caused, transitive)

Coffee poured out of the pot (Process-focus, internally caused, intransitive)
They poured coffee out of the pot (widened-focus, externally caused, transitive)

The bell rang (Process-focus, internally caused, intransitive)
Sally rang the bell (widened-focus, externally caused, transitive).

Semantically, the additional NP brings into the linguistic picture an external cause or trigger of the process of change – the process is no longer presented as self-generated. It is as if the additional NP brings into the linguistic picture the ACT component of the situation, which was suppressed without it:

ACT ⟶	PROCESS	STATE

Syntactically, the verb frame changes from intransitive (no NP complement after the verb) to transitive (one NP complement after the verb) – see Chapter 6. Not all Process-focus verbs, however, can widen their focus in this way, e.g.

The spider crawled along Sarah's arm (Process-focus, internally caused, intransitive)
*Alice crawled the spider along Sarah's arm (widened-focus, externally caused, transitive)

The chickens squawked (Process-focus, internally caused, intransitive)
*The fox squawked the chickens (widened-focus, externally caused, transitive).

We can now consider verbs with a wider focus, whose meaning includes both a process and a state component or an act that triggers a process (Section 8.3).

8.3 Wide focus verbs

Process with state

ACT ──────────────▶	PROCESS	STATE

The main difference between these verbs and the Process-focus ones is that the meaning of these verbs specifies a particular state as the end point of the process, e.g. *die, dissolve, freeze, melt, mature* (see Box 8.4 for examples). It is unsurprising, therefore, that so many of these verbs should be identical in form to a corresponding adjective, e.g. *clear, cool, slow, sober, sour, tense* (see Box 8.4 for examples). As usual, we can check that a state component is included by checking **whether or not it can be denied**, e.g.

*My hamster died *but it is alive and well*
*The chocolate has melted *although it is completely solid*
*I cooled down *but I am boiling hot.*

Like the more narrowly focused process verbs, these also present the situation as an internally generated process. The entity that undergoes the process is presented as changing of its own accord – any external causes that may trigger the process in 'reality' are kept out of the linguistic picture.

An external cause can be brought into the picture only by adding an NP, as in the case of the verbs that focus only on the process (see Section 8.2 above), e.g.

His ideas developed quickly
He developed his ideas quickly

Bill has aged
The illness aged Bill.

Box 8.4 Wide focus verbs

Process with state:

- Verbs of appearance, disappearance and occurrence: *appear, arise, awake, develop, die, disappear, evolve, expire, form, grow, happen, lapse, materialize, occur, perish, result, rise, vanish, wane, wax*
- Verbs of quantity or quality change: *age, alter, change, decrease, diminish, heal, divide, ease, expand, fade, fill, flood, improve, increase, mature, multiply, quadruple*
- Verbs of temperature or composition change: *burn* (in the sense of being consumed by fire), *char, chill, clog, collapse, corrode, decompose, defrost, dissolve, erode, explode, fray, freeze, heat, ignite, melt, thaw*
- Verbs of breaking: *break, crack, crumble, chip, rip, shatter, smash, snap, splinter, split, tear*
- Verbs of shape change: *bend, crease, crinkle, crumple, (un)fold, stretch, shrink, shrivel, warp, wrinkle*
- Verbs of colour change: *blacken, brown, gray, green, redden, tan, whiten, yellow*
- Verbs of state change where the end state corresponds to that specified by a related adjective:
  - with no suffix: *clear, cool, double, dry, empty, loose, mellow, narrow, open, pale, shut, slack, slow, sober, sour, tense, thin, warm*
  - with *-en*: *awaken, brighten, broaden, coarsen, darken, deepen, freshen, harden, flatten, lengthen, lessen, lighten, quicken, shorten, sicken, soften, stiffen, straighten, sweeten, thicken, weaken, widen*

Features:

- A specific change state is implied and cannot be denied
- Intrinsically controlled process
- External cause of process only with additional NP

The bath filled with water
Sarah filled the bath with water

The fridge defrosted quickly
Bill defrosted the fridge quickly

Her jeans shrunk
She shrunk her jeans

The cup broke
The child broke the cup.

In these cases too, the additional NP brings into the picture an ACT component that was not present before:

ACT ──────────▶	PROCESS	STATE

Syntactically too, the additional NP changes the verb frame from intransitive to transitive (see Levin and Rappaport Hovav 1995). Syntactically speaking, therefore, some of these verbs end up in exactly the same frames as verbs that are semantically quite different – the Act-focus ones, for example. But the syntactic similarities should not make us forget the meaning difference. Let's reconsider some of the examples we have just seen, where the verb focus has been widened by adding an NP, e.g.

Bill defrosted the fridge
She shrunk her jeans
Alice opened the door
The child broke the cup

and compare them with some Act-focus verbs that occur in the same syntactic frames, e.g.

Bill patted the cat
She kissed her friend
Alice stroked my arm.

With the Act-focus verbs, the entity expressed by the first NP always acts in a way specified by the verb. The verb meaning specifically tells us what action was involved. With the 'widened' Process-focus verbs, on the other hand, the first NP can act in many different ways to bring about the change in the second NP. The verb specifies only the nature of the change rather than what the first NP does. In fact, we do not necessarily know what the first NP did to trigger the change – the verb does not tell us. If someone said

The child broke the cup

it would not be unreasonable to ask how they did it, while it would be odd, or at least unusual, to follow up a statement like

Bill patted the cat

with the question 'How did he do it?'

8.4 Wide focus verbs that include ACT

The last types of verbs we deal with are those where an ACT component is included in the meaning of the verb itself. Here, the ACT triggers a process, or a process that results in a specified state

ACT ——————▶	PROCESS	STATE

ACT ——————▶	PROCESS	STATE

We will deal with both these possibilities together as most of the verb classifications you will encounter in the clinical and psycholinguistic literature tend to cut across them. The crucial thing is to understand how the ACT component connects to the PROCESS, irrespective of whether or not a STATE is included in the verb's focus.

Let's remind ourselves of the semantic structure of ACT situations expressed by narrow focus ACT verbs. We said that the semantic structure of these situations could involve two participants, one acting towards another and, in some cases, with actual contact between them. So we could think of the first participant (X) exerting force or applying pressure on the second participant (Y)

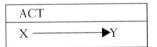

ACT	
X ————————▶Y	

With the narrow Act-focus verbs, that is where the situation ended. The verb meaning did not include any changes or effects on the second participant (see Section 8.2.). With these wide focus verbs, however, the first participant's action triggers a process of change in the second participant. There is a causal chain that we might represent as

ACT ——————▶	PROCESS
X acts	Y changes

As we have seen, the semantic structure of processes in general involves something or someone changing, a beginning point of the change, an end point of the change and a trajectory or path of the change. Any of these aspects of the PROCESS may be specified as part of the verb's meaning and/or expressed as separate phrases (see Section 8.2 above) and that

---

Box 8.5 Wide focus verbs with ACT

- Caused motion: *bring, carry, cart, chuck, convey, ferry, fling, hand, hurl, put, place, position, raise, remove, send, store, take, throw, transport*
- Caused motion with substance specified: *butter, dust, flour, milk, oil, paint, paper, salt, shampoo, sugar, tile, varnish, water, wax*
- Caused motion with end point specified: *bottle, box, can, file, pocket, pot*
- Transfer or transaction: *acquire, attain, borrow, buy, collect, donate, earn, feed, gain, gather, get, give, hire, lend, let (in the 'rent' meaning), lose, obtain, present, (re)pay, recover (in the 'retrieve' meaning), rent, retrieve, rob, sell, show, steal, supply, win*
- Communication: *acknowledge, address, admit, advise, announce, answer, argue, assure, complain, consult, convince, declare, demand, deny, discuss, encourage, explain, express, inform, mention, note, offer, phone/ring, promise, propose, publish, quote, read, remark, reply, report, respond, reveal, say, state, suggest, swear, teach, tell, threaten, urge, warn*
  - Caused change of state:
    - Cutting: *axe, cut, dice, hack, hew, lop, sever, shear, slash, slice*
    - Destruction and defeat: *annihilate, bulldoze, defeat, demolish, destroy, dismantle, overthrow, raze, ruin, wreck*
    - Consumption: *devour, drink, eat, fritter, gobble, guzzle, swallow, waste*
    - Bringing into existence: *draw, knit, paint, sew, sketch, weave, write*

---

applies in exactly the same way to wide focus verbs of this type. So the semantic structure of each component situation remains the same. The only difference is that the act that triggers the process is explicitly built into the verb's meaning, rather than being blurred out of the linguistic picture or inferred indirectly from context or through the addition of a phrase. Recall the comparison between the narrow Act-focus verb *push* and the verb *throw*, exactly the kind of verb we are dealing with here.

While with *push* we can deny that any change in the second participant had occurred:

X pushed Y but Y didn't budge

we cannot do the same with *throw*:

*X threw Y but Y didn't budge.

With *throw*, the application of force by X to Y has consequences beyond the act itself – it triggers a process as its consequence.

The process may not just be oriented towards some end point but actually require the reaching or achievement of that end point. A STATE component may also be specified so that the causal chain is made longer and more complex

ACT ⟶	PROCESS	STATE
X acts	Y changes	Y is in Z

We can check that all three component situations are included in the meaning of a verb by using the usual denial test. Take the wide focus verb *kill*. We cannot deny without contradiction the resulting state, the process or the act:

*George killed my hamster *but it is alive and well* (denial of STATE)
*George killed my hamster *but it didn't change at all* (denial of PROCESS)
*George killed my hamster *although he did not do anything to make it die* (denial of ACT).

Second, we can add an adverb phrase and check whether it can modify each of the component situations. For instance, the sentence

George *almost/nearly* killed my hamster

is ambiguous: it can mean that George was about to do something that could have resulted in the death of my hamster but he refrained – the adverb phrase modifies the ACT. Or it can mean that George did something that almost/nearly had fatal consequences for my hamster – the adverb phrase modifies the STATE. If we add the adverb phrase *slowly* to a sentence with *kill*:

George killed my hamster slowly

we will get an ambiguity again; this time the adverb phrase could modify the ACT or the PROCESS. When this sort of adverb phrase is combined with narrow focus verbs, no such ambiguities arise, e.g.

George almost/nearly laughed/coughed/cried

(see Section 8.1 above and Pustejovsky 1995).

Wide focus verbs are semantically more complex in three ways: first, they involve connected situations while the narrow focus verbs only involve one situation. Second, when an ACT component is included, the connection between situations becomes causal (that is why this type of verb is often referred to as causative) and cause-effect relations are also involved. Third, each situation contributes different participants and aspects of the situation that can be specified to distinguish a verb from another verb of similar focus and semantic structure.

Consider, for instance, the verbs *put* and *give*. They are wide focus verbs of this type so they involve a more complex causal chain than, say, narrow focus verbs like *pat* (Act-focus) or *go* (Process-focus). They involve an actor triggering a second participant's change of location or possession. The nature of the act, the properties of the participant that changes, the final position or recipient of what changes, or any other aspect of the linked situations remains unspecified. Anybody can put or give something; it can be anything at all with no restrictions on how the change takes place. Any final location or recipient will do. Now compare *put* with the verb *bottle*, which is also a wide focus verb of this type and thus equally complex in terms of the number of situations that are packaged together in a single verb. Both verbs involve an act that can be carried out by any kind of actor. The process triggered in both cases is quite similar – hence the fact that *put* can be used to paraphrase *bottle*, e.g.

John bottled the wine
John put the wine in bottles.

The main difference is that the verb *bottle* requires a particular end point – what moves must end up in the particular container the noun *bottle* identifies. *Put* is not restricted in this way.

Now compare *give* with another verb with wide focus and caused transfer such as *sell*. These are almost identical except that *sell* requires money as part of the transfer, while *give* does not – the process of change is different. But the difference could be in what end of the process is highlighted – the beginning of the transfer, as for *sell* and *remove*, or the end point of the transfer, as for *buy* and *store*.

The causing act itself could be a source of semantic contrast. Consider the wide focus verbs *kill*, *murder* and *assassinate*, which are all more complex than the related narrow focus process verb *die* (see Section 8.1 above). While *kill* does not require the act to be intentional, *murder* and *assassinate* do, as can be seen from the fact that intention cannot be denied:

George killed his friend *by accident*
*George murdered/assassinated his friend *by accident*.

But both *kill* and *murder* contrast with *assassinate* in the type of entity that undergoes the change: *kill* is completely unrestricted; with *murder* it is usually a human being that dies, while *assassinate* not only requires a human being but also someone famous and of public importance, e.g.

??George murdered/assassinated my hamster.

The nature of the entity that changes can also be the source of contrast between wide focus verbs, such as those of consumption. The verbs *eat* and *drink* involve quite similar acts, with similar parts of the actor's body involved, but the entity that is consumed is either solid (*eat*) or liquid (*drink*) – hence the quandary about whether you eat or drink soup.

Finally, consider the wide focus verbs *axe*, *saw*, *dice* and *slice*. They all involve someone acting in a way that triggers a process of change in some other entity. *Axe* and *saw* require particular and different instruments to carry out the act and, therefore, require different kinds of actions. *Dice* and *slice*, on the other hand, can be done with any kind of appropriate implement but specify the final shape of the entity that undergoes the change.

So we see that wide focus verbs not only incorporate two or three situations but may be particular about different aspects of those situations. The myriad ways of specifying these gives rise to the myriad range of verbs we have to talk about causal chains.

8.5 Summary of situation types

We have concluded our survey of the types of situations expressed in language and, in particular, in English. We have seen that the linguistic representation of situations is strongly constrained in two main ways. First, the number of situations that can be brought together into a single sentence with a single main verb is limited to the three types we have discussed – ACT, PROCESS, STATE. We can *think* about longer causal chains but we cannot package all the meanings into one verb and express them linguistically with one sentence.

Second, the semantic structure of each of the situations that make up the causal chain is highly constrained. Only a limited number of participants or aspects of the situation can be foregrounded and included in the meaning of the verb or expressed by the complements of the verb.

These two aspects of meaning – how wide or narrow the focus of the verb is and which aspects of a situation are foregrounded – are particularly important linguistically. As we have already mentioned in Chapter 6 and in Section 8.2 above, they affect parts of the syntactic structure that other aspects of meaning can't reach. We will come back to this in the next two chapters.

As we have pointed out in Chapters 2 and 7, language, like all forms of representation, abstracts away from the mass of information that is present in 'real' situations and concentrates on only a few aspects. When we look across the situations we have discussed in this chapter, we can see that:

- One participant is always foregrounded – the one that acts, changes or is located. The situation is then presented from the perspective of this participant.
- Another participant may be picked out – the one towards which the act, the process of change or the state is oriented.

So the 'core' of linguistic situations can be boiled down to an act or process involving just one participant, or an act, process or state involving two participants.

It is only with processes, which are represented as changes of position, that other 'core' components or participants are foregrounded: the initial position where the change starts and the trajectory or path it takes. We have seen, however, that very few verbs foreground all four aspects simultaneously. That is, there are not many verbs like *go* where all four can be expressed, e.g.

Mary went [from her school] [along the river] [to the park]
Mary: participant that changes
from her school: beginning point of the change
along the river: trajectory of the change
to the park: end point of the change.

In English, there are no verbs that require all four to be expressed – usually only two, or at most three, components have to be expressed (see also Chapter 6), e.g.

*Went
Mary went   (participant that changes must be expressed)

Mary went to the park   (participant that changes and end point)

Mary went along the river   (participant that changes and trajectory)

Mary went along the river to the park   (participant that changes, trajectory and end point).

Rather than being expressed by a separate phrase, some of these 'core' components may be incorporated into the meaning of the verb, e.g. the verb *pale* incorporates the end point towards which the process is oriented (e.g. Mary paled); verbs like *drop* or *rise* incorporate part of the path (e.g. The poster dropped on the floor/off the wall; Smoke rose from the house).

We can see the similarities in semantic structure of the component situations in the wider causal chain by comparing the diagrams we have used throughout this chapter:

ACT FOCUS	PROCESS FOCUS	STATE FOCUS
X acts towards Y	X changes towards Y	X is in Y

$$\longrightarrow$$

Beginning point	Path	End Point

If X is not just oriented towards Y but exerts some sort of force on it that makes Y change, then all the situations can be linked into a continuous causal chain:

ACT $\longrightarrow$	PROCESS	STATE
X acts	Y changes towards Z	Y is in Z

$$\longrightarrow$$

Beginning point	Path	End Point

As we have seen in this and the previous chapter, there are various ways of distinguishing verbs and determining their situational focus. The boundaries between situations, however, are not always clear-cut and verb meanings can often straddle two situations. We have seen, for instance, that verbs of spatial configuration like *sit*, *stand* and *lean*, can be interpreted as processes or states (see Chapter 7). Furthermore, while the meaning of the verb focuses the linguistic zoom lens on one situation, the meaning of its complements may readjust the situational focus of the whole sentence. For example, Process-focus verbs of motion can appear more act-like if they are combined with NPs that refer to a human being, e.g.

NP[*John*] slid down the hill
NP[*The lump of rock*] slid down the hill.

The situational meaning of the whole sentence is therefore the product of a complex interaction between the meaning of the verb and the meaning of its complements, together with additional meaning effects provided by the syntactic structure of the whole sentence, as we will see in Chapters 10, 12 and 13.

8.6 Why we need these concepts

The detailed analysis of verb meanings we have gone through is clearly necessary from a linguistic point of view: it is a crucial building block to describe the meaning of whole sentences. But why bother with the semantics of situations from a clinical point of view? Because our common sense understanding of how things and people interact in the world is not enough. Without this kind of analysis, we would not understand how complex talking about situations really is. As we have repeatedly pointed out, language does not simply copy or reflect experience, so what might be experientially simple can be linguistically complex.

Consider, for instance, how Travis, a six-year-old boy with specific language problems, talks about transfer situations pictured below (see Chiat 2000).

Travis: Monkey – panda wanta a pear – monkey want money (Evelyn 1996; Chiat 2000).

Figure 8.5 (Source: Chiat, S. *Understanding Children with Language Problems* (Cambridge, Cambridge University Press, 2000: 174).)

Travis: Pig want – pear in basket – sheep give it pig – pig want pear – um basket and sheep and he give it and a lot – lot of 5p (Evelyn 1996; Chiat 2000).

Figure 8.6 (Source: Chiat, S. *Understanding Children with Language Problems* (Cambridge, Cambridge University Press, 2000: 176).)

He clearly knows what the situation involves, what its main components are and what the participants desire; yet he cannot bring them together and package them appropriately into a single verb of transfer involving money (*buy* or *sell*), foregrounding and connecting the main participants in the way English requires. Other times, he seems to focus on only one sub-situation within a more complex causal chain – for instance, he says

Target: Pouring sugar into the bowl
Travis: Sugar in the pot   (focus on the end point of the motion)

Target: A top spinning
Travis: Round   (focus on the direction of the motion)

Target: Dropping apples
Travis: Fruit on the floor   (focus on the end point of the motion).

Translating an experienced situation or a pictured scene into language can be highly problematic even after language has been fully acquired, if the relevant mechanisms have been disrupted by a stroke or head injury. For instance, CP, a young woman who had suffered a stroke, describes the following video scenes as

Target	*Response*
1. A woman tickling a child	Child giggling
2. A woman dressing a boy	Boy has jumper
3. A boy tripping up a girl	Girl falls
4. A man giving books to a woman	Woman holds the books
5. A woman lifting a child up	Child in the air.

CP too focuses only on one component of a complex situation, a bit like Travis. Where the target situation would typically be described with wide focus verbs that include ACT, PROCESS and STATE as part of their meaning, CP tends to talk about the end point or outcome of the causal chain (1, 2, 4, 5) or the process (3) leaving out the ACT component of the situation altogether.

In CP's case, her syntactic resources would often be enough to give full expression to the whole causal chain. For example, the probable target for scene number two involves a verb and two NPs; CP's response also includes a verb and two NPs, though not the two NPs that would express both 'core' participants in the target scene. For people like CP, therefore, it's not just a question of finding the right words or the structure to express the situation she wants to talk about. Deciding what to focus on and what to give prominence to can be a problem in itself (see Dipper, Black and Bryan, submitted).

Keeping in mind the semantic differences we have discussed in this chapter might be particularly useful in assembling clinical materials. For example, the types of pictures you might look for to test comprehension of verb meanings might vary depending on the verb focus. For narrow focus Act verbs such as *kiss* or *kick*, a single picture might do, while for wide focus verbs, such as *buy* or *sell*, you might need a picture sequence or a composite picture. Similarly, if you are working with someone who can only use gesture or drawing to communicate situations, it might be helpful to think about the number and types of sub-situations and which of those would be more crucial for communicating.

Most of the time, we are unaware of how complex the process of putting our thoughts into words really is (see Black and Chiat 2000), although we all experience something akin to CP's problems in many situations. For instance, when we write, we become much more conscious of the difficulties of conveying our perspective on a situation, making some aspects more prominent than others. Even when we talk, we often have to rethink and rephrase what we say, if it becomes clear that the focus and relative prominence we have expressed has led to misunderstandings. We often have to engage in a cycle of clarification and rephrasing, which is much easier if our partners in the communication are careful listeners who are willing and able to guide us through the possible misunderstandings. Part of the therapist's role is also to act as a specialist listener who can help the client refocus and adjust their communication, as well as advise their regular communicative partners in how they might adapt their own communication to the person with the language disability.

Exercises

1. Identify the main verb in each of the following sentences. Decide what type of situation it expresses and whether it has wide or narrow focus.

    1. The baby crawled across the floor.
    2. She yawned every two minutes.
    3. She is mending the bike.
    4. The boy squirted ink all over the page.
    5. She got the money from Sarah.
    6. They delivered several parcels to our door.
    7. She winked at her friend.
    8. Bob mumbles all the time.
    9. A man coughed during the concert.
    10. Dominic returned to Africa.
    11. I returned the books to the library.
    12. He slid the note under the door.
    13. Your train departs from platform one.
    14. We marched across the fields.
    15. The general marched his troops into battle.
    16. She passed me the newspaper.

17. They supplied the chemical weapons to the dictator.
18. The women fetched water from the well.
19. The agent rented that flat to Sally.
20. The heat of the sun melted the snow.

2. You want to test comprehension of Act-focus verbs with a picture selection task. Using available clinical materials or your own pictures, put together a set of 12 target pictures that would be suitable for this task. You can decide whether the task is for a child or an adult with language impairment.

3. The following is a set of instructions for a chemistry experiment, taken from teaching materials (Fullick, Richardson, Sang and Stirrup 1996: 73). Decide the focus of all the verbs in bold.

Making copper sulphate
1. One third **fill** a test tube with sulphuric acid.
2. **Add** a spatula of black copper oxide.
3. **Warm** the tube carefully over a medium Bunsen burner flame.
4. What do you see **happening** in the tube?
5. If all the black powder **dissolves**, add a little more.
6. **Put** the tube in the rack. **Set** up a filter funnel with filter paper as shown.
7. **Pour** the blue liquid into the filter paper. **Collect** the filtrate in a small beaker.
8. **Label** a Petri dish with your name and 'copper sulphate'.
9. Pour the filtrate into the Petri dish.
10. **Leave** the dish out in the laboratory until next lesson so that the water can **evaporate**.

4. Imagine you are working with a man who has acquired aphasia. He wants to learn to cook for himself – something he never had to do before his stroke. He has picked out a recipe he likes because the ingredients are simple, the recipe is short, and the result healthy. There is just one drawback: he has comprehension problem with verbs, and adjectives related to verbs, that have wide focus and include ACT. Underline all the verbs or adjectives he might have problems with in this recipe (from *Jane Grigson's Vegetable Book*, 1980: 297).

8 small leeks, topped and tailed
3 tablespoons of butter
¾ kg mushrooms, quartered
250 ml vegetable or chicken stock
½ teaspoon brown sugar
pinch saffron

½ teaspoon fresh ginger root, chopped small
2 tablespoons butter mashed with 2 tablespoons flour
salt, pepper

Slice the leeks and fry them in the butter until they collapse. Then add the mushrooms and stir them about thoroughly. Add stock, sugar, saffron and ginger. Cover and leave a few minutes until the vegetables are cooked. Add the butter and flour in little bits to thicken the juices, keeping the liquid under boiling point. Stir all the time. Season to taste and serve.

|9|

Shaping situations: selecting participants

9.1 Introduction

As we saw in the previous chapter, language reduces situations to a 'core': an action, a process, a state or a combination of these (see especially *Summary of situation types*). The number of participants in each situation type is also limited: at least one participant but not more than five.

So far, we have used variables like X and Y and descriptions like 'the beginning point', 'trajectory' and 'end point' to talk about the participants in each type of situation. In many linguistic theories, as well as some traditional grammars, the different participants have been distinguished by means of descriptive labels – so-called Thematic Roles. We will do the same here, as a convenient shorthand to refer to and distinguish 'core participants' in the different types of situation.

Thematic roles have been central to analyses of verb and sentence meaning. Their importance, however, has diminished or has been challenged in more recent accounts (see Butt and Geuder 1998; Dowty 1991; Jackendoff 1990; Tenny and Pustejovsky 2000). In the analysis we have adopted in this book, thematic role labels are just a quick and convenient way of talking about situation participants. They do not add anything of substance to the analysis. Nevertheless, they come in handy in describing both the general semantic structure of situation types and that of specific verbs, as we will demonstrate in the next section.

9.2 How to apply thematic role labels

We can use thematic role labels to label the participants in narrow focus Act events as follows:

Act-focus events: X Acts (towards Y)

Actor = the X that acts
Goal = the Y towards which the act is oriented.

For instance, we can say that the sentence

John smiled

expresses an Act-focus event – the specific action expressed by the verb
smile – and the Actor of this action is whoever *John* refers to when the sentence is uttered or written. The sentence tells us nothing about whether John's
action was directed towards anyone but if the sentence had been

John smiled *at the baby*

we would also know who the Goal of John's action was. As long as we kept
the verb *smile*, we could plug other noun phrases before the verb and they
would still be interpreted as Actor, e.g.

I smiled at the baby
My friend smiled at the baby
The candidate smiled at the baby.

Similarly, we could plug other noun phrases into the prepositional phrase, and
the result could still be interpreted as expressing the Goal. Or we could substitute the verb *smile* with other Act-focus verbs (see Chapter 8, Section 8.2),
and the phrases around the verb could still be interpreted as Actor and Goal
respectively, e.g.

John *laughed* at the baby
John *frowned* at the baby
John *winked* at the baby.

We can think of all Act-focus verbs as expressing an action that involves one
entity (the Actor) or connects two entities (an Actor and a Goal), e.g.

John touched/patted/kissed/cuddled the baby.
Actor   Goal

These participants, whose role in the event is differentiated by the thematic
role labels, are intrinsically bound up with the meaning of the verb. If we
understand the meaning of this type of verb, we also understand that it
involves semantically an Actor or an Actor and a Goal. The general semantic structure of all Act-focus events can then be expressed as

Actor acts towards Goal.

We can use the same reasoning in applying thematic role labels to the participants in a narrow focus Process event:

Process-focus events: X changes towards Y
Theme = the X that changes.
Goal = the Y towards which the change is oriented (i.e. the intended end-point).
Source = the beginning point of the change.
Path = the trajectory of the change.

Consider, for instance

John went *to the park/home*
John went *pale*
John went *into a rage*.

where the different phrases after the verb express different kinds of end points – a place, a physical property, a psychological state. Yet, as we have already seen, we can treat them all as end-points of a process and give them all the same thematic role label – they are all Goals. Similarly, even though the precise nature of the processes is different, John is involved in the same way as the participant that undergoes the process and necessarily changes either spatial location, physical property or mental state.

In the sentences below, *John* always expresses the participant that changes (the Theme) but different points of the process are specified, e.g.

John left *home* (NP = Source, where the process begins)
John escaped *from prison* (PP = Source)
John walked *from work* (PP = Source)
Water was leaking *from the pipe* (PP = Source, water = Theme)
The pipe was leaking water (NP = Source, water = Theme)

John walked *around the lake* (PP = Path)
John strolled *along the seafront* (PP = Path)
John went *down the road* (PP = Path)
John strolled *in* (PP = Path).

As we have seen in Section 8.2 of the previous chapter, each point in the process of change may be expressed in a sentence, so that we could rewrite the schema for the semantic structure of Process-focus events as:

Theme changes from Source via Path to Goal.

Wide focus Act events, which bring together ACT and PROCESS or ACT, PROCESS and STATE, potentially involve all the thematic roles of the situations they include:

Wide focus Act events: X Acts, Y changes towards Z, Y is in Z
Actor = the X that acts
Theme = the Y that changes
Goal = the end point of the change
Source = the beginning point of the change
Path = the trajectory of the change.

For instance, in sentences expressing a caused change of position, possession or state (see Chapter 8, Section 8.4), the core participants can be identified as:

George put the box on the table
Actor   Theme   Goal

George loaded the car with bags
Actor   Goal   Theme

George loaded the bags into the car
Actor   Theme   Goal

They took the child into care
Actor   Theme   Goal

They took the child from her parents
Actor   Theme   Source

George gave the box to Bill
Actor   Theme   Goal

George took the box from Bill
Actor   Theme   Source

George killed my hamster
Actor   Theme

George demolished the shed
Actor   Theme

Transactions involving communication and all other events discussed in Section 8.4, Chapter 8 can also be analysed in this way, e.g.

His boss mentioned the rumour to Alistair
Actor   Theme   Goal

Bob told the joke to his mates.
Actor   Theme   Goal

The meaning of the verb tells us specifically about the action that caused the change, or something about the particular process of change or both. The thematic roles, on the other hand, label and distinguish the participants involved in the causal action or the process of change. Again, we can think of the semantic structure of this type of event as a combination of the general structure of the sub-situations that make it up:

Actor Act $\rightarrow$ Theme changes from Source to Goal via Path.

For states, the relevant thematic role labels are:

- Locational states: X is located in Y
  Theme = the X that is located
  Location = the physical place, time, or property involved.

So the first noun phrase in each of the following sentences would be labelled the Theme, while the different phrases after the verb would all be labelled Location:

The cup is on the table
Theme   Location

The shop is across the road
Theme   Location

The meeting is at two o'clock
Theme   Location

Our film is after the documentary
Theme   Location

The soup is hot
Theme   Location

Stuart is tall
Theme   Location

Bill looks depressed.
Theme   Location

With verbs that express possession, the possessor is always treated as the Location (see Chapter 8, Section 8.2) and the possessed as the Theme, e.g.

Mary has/owns that large house
Location   Theme

That large house belongs to Mary.
Theme   Location

- Psychological states: X is in a psychological state with respect to Y
  Experiencer: the X that is in perceptual, mental or emotional state
  Stimulus: the Y that specifies the content or the trigger of the state.

For instance:

I   like that idea
Experiencer   Stimulus

Mary fancied the red dress
Experiencer   Stimulus

The present delighted Mary
Stimulus   Experiencer

That possibility frightens me.
Stimulus   Experiencer

Apart from being convenient in specifying the general semantic structure of situation types, thematic role labels can come in handy in describing the semantic structure of particular verbs – also known as the **thematic or argument structure** of that verb (see Section 9.3 below). This thematic or argument structure makes clear which participants, out of the set allowed by the situation type the verb corresponds to, are selected by the verb. For instance the verbs *sneeze, laugh, arrive, put, remove, store, be, own, like* can be given the following thematic or argument structures:

sneeze [Actor]
laugh [Actor Goal]
arrive [Theme Goal]
put [Actor Theme Goal]
remove [Actor Theme Source]
store [Actor Theme Goal]
be [Theme Location]
own [Location Theme]
like [Experiencer Stimulus].

Thematic role labels make it easier to specify what each verb shares with other verbs of that type. For instance, *laugh, kick* and *kiss* express different actions, yet they share situation type and involve the same sort of participants. Their thematic or argument structure makes these similarities apparent:

laugh [Actor Goal]
kick [Actor Goal]
kiss [Actor Goal].

The verbs *remove* and *store* have similar but not identical thematic structures:

remove [Actor Theme Source]
store [Actor Theme Goal].

They correspond to the same event type but foreground different ends of the process undergone by the Theme. *Store* foregrounds the end point of the process (the Goal) and ignores where the Theme has started out from (the Source). *Remove* foregrounds the motion away from the Source and ignores where the Theme might end up as a result of the motion (the Goal) – see also Section 8.4 of the previous chapter.

Verbs with similar thematic structures will tend to occur in similar syntactic frames. But the correspondence between syntactic and semantic structure is only partial. Verbs that correspond to different situation types involving different participants can end up in similar syntactic structures. For instance, narrow focus Act verbs with an Actor and Goal participant can slot into the same types of frames as psychological state verbs involving participants like Experiencer and Stimulus, e.g.

$_{NP}$[Mary] _____ $_{NP}$[her friend]
     kicked
     kissed
     liked
     annoyed

Conversely, phrases of the same syntactic type (e.g. noun phrases or prepositional phrases) occurring in apparently similar positions in the sentence can express different types of participants in the situation or make a completely different contribution to the meaning of the sentence – not express participants at all. In the next section, we will consider how to tell apart phrases that express participants (also called argument or complement phrases) from those that do not (so-called non-argument or adjunct phrases).

9.3 How to tell complements and adjuncts

Imagine we were faced with a verb whose meaning we did not know, something like

Mary *flixed* her friend.

We could interpret the verb as expressing an act involving an Actor and a Goal, like *kick* and *kiss* – *flix* could mean something like 'touch lightly with a flick of the wrist'. Or it could be interpreted as a psychological state such as *like* and *annoy* – something like 'experiencing an ambivalent feeling towards someone'. Perhaps *flix* could express an act that triggers a process of change, something like *feed* or *rob*, or a possessional state such as *have* or *possess*. We can make some informed guesses about the roles of the two noun phrases around the verb but we cannot know for sure without knowing the specific meaning of the verb. This shows what a close relationship there is between the verb and the phrases that express the participants linked by it – the verb's arguments or complements.

Other phrases in a sentence will have a less intimate relation with the verb and its meaning – these are non-arguments or adjuncts. Consider, for instance, how we would interpret the emboldened phrases below:

Mary flixed her friend *on Sunday*

Mary flixed her friend *for no good reason*
Mary flixed her friend *with her careless remarks.*

Even if we do not know the meaning of the verb and how the other phrases are linked to it, we have a pretty good idea of how the non-arguments or adjunct phrases are to be interpreted. They provide a kind of setting in space or time (e.g. *on Sunday*) and add further details about the situation but do not express the central, focused action, process or state, nor the participants in that situation.

Which criteria can we use to distinguish arguments or complements from non-arguments or adjuncts? A number of semantic and syntactic properties can be used to decide whether a phrase is a complement or an adjunct – from now on, we will use only the terms complement and adjunct to keep terms to a minimum.

First, as we have seen, complements make a different semantic contribution to the sentence and are semantically bound to the main verb. Complements express participants in the situation in the sense discussed in Chapter 8. Using thematic role labels as a shorthand, we can say that a phrase is a complement if it expresses an Actor, Goal, Theme, Source, Path, Location, Experiencer or Stimulus. If it does not, then it is an adjunct. This is not a difficult criterion to apply but it requires a little care. Consider, for instance, the difference between the phrases *at her niece* and *in her sleep*, both of which are prepositional phrases occurring in the same position in the sentence:

She smiled *at her niece* (complement)
She smiled *in her sleep* (adjunct).

In this case, it is clear that the first PP expresses the Goal towards which the act of smiling is directed, while the second PP expresses the setting of the act of smiling – where or when the act takes place. The semantic content of the PPs themselves help us in assessing their semantic contribution to the sentence – how they are to be interpreted in relation to the verb and any other complements. The preposition *at* is much more likely to express Goal than the preposition *in*, and the noun *niece* is a more likely Goal for the verb *smile* than the noun *sleep*. Similarly, it should be fairly straightforward to decide that the noun phrase *wine* is a complement in the sentence

She drank *wine* (complement)

as it expresses a core participant in the event, the Theme, while the noun phrase *all night* in the sentence

She drank *all night* (adjunct)

is an adjunct since it tells us when the event of her drinking took place rather than what she drank.

There are, however, cases where the same phrase with the same semantic content can contribute differently to the meaning of the sentence depending on the verb it combines with. So, we cannot just rely on the meaning of the phrase or part of the phrase to decide whether it is a complement or an adjunct. The meaning of the verb, as we have stressed many times, is a crucial factor. Consider, for instance:

She went *upstairs* (complement)
She slept *upstairs* (adjunct).

Here the same prepositional phrase, with the same meaning, contributes differently to the meaning of the whole sentence – the meaning of the verb pushes us towards a different way of linking them. In the first sentence, the verb *go*, a Process-focus verb that expresses motion towards an end point or along a trajectory, allows us to interpret *upstairs* as either the Goal or the Path. In the second sentence, the verb *sleep*, an Act-focus verb with no orientation and no Goal, does not allow for this way of interpreting the PP. We can only interpret it as expressing the setting of the whole event – the place where her act of sleeping took place.

We can see a similar type of contrast in the following pairs of sentences:

She put her dinner *in the kitchen* (complement)
She ate her dinner *in the kitchen* (adjunct)

She threw the shirt *in the sink* (complement)
She washed the shirt *in the sink* (adjunct).

In the first sentence of each pair, the prepositional phrases express where the Theme (*her dinner* and *the shirt*) ends up as a result of her actions. The prepositional phrases express core participants, essential elements of the semantic structure of situations – complements. In the second sentence of each pair, on the other hand, the prepositional phrases express the setting of the whole event, the place where her eating of her dinner or her washing of the shirt took place. The prepositional phrases give additional information about the event but do not express core participants or components of the semantic structure of the situation.

Even when we are dealing with the same main verb and the same preposition heads the prepositional phrase, we still have to think carefully before deciding whether the phrase in question is a complement or an adjunct. Consider the following pair of sentences:

He loaded the cart *with hay* (complement)
He loaded the cart *with the pitchfork* (adjunct).

The verb *load* expresses an act that triggers the movement of a substance or an object to some container. Using the thematic role labels, we can say that *load* involves three core participants: an Actor, a Theme and a Goal. In the first sentence, the prepositional phrase expresses the Theme, the substance that ends up in the cart (the Goal) as a result of his action. In the second sentence, on the other hand, the prepositional phrase gives additional information about the instrument he employed to move some unspecified thing into the cart. So, be careful when you apply the first test to distinguish complements from adjuncts:

Semantic test 1: Only phrases that express core participants in the semantic structure of a situation are complements. That is, only phrases that can be labelled Actor, Theme, Goal, Source, Path, Location, Experiencer or Stimulus are complements.

Semantic test 2: Phrases that are adjuncts are more likely to make the following semantic contributions to the meaning of the sentence:

1.   They express the place or time of the *whole situation*, e.g.

     Mary giggled *in class*. (adjunct)
     Sue met Alice *at the cinema yesterday* (adjuncts)
     John coughed *during the concert* (adjunct)
     Tom was ill *in Leeds last week* (adjuncts).

     Time adjuncts tend to express:

     •   Time location: the phrase tells you when the whole situation took place (relative to some reference time such as the time of the utterance), e.g.

         Sue met Alice *yesterday/last week/two months ago*.

     •   Duration: the phrase tells you how long the situation lasted, e.g.

         Sue met Alice *for an hour*
         Sue slept *from Monday evening until Tuesday afternoon*.

     •   Frequency: the phrase tells you how often the event occurred or the state obtained, e.g.

         Sue sings *quite often/three times a week/once a month*
         Sue is in Berlin *at least twice a week*.

     •   Completion: the phrase gives the time span required for the completion of a particular event, e.g.

         Sue wrote the article *in a couple of hours*
         The train got to Glasgow *in 6 hours*.

2.   They express other measures apart from time, e.g. amount, size, length:

     Sue has grown *two inches*
     Could you shorten these trousers *a little*?
     Your plans interest me *considerably*.

3. They give additional information about the situation by specifying the manner, means or instrument involved, e.g.

    John left the room *in a hurry* (manner)
    John amused the children *by telling them silly jokes* (means)
    John cut the cake *with a sharp knife* (instrument).

4. They provide information about the purpose, intention or reason for a situation, e.g.

    John coughed to *attract my attention* (purpose)
    John dropped the vase *accidentally/deliberately* (intention)
    John is depressed *because of the state of the world* (reason).

5. They specify something or someone that accompanies or co-occurs with the main situation, e.g.

    John walked around *with a gloomy expression*
    John went to the races *with a friend*
    John watched the movie *with his children*.

Some of the semantic differences we have discussed also surface as syntactic differences, so we can also use some syntactic tests to distinguish complements from adjuncts:

Syntactic test 1: Only complements are syntactically obligatory, that is the sentence is not well-formed without them. Adjuncts are *never* obligatory – the sentence is well-formed although some additional information might be lost if the phrase is not there. For instance, we cannot omit the complement noun phrase *cats*, which expresses one of the core participants – the Stimulus – in the following sentences.

George likes *cats* very much
*George likes very much

but we can omit the adjunct adverb phrase *very much*:

George likes cats.

Similarly, we can omit the prepositional phrase *in the kitchen* in the second sentence but not in the first:

She put her dinner in the kitchen → *She put her dinner
She ate her dinner in the kitchen → She ate her dinner.

This test works well with states where the two core participants (Theme and Location or Experiencer and Stimulus) are *always* syntactically obligatory. They are not only core components of the semantic structure of the situation but they also cannot be left 'implicit' or 'understood' – they have to be actually there in the sentence, e.g.

The vase was on the table → *The vase was
That drink contains sugar → *That drink contains
George owns two houses → *George owns
George loves hip hop music → *George loves
That idea intrigues me → *That idea intrigues.

With events, however, this test only works in some cases. While it is true that if a phrase is obligatory, it is a complement, the converse is not true. This is because there are *optional* complements, phrases that express core participants in the semantic structure of the event but can be left out syntactically. Any of the following complement phrases can be left out, depending on the particular verb (see also Chapter 8):

- the Goal, with any event type, e.g.

  Mary smiled *at Sue* → Mary smiled
  Mary ran *home* quickly → Mary ran quickly
  Mary poured the wine *into the glasses* → Mary poured the wine

- the Theme with some wide focus Act events, e.g.

  He was eating *cakes* → He was eating
  He cooked *the meal* → He cooked
  He is knitting *a jumper* → He is knitting

- the Source or the Path with the types of events that involve a PROCESS, e.g.

  He left *the office* → He left
  He walked *down* to his neighbour's flat → He walked to his neighbour's flat.
  He lifted the box *up* above his head → He lifted the box above his head.

So this test *only* works if the phrase is obligatory. If the phrase is optional, you still need to apply the semantic tests and/or some of the other syntactic tests.

Syntactic test 2: If the phrase is relatively more independent of the verb, it is more likely to be an adjunct. Here syntactic independence reflects greater semantic independence. As we have seen above, complements are more closely linked with the main verb and this is reflected in the fact that they are less likely to be placed away from the verb and other complements within the verb phrase. Adjuncts, on the other hand, can move more freely, e.g.

John spoke *to Sue* (Goal, complement)
To Sue John spoke (without emphatic or contrastive intonation)
John spoke to Sue *on Sunday* (Time location, adjunct)
On Sunday John spoke to Sue
John looked *at Sue* (Goal, complement)

??It was *at Sue* that John looked
John ate *at two o'clock* (Time location, adjunct)
It was *at two o'clock* that John ate.

Syntactic test 3: If the proform *do so* refers to or replaces the phrase as well as the verb, the phrase is a complement (see also Chapter 4, Section 4.4). Consider, for instance

She laughed *at the joke* (Goal, complement)
*She did so *at the joke*
She laughed *in the pub* (place setting for the whole situation, adjunct)
She did so *in the pub*.

She put the apples *in the kitchen* (Goal, complement)
*She did so *in the bowl*
She ate the apples *in the kitchen* (place setting for the whole situation, adjunct)
She did so *in the kitchen*.

It should be clear by now that the meaning of a sentence is more than the sum of the meanings of the individual words or phrases it contains. How word and phrase meanings combine is crucial and we need concepts to distinguish different kinds of combination. In the next section, we will consider how thematic role labels and the complement/adjunct distinction may be used in clinical assessment and therapy.

9.4 Why we need these concepts in the clinic

Thematic roles can also be a useful shorthand in planning therapy. Supposing a language sample from a child consists of very short utterances, often with incomplete verb structures. We could easily decide that the child's syntax is limited, and that therapy should aim to build up sentence structure. This might lead us to target the prototypical English sentence structure NP-V-NP. More than likely, we will fill these syntactic slots with prototypical situation types – those involving an Actor and a Theme:

Mummy is washing the car
The boy is throwing the ball.

By modelling these structures, we might hope to elicit at least a V-NP structure, if not the full NP-V-NP. This may be a perfectly appropriate goal. As we have seen, though, the syntactic structure NP-V-NP doesn't just convey the prototypical situation of wide focus event with ACT. If we are promoting sentence structure to talk about situations that are important to the child, it would be wise to think about other types of situation involving other thematic roles. For example, we might target:

Situations involving Actor-Goal: touch, kiss, hug, tickle
Situations involving Experiencer-Stimulus: see, hear, want, like, hate
Situations involving Stimulus-Experiencer: surprise, upset, annoy, bother.

Notice that the target syntactic structure can stay the same, with the different thematic roles always taking the form of NPs preceding and following the verb. The advantage of targeting a range of thematic roles is first that it may enable the child to talk about different types of situations – as children normally do from the earliest stages of language development. In addition, we are consolidating the general structural patterns that English uses to convey situations, and laying the foundations for further verb learning.

An understanding of thematic roles can also contribute to therapy with adults with acquired language impairments. We have already seen several examples where a person with aphasia is unable to produce verbs (see Chapters 3 and 6) and therefore cannot talk about situations. Although some people with these symptoms can produce the relevant phrases for the participants in the situation (the complements of the verb which is itself missing), others produce phrases that do not refer to core participants. For instance, when trying to describe a picture of a man reading a book, MM (Marshall, Pring and Chiat 1993) would say:

man ... chair ... b o o k

where only *man* and *book* pick out participants in this reading event, while *chair* conveys additional information about the position of the man or is irrelevant. Similarly, AER (Nickels, Byng and Black 1991) would tend to include in his picture description phrases that referred to objects or people present in the picture but not necessarily involved in the target event or state. For instance, when he tried to talk about a girl painting a picture, with a boy watching in the background, he would include both the girl and the boy in his description, making it difficult for the listener to know who was engaged in painting or whether both people were. Although this kind of language production is often labelled 'telegrammatic', it is quite unlike a telegram since, in a telegram, one mentioned only the most important aspects of a situation – everything else was an unnecessary expense.

There are many different explanations as to why people with aphasia produce these kinds of utterances (see Marshall, Black and Byng 1999). Irrespective of the explanation, however, quite similar therapeutic approaches have been taken to treating this sort of problem. For instance, therapists often start by working on the core situation – the action, process or state and the core participants, avoiding information about the place or time setting of the situation or the reason for the situation – the type of information conveyed in language by adjuncts:

- The therapist might select pictures that depict situations of the same type, involving participants with the same thematic roles – e.g. Actor and Goal, or Actor and Theme. Pictures depicting the same situation type are worked on before another set of pictures relating to a different situation type is selected. In this way a range of situation types is covered.
- Alternatively, pictures of the same situation are selected, varying one of the core participants. For instance, the person with aphasia and the therapist would work through pictures of a man writing a letter, a woman writing a letter, a child writing a letter, maintaining the same action and Theme but changing the Actor. Or the Actor and the action would be the same but the Theme would be varied. The person's attention would be focused on the core participants and what links them into the action.
- The person with aphasia might be given a spoken or written verb (or a gestured action) and asked to select appropriate objects, pictures, words or phrases that could express participants in that situation. They may, for instance, be given different kinds of psychological state verbs (e.g. *like, hate, admire, fear, interest*) and be asked to select items that would be appropriate Stimuli with different Experiencers.

So the analytical tools that we have covered in this and the preceding chapter are helpful in thinking about situations and breaking them down into manageable, linguistically relevant chunks to be targeted in therapeutic tasks.

Box 9.1 Terminological note

A variety of definitions of thematic roles are used in the linguistic, psycholinguistic and clinical literature. This can be confusing, although the thematic roles we use in this book are defined fairly similarly in the majority of analyses, especially more recent ones.

The main difference you will find is that some analyses (especially in the clinical and developmental literatures) use the thematic role of Patient. In our analysis, this label is not necessary and has not therefore been included in the set. In other analyses, a complement phrase may be labelled Patient if:

- it expresses the participant 'affected' by the action of the Actor e.g. instead of calling the second participant Goal in ACT-focused situations, it would be called Patient
- it expresses the participant that changes in a wide focus event with ACT – instead of calling it Theme, it would be labelled Patient.

(continued)

This usage has the disadvantage of not distinguishing between a second participant that does not change and one that does – both get labelled Patient.

Some analyses use a much larger set of thematic role labels – not only Patient but also Beneficiary, Instrument and many others. This is partly because people were using thematic roles to capture all aspects of situational meaning (see the next chapter). In more current analyses, such as those brought together in this book, thematic roles are purely a shorthand and the set is kept as small as possible. Other aspects of situational meaning are analysed with other concepts.

Box 9.2 Predicates and arguments

The semantic characteristics of verbs make them an archetypal example of **predicate** terms. These are terms that assert something about one or more individuals, known as their **arguments,** and provide places which these arguments slot into. A one-place predicate asserts something about just one individual, and therefore offers just one slot, as in the case of intransitive verbs (see Chapter 6, Section 6.3):

[Actor] yawn
            ↓
       one-place
       predicate

At the other extreme are five-place predicates, for example:

[Actor] carry [Theme] [Source] [Path] [Goal]
            ↓
       five-place
       predicate

But verbs are not the only predicate terms. From a syntactic point of view, we saw that other categories apart from verbs can take complements (Chapter 6, Box 6.1); semantically, these categories are also predicate terms.

Take the case of nouns that are derived from verbs:

[Joe's] *love* [of music]
[the world's] *hope* [for peace]
[the therapist's] *management* [of the meeting]
[the hitchhiker's] *acceptance* [of a lift] [from the truck driver].

(continued)

Like the verbs from which they derive, each of these nouns asserts a situation involving two or three participants. Some nouns share the predicate structure of the verbs from which they derive, but carry a narrower meaning. *Gift*, for example, takes the same arguments as *give*:

[Sue's] *gift* [of a painting] [to the museum]

but conveys a very specific type of giving. Some nouns that act as predicates are not related to verbs at all, for example:

[Dan's] *gratitude* [to his friend] [for the idea]
the *idea* [of a long holiday]
[Shakespeare's] *story* [about Romeo and Juliet].

When adjectives follow verbs (see Chapter 6, Section 6.3), they too act as predicates. Here, the verb asserts a state, and the adjective specifies what that state is. Predicate adjectives take up to two arguments:

fond [of iced coffee]
brilliant [at sport]
grateful [to his friend] [for the idea].

Prepositions, when they convey location in space or time, are predicate terms taking up to two arguments:

on [the floor]
across [the road] [from the station]
after [the meal].

Exercises

1. The following sentences express different situation types which you have already analysed in Exercise 1, Chapter 8. Now, for each phrase in the sentence (inside or outside the verb phrase) say

   (i)   whether it is a complement or adjunct
   (ii) if it is a complement, which thematic role label would fit it best
   (iii) if it is an adjunct, what semantic contribution it makes to the sentence.

   1. The baby crawled across the floor.
   2. She yawned every two minutes.
   3. She is mending the bike.
   4. The boy squirted ink all over the page.
   5. She got the money from Sarah.
   6. They delivered several parcels to our door.
   7. She winked at her friend.
   8. Bob mumbles all the time.

    9. A man coughed during the concert.
  10. Dominic returned to Africa.
  11. I returned the books to the library.
  12. He slid the note under the door.
  13. Your train departs from platform one.
  14. We marched across the fields.
  15. The general marched his troops into battle.
  16. She passed me the newspaper.
  17. They supplied the chemical weapons to the dictator.
  18. The women fetched water from the well.
  19. The agent rented that flat to Sally.
  20. The heat of the sun melted the snow.

2. Imagine you are working with a child who frequently does not express some of the participants in situations. You want to check his comprehension of the role that different participants play in situations using an acting out task. Create 12 sentences that the child could act out with toy figures. You need to:

- make sure your sentences are balanced for syntactic structure, e.g. you control for the structure of the verb phrases
- make sure your sentences include a range of thematic roles.

3. A woman with aphasia produced the following descriptions of pictures (adapted from Marshall *et al.* 1993). Keeping in mind that she has difficulties in producing verbs, how would you describe the phrases that she produces? Is she able to identify participants in the situation, and if so, which ones? What might lead you to think that she is not focusing on the core aspects of the situation in the picture?

Target	*Production*
1. A woman driving a car	My car ... Ford Escort ... blue
2. A man smoking a pipe	Man ... pipes ... jumper
3. A woman dusting a shelf	Woman ... books ... duster ... blue ... shoes
4. A man cutting bread	Man ... yellow ... shirt
5. A woman giving a boy a present	Boy ... woman ... dress ... good

|10|

Shaping situations: foregrounding participants

10.1 Introduction

We have already seen in the previous chapter that the semantic distinction between participants (complements) and non-participants (adjuncts) has syntactic consequences. For instance, we saw that the closer semantic relationship between a verb and its complements results in the complements staying closer to the verb than any adjuncts. Indeed, we used this as a syntactic test (see Chapter 9, Section 9.3) to tell complements and adjuncts apart. Consider the ambiguous sentence

Tom baked a cake *for Susan*

whose ambiguity hinges on the complement or adjunct interpretation of the prepositional phrase *for Susan*. We can either interpret it as a Goal complement, the intended recipient of the cake (the Theme) that was made by Tom (the Actor), e.g.

Tom baked a cake for Susan as a present for her birthday.

Or we can interpret it as an adjunct, something like 'instead of Susan' or 'on Susan's behalf', e.g.

Tom baked a cake for Susan as she was too busy to bake one herself.

If, however, the phrase occurred closer to the verb, as it can with *bake*, the Goal interpretation would become the most likely, or even the only, interpretation, e.g.

Tom baked Susan a cake as a present for her birthday
?Tom baked Susan a cake as she was too busy to bake one herself.

Staying closer to the verb means that complements tend to come before adjuncts – before in time in spoken language and before in space in written language. Within the verb phrase, therefore, complements and adjuncts will tend not to swap places, all other things being equal, as can be seen from the ungrammaticality of the sentences below where the adjuncts *yesterday* and *in the morning* are placed before the complements *a cake* and *to Susan*:

Tom baked a cake *yesterday*
*Tom baked *yesterday* a cake

Tom talked to Susan *in the morning*
*Tom talked *in the morning* to Susan.

So part of the linear order of the phrases in a verb phrase is determined by whether the phrase is a complement or an adjunct, with complements before adjuncts. But what about phrases that are complements? How are these phrases arranged in a sentence? The answers to these questions are extremely complex and depend on the theoretical approach one takes (see Butt and Geuder 1998; Tenny and Pustejovky 2000; Tenny 1994; Goldberg 1995). Here we will somewhat simplify things and say: it largely depends on how the speaker wants to present the situation, the verb chosen, and the linguistic devices available to make some participants more prominent.

All languages treat certain positions in sentences as special or privileged: phrases placed in these positions are conferred a special status simply by virtue of being in those privileged positions. These special positions are usually called the Subject and the Object of a sentence.

10.2 Subjects and Objects in English

Although there is no generally agreed or universally applicable definition of Subject or Object, most linguists would identify the positions marked below as the Subject and Object of an English sentence:

$_S$[$_{NP}$[Subject] $_{VP}$[V $_{NP}$[Object]]]

In English, the Subject is:

- the phrase (usually the Noun Phrase) that is outside the Verb Phrase and precedes it;
- an obligatory component of the sentence in that the sentence would usually not be well-formed without it;
- the phrase whose head determines the person and number features of the verb and any other relevant elements inside the VP.

  It has a special form (so-called case-marking) that distinguishes it from other phrases. In English this special form is visible only with some pronouns – we use *I, s/he, we, they* in Subject position and *me, her, him, us* and *them* everywhere else.

For instance, in the sentence

George VP[loves cats]

George is the Subject:

- It is outside and before the VP.
- Without it the sentence would be ungrammatical, e.g.

  *S[loves cats].

- It determines the third person singular marking on the verb – we say *loves* cats not *love* cats.
- If we substituted a pronoun, we would say

  He loves cats rather than *Him loves cats*.

In contrast, the Object:

- immediately follows the V inside the VP;
- can be optional or obligatory depending on the verb it combines with, the speaker's perspective on the situation and other contextual factors;
- does not affect the person and number of the verb and other elements in the VP;

  For instance, *cats* in the sentence above is the Object: because of its structural position (is inside the VP) and linear position (immediately follows the V):
  - It is obligatory with the verb *love* but would not be required by many other verbs, e.g.

    George slept/sneezed/laughed
    George is running/leaving/cooking

    are all grammatical without an Object.
  - The appropriate pronoun for *cats* in this position would be *them* rather than *they*, e.g.

    George loves them
    *George loves they.

Although phrases that are made the Subject or the Object of a sentence are imparted greater prominence than other complements or adjuncts, there are also differences between them. The Subject is a position of primary prominence or focal attention (Langacker 1998), while the Object is relatively less prominent. The Subject is 'a starting point to which other information is added' (Chafe 1994: 92). It gives the listener a kind of viewing point or perspective from which the situation has to be understood. By making a phrase the Subject of a sentence we are implicitly instructing our listeners to attend to that entity first, before we attend to any Objects, and then any other complement or adjunct. Given that sentences are constructed and heard in time, what we place or hear first tends to affect what we do next – we construct what cognitive linguists have called a 'focus chain' (Langacker 1998), where positions of greater prominence are the main links in the chain that guides our attention.

The primary prominence of Subject is reflected in its tendency to occur before the Object. Cross-linguistically, the most common ordering of Subject, Object and verb are: SOV, SVO (like in English) and VSO, while the other possible orderings (VOS, OVS, and OSV) are much rarer (Greenberg 1963; Pullum 1986; Trask 1993).

Differential prominence is also suggested by the relationships between noun phrases and pronouns or possessive determiners in a sentence. For instance, both Subject and Object can function as the antecedents of pronouns and possessive determiners elsewhere in the sentence, e.g. in

George likes *his* mother

we understand *his* to refer to the same person as *George*, the Subject, at least on one interpretation. But a noun in Object position, or part of the Object NP, cannot control the reference of a pronoun in Subject position, e.g. in

He likes *George's* mother

George can no longer control the referent of *he* – *George* and *he* can no longer refer to the same person.

A similar pattern of relationships can be seen with respect to Objects, in comparison to other complements or adjunct phrases. For instance, in the sentence

George put the *kitten* in *its* basket

we understand *kitten* and *its* to refer to the same animal – the Object NP controls the referent of the Det in the Goal PP. But the converse does not hold, for example in

George put *it* in the *kitten's* basket

it and *kitten* cannot any longer refer to the same animal. So the more prominent links in 'focal chains' also act as the crucial links in chains of reference (see Langacker 1998).

10.3 Where participants end up

Although speakers can choose how to present a situation and a verb to express it, their choices about foregrounding one of the participants are fairly restricted. Let us consider first which participant can end up in the Subject position, with the greatest degree of prominence.

As Subject

In the two event types that involve an Actor (the narrow and wide focus events involving ACT) the Actor always ends up as the Subject, e.g.

$_s$[$_{NP}$[Actor] VP]

$_s$[$_{NP}$[*Bill*] $_{VP}$[cried/yawned/laughed]]
$_s$[$_{NP}$[*They*] $_{VP}$[kissed the children]]
$_s$[$_{NP}$[*We*] $_{VP}$[cooked the dinner]]
$_s$[$_{NP}$[*My brother*] $_{VP}$[sold our house]]
$_s$[$_{NP}$[*I*] $_{VP}$[told a story to the children]]
$_s$[$_{NP}$[*The hurricane*] $_{VP}$[destroyed several villages]].

Having chosen these types of situations and these types of verbs, there is no alternative to placing the Actor in Subject position. There is no English verb that would allow us to express the same situations from 'the point of view' of the Goal or the Theme. If we want to make the Goal or the Theme more prominent and place it in Subject position, we have to use a different construction such as the passive:

The children were kissed by them
The dinner was cooked by us
Our house was sold by my brother
The children were told the story by me
Several villages were destroyed by the hurricane.

This regular placing of the Actor in Subject position is not just a pattern in English but is a universal tendency. Because of this tendency, the Subject has often been defined as 'the doer' or the Actor – for instance, in some traditional grammars and in some of the clinical literature. However, it is a one-way implication only: Actors become Subjects but not all Subjects are Actors. We cannot therefore define Subject by reference to the thematic role of the phrase in that position.

If there is no participant with the thematic role of Actor, another participant will be foregrounded and occur as the Subject. With Process-focus verbs, it is usually the Theme that ends up as the Subject, e.g.

Sarah went to the park
George became very agitated
The kite was flying high
Water dripped/leaked from the pipe
A strong light emanated from the planet
The door opened
The cup broke
The candles melted away.

With emission verbs (see Chapter 8, Section 8.2) the Source can also be the Subject, e.g.

The pipe was dripping/leaking water
The planet emitted a strong light.

With locational states, it is usually the Theme that is realized as the Subject while the Location remains inside the VP, e.g.

The vase was on the table
The meeting is at two o'clock
Your argument seems weak
Janet is upset
This book belongs to Mary.

With some state verbs that express possession, however, the Location (the possessor) is given greater prominence and mapped onto the Subject, e.g.

Mary owns this house
I have a new coat.

With psychological state verbs, both the Experiencer and the Stimulus can become the Subject, depending on the verb, e.g.

She loves jazz (Experiencer = Subject)
Exams worry her (Stimulus = Subject).

Participants with a variety of thematic roles can therefore be realized as Subjects, although some thematic roles are more likely than others to be given greater prominence and be mapped onto the Subject. By being singled out in this way, a participant can be made to appear more in control, more determining or influential in the situation – it appears as 'the doer' even when no 'doing' is involved, as in states.

As Object

Which participants end up as the Object? Again, it largely depends on the type of situation and the meaning of the verb involved. For Act-focus situations, the Goal is usually the Object, that is the noun phrase closest to the verb inside the verb phrase (see Section 10.2 above). The Goal is placed in Object position with verbs that express direct physical contact, e.g.

Mary ᵥₚ[patted ₙₚ[*the child*]]
Mary ᵥₚ[kissed ₙₚ[*her friend*]]
Mary ᵥₚ[stroked ₙₚ[*the cat*]].

On the other hand, if the act is only oriented towards the Goal but no contact is involved, the greater 'distance' between the Actor and the Goal is reflected linguistically in that a preposition intervenes between the verb and the Goal, e.g.

Mary ᵥₚ[winked ₚₚ[at ₙₚ[the child]]]
Mary ᵥₚ[smiled ₚₚ[at ₙₚ[her friend]]].

In these cases, the Goal is within the PP and no longer qualifies as the Object, in the sense defined in Section 10.2 above.

For the wider-focus events involving ACT, the Theme tends to occur as the Object, e.g.

s[ₙₚ[We] ᵥₚ [cooked *the dinner*]]
s[ₙₚ[My brother] ᵥₚ [sold *our house*]]
s[ₙₚ[I] ᵥₚ [told *a story* to the children]]
s[ₙₚ[The hurricane] ᵥₚ [destroyed *several villages*]].

The Goal, however, can be relatively more prominent and be mapped onto the Object with some of these verbs – compare

He loaded *the car* with bags (Object = Goal)
He loaded *the bags* into the car (Object = Theme).

Although these two sentences express the same situation, turning either the Theme or the Goal into the Object has subtle meaning effects. With the Goal in Object position, so that the Goal is foregrounded, the implication is that the car is completely full. On the other hand, when the Theme is the Object we do not get this effect – there is no indication of how full the car is. Participants in Object position appear more, or more completely, affected, at least in the sense that more attention is focused on that effect than any other (see Pinker 1989). Because of this, mapping choices are often constrained by the meaning of the verb itself. Consider the pattern of possible and impossible mappings with verbs like *pour* and *fill*, e.g.

He poured *wine* into the glass (Object = Theme)
He filled *the glass* with wine (Object = Goal)

*He poured the glass with wine (Object = *Goal)
*He filled the wine into the glass (Object = *Theme).

Both verbs can be used to describe quite similar situations, involving similar participants. The verb *pour*, however, foregrounds the transfer of the Theme, while *fill* foregrounds the state of the Goal that results from the transfer of the Theme. These meaning differences are reflected in the foregrounding of different participants and the related mapping possibilities: only the Theme can be made the Object with the verb *pour*, while only the Goal can become the Object with *fill*. Similarly contrasting patterns can be observed with pairs of semantically related verbs such as *steal/rob*:

Bill stole *her savings* from Mary   (Object = Theme)
Bill robbed *Mary* of her savings   (Object = Goal)
*Bill stole *Mary* of her savings   (Object = *Goal)
*Bill robbed *her savings* from Mary   (Object = *Theme).

Again, the type of situation expressed by the two verbs and their participants are very similar. Both verbs give most prominence to the Actor, which ends up as the Subject. The main difference between the two verbs is that they give secondary prominence to different participants – *steal* to the Theme and *rob* to the Goal.

Apart from the meaning of the verb, possible mappings are also constrained by the meaning of the phrases that express participants. The Goal, for instance, can only become the Object if the phrase refers to an entity that can be affected in the relevant way required by the verb:

Alice sent the parcel *to Mary* (Goal not Object)
Alice sent the parcel *to London* (Goal not Object)

Alice sent *Mary* the parcel (Object = Goal)
*Alice sent *London* the parcel (Object = *Goal).

With many verbs of transaction and communication, both the Theme and the Goal can become Objects, in the sense that both the Theme and the Goal become NPs inside the verb phrase:

He $_{VP}$[sold $_{NP}$[Mary] $_{NP}$[the house]]
He $_{VP}$[told $_{NP}$[me] $_{NP}$[the news]].

This is why these sentences are often called 'double object constructions' and these verbs are labelled 'ditransitive' (see also Chapter 6).

As we can see from the patterns summarized above, one participant in each sentence must be given primary prominence – the situation must be seen from a particular point of view. Secondary prominence, on the other hand, may or may not be given to another participant: there may or may not be an Object depending on the meaning of the verb and the phrases involved.

10.4 Why we need these concepts

It is almost impossible to read any of the literature on typical and atypical language development, language processing and acquired language impairments, without coming across the terms Subject and Object. For example, you will often hear therapists working with children say things like 'This child is only using Verb-Object, and we are working on Subject-Verb-Object in therapy'. Here, the therapist is using the terms Subject and Object to capture the basic sentence frames that occur in a child's utterances (see Chapter 6). This is how the terms are used in syntactic profiles of children's language. For example, the Language Assessment, Remediation and Screening Procedure (LARSP) (Crystal, Fletcher and Garman 1976) records the combinations of Subject, Verb and Objects that occur in a sample of the child's utterances. Similarly, the South Tyneside Assessment of Syntactic Structures (STASS) (Armstrong and Ainley) presents children with pictures that are designed to elicit these 'core' sentence structures.

As we have seen in this chapter, Subject and Object are crucial for looking at how we understand utterances. Imagine a friend rings you with the latest gossip, telling you that

Frank loves Alice.

Here neither the meaning of the verb by itself or the meaning of the noun phrases is enough to tell you 'who is loving whom' – the sentence is what people call 'reversible'. Your only clue is the order of the noun phrases with respect to the verb, with the Subject coming first – one of the main ways in which the Subject is privileged in English, as we saw in Section 10.2 above. You have to be able to identify Subject and Object to work out the intended semantics and extract the information that Frank is experiencing a certain feeling for Alice and not vice versa. In other languages, other cues will signal Subject and Object, directing listeners to the intended meaning.

Some comprehension assessments focus on this relationship between syntactic roles and thematic roles. The TROG (Test for the Reception of Grammar, Bishop 1993) for example, presents children with reversible sentences such as 'The girl is pushing the horse', 'The cup is in the box', along with four pictures which include the target and its reverse (girl pushing horse and horse pushing girl, cup in box and box in cup). The child has to point to the picture that matches the sentence. Here, the test is checking if the child notices the position of the nouns and can map these onto the thematic roles of Actor, Theme and Location.

Similar assessments are used to assess comprehension in acquired aphasia. For instance, some adults with aphasia have difficulties in comprehending reversible sentences but not sentences where the meaning of the verb and of the phrases it combines with is enough to constrain interpretation. For instance, they may be able to match to an appropriate picture sentences like

The boy is kicking the wall
The girl loves books

or distinguish appropriately those sentences from unacceptable counterparts like

??The wall is kicking the boy
??Books love the girl

but not be able to interpret correctly in picture selection and judgement tasks reversible sentences such as

The boy is kicking the horse
The girl loves the boy

(see Marshall *et al.* 1999; Mitchum and Berndt 2001).

In contrast to people who have difficulty sorting out the connection between syntactic and thematic roles, some people with dementia or acquired aphasia show a surprising ability to use this information. WL is one such person (Schwartz, Marin and Saffran 1979). WL had difficulty with single nouns, so that she could not, for example distinguish between cat and dog. However, when she was shown a picture of a dog chasing a cat and was told 'the dog is chasing the cat, show me the cat', she could identify the cat correctly. This showed she could identify *cat* as the Object of *chase*, knew the Object was the one being chased, and could use this to identify *cat*. RG is another person who had difficulty understanding nouns, but could use the syntactic position of a noun to identify it (Marshall *et al.* 1996). Even when he was given a nonsensical sentence such as 'Toft is shocked by Brighton', RG was able to identify Toft, saying 'forget the names, just look at who's being shocked'.

As we have seen in this chapter, the syntactic roles of Subject and Object are also important in conveying our perspective on the participants in a situation. Consider, for example, the following descriptions of one of the RAPT pictures (Renfrew 1997):

Figure 10.1 Action picture test. (Source: Renfrew, C. Action Picture Test (Bicester, Winslow Press Ltd., 1988))

Child A: Man jumping over the fence
Child B: Horse jumping over the fence
Child C: Man is on the horse
Child D: Fence is under the man.

All of these descriptions are identical in terms of phrasal structure: they all have an initial NP followed by a VP that contains a verb and a prepositional phrase. Semantically, however, the first two descriptions differ from the others: Child A and B describe the scene as an event, the motion of a particular entity, while Child C and D treat it as a state where one entity is located with respect to another. This semantic difference is apparent from the verbs the children have used – a verb of motion (*jump*) as opposed to a state verb (*be*). But, even when the scene is described as the same type of situation, there is still a difference: each child has foregrounded a different participant and has presented the situation from that participant's perspective. How do we know that? Because a different participant has been made the Subject of the sentence. This aspect of sentence organization tells us about the intended semantics. Without this concrete clue, we would only be guessing what the child is focusing on and how she 'sees' the scene. We can then ask whether the child's perspective on the scene is fairly typical or not.

For instance, one intuitively feels that there is something 'odd' about Child D's description. Its phrasal structure is perfectly grammatical, with the required phrases and words in the right order – its structure is, after all, identical to that of the other, more 'natural' descriptions. There is nothing wrong with its semantic structure either: a thing is located with respect to something else using an appropriate state verb and, in this respect, it is just like Child C's description. We need to ask: what has the child achieved in putting the sentence together? To pin down our impressions that something is 'odd', we have to look at what the child has turned into the Subject of the sentence. This is why this level of sentence organization is given particular importance in many procedures for analysing children's and adults' utterances.

Exercises

1. Shel is a 2½ year old who is acquiring Standard English. As illustrated in the following examples, her use of pronouns differs in certain respects from the adult use of pronouns in Standard English (though not necessarily in other dialects of English):

      (i)   Put him in the swing.
      (ii) She's got pants.
      (iii) They go faster.
      (iv) Him go on slide.
      (v)   Put she on that chair.
      (vi) Them sit down now.
      (vii) Think her will stand on that.
     (viii) Her have a ride.
      (ix) Get she in a cot.
      (x)   I dropped she to get out that way.
      (xi) Can you open them?
      (xii) [anə] put them back in.
     (xiii) She just falled over.
      (xiv) Hope they're not too big for me.
      (xv) Let she kiss her better.
      (xvi) Him's gone.
     (xvii) He want mummy.
    (xviii) Him want mummy.

   Describe the syntactic distribution of the forms *he/him, she/her, they/them* in the data. What characteristics of Subject and Object in English enable us to identify the syntactic role of Shel's pronouns despite the errors she makes?

2. Imagine you are working with an adult with aphasia who seems to have difficulties in comprehending reversible sentences (see Section 10.4 above). You want to make up a sentence-picture verification task to check this out (see Mitchum and Berndt 2001). The task involves showing him a picture and asking him whether or not it matches the sentence he has heard or read. You need to:

   • select 20 sentences all with the structure NP $_{VP}$[V NP]
   • control for the semantic type of the verb – whether it is wide or narrow focus, and what type of situation is involved
   • imagine the types of scenes you are going to photograph in his home to use as the pictures in the task
   • think about any problems you might encounter in assembling your materials and in selecting suitable stimuli.

IV

Syntax – semantic links:
time and modality

|11|

The auxiliary system

11.1 Introduction

Consider the following sentences:

The student go for a job interview. She feel very anxious. But the manager offer her the job.

You can probably visualize the situations in these sentences clearly enough. Yet you are bound to feel dissatisfied with them. You can't help wondering *when* the situations occurred. But why should this matter to you when you don't know who we are talking about, and have no reason to worry what happened to her let alone when it happened? The reason, of course, is that language makes it matter. Language cares about time. So let's try adding some times to see if this solves the problem:

On Monday, the student go for a job interview. She feel very anxious in the morning. But the manager offer her the job later in the day.

There is still something missing. The problem is that language is fussy about time, demanding that we mark certain time distinctions in certain ways. English is particularly fussy in this respect, insisting on a complex of time distinctions that are marked by **auxiliary verbs** and **verb inflections**. Once we add these forms to the above sentences, they are fine:

The student went for a job interview. She felt very anxious. But the manager offered her the job.

Or:

The student has gone for a job interview. She is feeling very anxious. But the manager may offer her the job.

We could include PPs specifying times as well:

(On Monday) the student went for a job interview. She felt very anxious (in the morning). But the manager offered her the job (later in the day).

But these – unlike the auxiliary markers – are optional extras.

In this chapter, we introduce the tense and auxiliary system of English, focusing on their syntactic organization. We also look at the vital role auxiliaries play in forming negative and question structures. This syntactic analysis of auxiliaries provides a springboard for looking at the particular range of time distinctions English imposes on us when we talk about situations.

11.2 Why we need to look at tense and auxiliaries

Tense and auxiliaries are a challenge for normally developing children. They certainly do not feature in children's earliest utterances. This is evident when we look at early forms of questions and negatives – auxiliaries are typically missing:

No singing song	See hole?
No play that	Mommy eggnog?
No fall (putting out hand in warning)	Sit chair?
No heavy	What doing?
No want stand head	Where milk go?

Gradually, they include more auxiliary verbs, but these are not always fully correct:

I can't see it	Oh, did I caught it?
I didn't did it	What did you doed?
You didn't caught me	Where my spoon goed?
They not cold	What he can ride in?
I not hurt him	Why kitty can't stand up?

(Examples taken from Klima and Bellugi 1973).

While most 4-year-olds have sorted out the intricacies of the auxiliaries, children with language problems may grapple with them over a much longer period. Even when their language has become quite complex, and they are using a range of auxiliary elements, they may continue to miss some out – as illustrated by the following speech sample from 8-year-old James, who has mild language problems and is struggling to learn to read:

And now they probably tipped the boat over. And the current is pulling them on. But they don't know there going to be a waterfall. The boat will turn over. All the air inside it keep you afloat. And if you fell out from a boat um um there this position and it called the [hiʔ ɪxpaɪwɪ lɪtəwɪ xɪðən] (= heat expiry lifting position). It keep you um hot.

Some people with acquired aphasia develop particular problems with auxiliaries and tense markers, either because they cannot recognize and comprehend particular types of auxiliary verbs and inflections or because they are unable to produce them (Berko Gleason, Goodglass, Green, Ackerman and Hyde 1975). For instance, they might omit third person singular non-past markers on verbs, e.g.

Target	*Response*
The baby cries	Baby cry
The dog chases the cat	Dog chase cat

or omit auxiliary *do* in certain contexts, e.g.

Target	*Response*
Where did you put my shoes?	Where put shoes?

while producing it in others, e.g.

Target	*Response*
Did you call?	Did you call?

The auxiliary system seems particularly vulnerable to breakdown, and problems with different aspects of it have been documented in many languages apart from English (see Paradis 2001). It is therefore necessary to be familiar with its properties and with the meanings that can be expressed through it. In many cases, omission of an auxiliary verb, tense or agreement marker will make little difference to someone's ability to communicate. In other cases, however, the omissions and substitutions could create considerable problems. Imagine what would happen if you left out auxiliaries expressing negation or substituted one modal verb for another during an interchange with your adolescent son. You might say:

I give you more money; you go to that club; you may come back by 11 p.m.

Although a speech and language therapist will not necessarily decide to work on these types of problems directly, analysis of the forms and meanings involved will be a necessary component of the psycholinguistic profile of a client, and important in targeting therapy or compensatory strategies.

11.3 The auxiliary system

Tense

The sentence

She borrow lots of old videos

is not acceptable. This is because, at the very least, English requires us to make a tense distinction on the main verb in a sentence. This sentence contains a 'bare' verb – to right it, we need to add one of the tense markers English requires:

Past: She borrowed lots of old videos
Non-past: She borrows lots of old videos.

There are a number of things to note about this syntactic category of tense:

- Tense refers specifically to this minimal marking of the verb. This syntactic category of tense must not be confused with the conceptual category of time, which can take many other forms (see following sections).
- In English, tense involves only a two-way contrast between past and non-past. Obviously, the past is so-called because it refers to past situations. Less obviously, the non-past is so-called because it spans a range of time references excluding the past. It can be used to refer to present and future situations:

  She sings every day
  She sings tomorrow evening.

  Non-past is therefore the most appropriate label for this tense. However, you will find it commonly referred to as the present tense for convenience.
- There is no future tense in English. Of course we can refer to future situations, as we have just seen. The point is that English, unlike many other languages, does not have a specific tense marker to indicate future. Compare Italian, where the future is marked by a verb ending, so that 'She sings tomorrow evening' translates as:

  Cant*erá* domani sera
  sing + future

  while 'She sings every day' translates as:

  Cant*a* tutti i giorni
  sing + non-past.

In English, we use a number of different categories to refer to the future. One is the non-past marker exemplified above. We will look at other categories used to refer to future situations and the subtle differences between these in Chapters 12 and 13.

The syntactic category of tense is always incorporated into a verb form. You may have noticed how the verb changed when tense was added:

Past: borrow*ed*
Non-past: borrow*s*.

The regular form of the past is *-ed*. The regular marking of the non-past is less straightforward, because it depends on the subject NP. Where the subject of the verb is third person singular (a NP with a singular noun as head, or pronouns *he, she, it*), the non-past is marked by *-s*:

My friend/she borrows lots of videos.

In all other cases, the non-past does not 'show up': there is no difference between the non-past form and the tenseless form of the verb:

I/You/We/My friends/They borrow lots of videos.

This relation between the subject and the verb inflection is known as subject-verb agreement.

The regular marking of tense is not without exceptions. The past tense takes an irregular form with certain groups of verbs or individual verbs – see Box 11.1 for examples. The non-past tense, on the other hand, shows just a few exceptions:

Box 11.1 Examples of irregular past tense forms

No overt marking: *put-put, cut-cut, set-set, hurt-hurt, spread-spread*

Vowel change: *do-did, get-got, come-came, sit-sat, give-gave, take-took, read/rid/-read/rɛd/, fall-fell, eat-ate, see-saw, know-knew, throw-threw, blow-blew, fly-flew, wear-wore, stick-stuck, run-ran, swim-swam, ring-rang, sing-sang, drink-drank, find-found, wind-wound, win-won, hide-hid, slide-slid, ride-rode, write-wrote, drive-drove, break-broke, steal-stole*

Consonant change: *have-had, make-made*

Vowel + consonant change: *think-thought, bring-brought, catch-caught, teach-taught*

Vowel change + consonant addition: *say-said, hear-heard, buy-bought, sell-sold, tell-told, feel-felt, sleep-slept, leave-left, keep-kept, lose-lost*

Whole word change: *go-went, be-was*

---

do: /dʌz/ not /duz/
have: /hæz/ not /hævz/
say: /sɛz/ not /seɪz/

apart from the verb *be* which is determinedly irregular across both tenses:

Non-past: I *am*
                you/we/they *are*
                he/she/it *is*
Past: I/you/we/they *were*
                he/she/it *was*.

Modals

Before the main verb of a sentence, we may find one of the following:

She *may* go out
She *can* go by bus
She *could* order a taxi
She *will* arrive late
She *would* be angry
She *shall* stay at home
She *should* watch television
She *must* finish her coursework.

These are known as modal verbs. Just one modal verb can occur in English. We cannot combine two even if they could make sense together:

*He may must see the doctor (Compare: He may have to see the doctor)
*She must can swim (Compare: She must be able to swim)

and would be possible in Italian:

Deve   poter nuotare
must+third person can swim.

Once a modal occurs, the main verb no longer carries a tense marker:

*She may goes out.

So what has happened to the tensing of the sentence which we claimed was obligatory? The answer is that the modal carries the tense. This is not obvious, because modals are not marked with past or non-past inflections and do not convey a past/non-past contrast. We know they are syntactically tensed, though, because they cannot occur in contexts requiring the tenseless form of the verb, for example in certain types of embedded sentence:

*I expect to *must* leave (Compare: I expect to have to leave)
*She'd like to *can* fly a plane (Compare: She'd like to be able to fly a plane).

Perfective aspect: have + *past participle*

have is another auxiliary verb that may occur before the main verb:

He has escaped
They have eaten.

When *have* occurs, it influences the form of the following verb. Rather than occurring in its bare form:

*He has escape

the following verb takes a form known as the past participle. In some cases, this is indistinguishable from the past tense, for example where it ends in *-ed*:

Past tense: He *escaped/walked/fainted/appeared ...*
Past participle: He has *escaped/walked/fainted/appeared ...*

Some verbs take the ending *-en* in their past participle form:

He has *eaten/given/taken/fallen/been ...*

while others combine this with a vowel change:

He has *spoken/written/woken/broken ...*

Many verbs, though, are irregular – see Box 11.2 for examples.

Box 11.2 Examples of irregular past participle forms

No overt marking: *put-put, cut-cut, spread-spread, hurt-hurt, set-set, come-come, run-run*
Vowel change: *sit-sat, get-got, read/rid/-read/red/, swim-swum, ring-rung, sing-sung, drink-drunk, stick-stuck, find-found, wind-wound*
Consonant change: *have-had, make-made*
Vowel + consonant change: *think-thought, bring-brought, catch-caught, teach-taught*
Vowel change + consonant addition: *do-done, say-said, hear-heard, buy-bought, sell-sold, tell-told, feel-felt, sleep-slept, leave-left, keep-kept, lose-lost*
Vowel change + *en/n*: *hide-hidden, ride-ridden, write-written, drive-driven, break-broken, steal-stolen, go-gone, fly-flown, wear-worn*

Notice that the past participle is not a tense. When *have* and the past participle occur, tense is still required, as the following example shows:

*He have escaped.

To right this we need to add a tense marker to *have* – either past:

He had escaped

or non-past:

He has escaped.

On the other hand, if we choose to include a modal verb, this appropriates the tense, returning *have* to its bare form:

He may have escaped
*He may has escaped
*He may had escaped.

Progressive be + *present participle*

The last of the auxiliary verbs figures in the following examples:

They were yawning
This is becoming very long.

The auxiliary verb here is *be*, which is hiding in the forms *were* and *is*. By now you can probably work out why *be* occurs in these forms – if you haven't clicked, we shall be revealing the reason for this in a minute. But first look at the verb following *be*. You will notice that this has *-ing* attached to it. This is because *be* must be followed by the present participle of a verb, and the present participle is formed by adding *-ing* to the verb. Happily, there is not a single exception in this case. Every verb takes *-ing*, even the verb *be* itself:

He is being silly.

Now let's go back to the form of the auxiliary. *Were* and *is* are tensed forms of *be*. As you might by now expect, where *be* occurs, it carries the tense – unless it is preceded by one of the other auxiliary verbs bearing the tense:

- Modal + *be*: He may be listening.
  Here, the modal *may* carries the tense, and *be* is fully recognizable in its now untensed form.

- *Have + be*: He has been smoking.

Here, *have* carries the tense, whether past *had* or non-past *has*. So how do we account for the form *been*? Since *have* is always followed by the past participle, if it is followed by *be*, this will occur in its past participle form *been*.

11.4 The full picture

We have taken a full few pages to present the auxiliary system of English when we could have summed it up in one line. We have seen that a sentence may contain up to three auxiliary verbs before the main verb, in the following sequence:

(modal) (have) (be) main verb.

Where *have* and *be* occur, they dictate the form of the following verb, giving:

(modal) (have + past participle) (be + present participle) main verb.

These auxiliary verbs are syntactically optional. Tense, on the other hand, is not. Where does tense fit in? You may have deduced this from the various combinations of auxiliaries above: tense attaches to the first verb in the sequence – modal if it occurs, otherwise *have*, otherwise *be*, otherwise the main verb. We can represent this pattern by placing tense at the start of the summary statement:

tense (modal) (have + past participle) (be + present participle) main verb.

You should find that any sentence of English you dream up contains one of the combinations allowed by this statement.

Except ...

This is not quite the full picture. There is one more auxiliary verb: the one that marks a sentence as passive – see Box 11.3.

Box 11.3 The passive auxiliary *be* + past participle

Recall that the passive structure, loosely speaking, reverses the NPs of the corresponding active (see Chapter 4, Section 4.4 and Chapter 6, Section 6.3):

NP[The mouse] ate NP[the cheese] → NP[The cheese] was eaten by
NP[the mouse].

(continued)

But how do we know that the NPs have been reversed, and that we should interpret the sentence as passive? How do we know that:

The house was flooded by the river

is passive, while:

The river flooded by the house

is not? The auxiliary verb is crucial. Passive sentences always contain the auxiliary verb *be*, this time followed by the past participle:

The house *was* flood*ed* by the river
The cheese *was* eat*en* by the mouse.

Notice that *be*, as the first auxiliary, takes the tense – as we would expect – and becomes *was*.

Where does the passive auxiliary occur in relation to the other auxiliaries? The following active sentence contains every possible auxiliary verb:

The spy may have been watching the student.

Try passivizing this sentence, and see where you put the passive auxiliary:

The student may have been *be*ing watch*ed* by the spy.

Here we have the modal *may*, followed by *have*, which takes the past participle of the following auxiliary *be*, which takes the present participle of the following auxiliary – the passive *be* which takes the past participle of the main verb *watch*.

So, to incorporate the passive auxiliary, we need to adjust our summary statement for auxiliaries as follows:

(modal) (have + past participle) (be + present participle) (be + past participle) main verb.

11.5 Auxiliaries and different sentence functions

As languages go, English has an unusually elaborate auxiliary system. Equally unusual is the way this system spreads its tentacles into certain sentence types. In contrast to many other languages, English draws on auxiliaries to perform a range of everyday sentence functions, using them to affirm and negate, to question and answer, and more. In each case, the use of the auxiliary does not alter the core structure or meaning of the sentence. The core sentence still consists of a NP and VP, and the VP still contains at least the verb and its complements. That core sentence still conveys a situation and the participants involved in that situation. The function served by the auxiliary applies to the sentence structure and meaning as a whole.

Auxiliaries as proforms for VP

When we introduced proforms which 'stand in for' constituents, we presented *do* or *do so* as the proform for VP, as in our examples:

You arrived late, *did* you?
Bob runs and *so does* Jill (Chapter 3, Section 3.3).
Madge left her purse in the bank and *so did* Sarah.
Madge *did so* too! (Chapter 4, Section 4.4).

Actually, this is not always the case. We oversimplified our description of VP proforms – precisely because we did not want to go into the complexities of the auxiliary system at that point. In fact, *do* is only the proform for a VP when the VP contains no other auxiliaries. If you look at the VPs in the above examples, you will find that they are carefully controlled:

You *arrived late*
Bob *runs*
Madge *left her purse in the bank*.

Not one contains an auxiliary verb. The only auxiliary element is therefore the tense-marking on the main verb. Under these circumstances, *do* stands in for the VP and carries its tense.

But look what happens when the sentence contains a tense-carrying auxiliary:

You *will* arrive late, *will* you?
Bob *is* running and *so is* Jill.
Madge *has* left her purse in the park and *so has* Sarah.

That tensed auxiliary now acts as the proform for the VP. English uses the tensed auxiliaries in a similar way to affirm a previous assertion:

A: This book looks riveting.
B: Yes, it *does*.

A: Summer has come to an end.
B: It certainly *has*.

A: It's raining.
B: So it *is*.

In each case, the response is an *elliptical* or shortened form of the sentences which replaces the subject NP with a pronoun:

the book → it.

and the VP with a tensed auxiliary:

looks riveting → does
's raining → is.

In effect, the elliptical structure echoes the original sentence (NP VP) in pro-forms. English uses this same elliptical structure in responses to questions. Where many languages use just *yes* or *no*, English provides this more complex alternative:

Will that piece fit in here? → Yes it will.
Is the phone working? → Yes it is.
Have you heard the latest? → Yes I have.

You might think about how many forms such elliptical responses can take – to work out all the possible combinations of pronoun subject and auxiliary verb, you need to multiply the number of auxiliary verbs by the number of pronouns. For any one question, just one of these elliptical forms – the one matching the subject- and auxiliary-marking in the question – will be appropriate:

Is the phone working? → Yes it is.
Is the phone working? → *Yes it has.
Is the phone working? → *Yes he is.

So, while we could use the word 'yes' in every case, if we go for the elaborate alternative that English offers, we must select just the right combination of pronoun and auxiliary.

Questions

We have just seen auxiliaries surfacing in responses to questions. They also surface in questions themselves.

To get a feel for how auxiliaries are manipulated to form questions in English, watch yourself turn each of the following statements into a question:

Box 11.4 Turning statements into questions

Statement	*Question*
They will wait	
They have waited	
They are waiting	
They will have waited	
They will be waiting	
They will have been waiting	
They waited	
All the girls in the band waited	
All the girls in the band are waiting	

In each case, the word order in the sentence changes. The tensed auxiliary that follows the subject NP in the statement precedes that NP in the question:

$_{NP}$[They] *will* wait → *Will* $_{NP}$[they] wait?
$_{NP}$[They] *have* waited → *Have* $_{NP}$[they] waited?
$_{NP}$[All the girls in the band] *are* waiting → *Are* $_{NP}$[all the girls in the band] waiting?

Only the tensed auxiliary moves in this way. Moving more than that auxiliary:

* Will have they waited?

or any other auxiliary:

* Have they will waited?

results in an ill-formed sentence.

What happens in sentences that do not contain an auxiliary verb? In English – unlike certain other languages – it is not possible to move the main verb to form a question:

*Wait they?
*Waited they?

Instead, *do* is recruited as a 'dummy' auxiliary verb:

They waited → *Did* they wait?

As soon as an auxiliary verb occurs, it appropriates the tense – in this case, *do* is marked as past *did*. The main verb is therefore stripped of the tense it carried in the corresponding statement:

They *waited* → *Did* they *wait*?

Neither

*Do they *waited*?

with tense on the main verb, nor

*Did they *waited*?

with tense on both verbs, is possible.

There are just two exceptions to this pattern. One is when *be* acts as a main verb (see Chapter 6, Section 6.3). If it behaved like other main verbs, we would expect *do* to be used to form a question. But it is not:

**Do they be angry?

This is because the main verb *be* behaves like its auxiliary counterpart, and moves in front of the subject NP:

Are they angry?

To appreciate its exceptional behaviour, compare the question form where the main verb is *seem* rather than *be*:

Do they seem angry?

and not

*Seem they angry?

The main verb *have* is less consistent in its behaviour. It may be treated like other main verbs, with *do* used to form a question:

They have a digital camera → *Do* they have a digital camera?

But it is also possible to treat it like an auxiliary, and move it to form the question:

Have they a digital camera?

However, this possibility only occurs when *have* is used to convey possession. Where it occurs in idiomatic combinations such as *have lunch*, *have a drink*, *have a go*, movement of *have* is distinctly odd:

*Had you lunch?
*Had you a go?

In British English, the idiosyncrasies of *have* are typically avoided by using *have got* to express possession, in which case *have* is an auxiliary and behaves like one:

Have they got a digital camera?

Negatives

The formation of negative sentences, like the formation of questions in English, hinges on the tensed auxiliary. In this case, the sentence function is marked by the negative particle *not* or its contracted form *n't*. Try negating the assertions in Box 11.4 above, and you will see that the negative particle attaches itself to the very same tensed auxiliary that moves to form the question:

They *will* wait → They *won't* wait
They *have* waited → They *haven't* waited
They *are* waiting → They *aren't* waiting
They *will* have waited → They *won't* have waited.

Attach *n't* to any other auxiliary and the result is way off:

*They will *haven't* waited
*They have *beenn't* waiting.

In some cases, the combination of auxiliary plus *n't* takes an idiosyncratic form – see Box 11.5.

Box 11.5 Idiosyncratic contracted negative forms

will + n't	→	won't
can + n't	→	can't
shall + n't	→	shan't
do + n't	→	don't
am + n't	→	ain't

In most varieties of English, there is no contracted negative with the auxiliary form *am*. The full form *not* must be used.

In the absence of another tensed auxiliary, just as in questions, *do* is used to carry the negative:

They *didn't* wait.

This removes the tense from the main verb:

*They *didn't* wait*ed*.

Just as in questions, even when *be* is a main verb, it behaves like an auxiliary and carries the negative:

They *aren't* angry
*They *don't* be angry,

and when *have* is a main verb expressing possession, both possibilities occur:

Like main verb: I don't have a watch
Like auxiliary: I haven't a watch.

The full form of the negative *not* is less constrained than its contracted partner. The neutral position for *not* is exactly the same, following the tensed auxiliary:

They will not wait
They have not waited
They are not waiting
They did not wait.

However, *not* may occupy other positions in relation to the auxiliary, with subtle effects on what is negated:

He may have not arrived (although we thought he had)
She may have not been joking (although we thought she was)
I may have not been working hard enough (as I should have).

The acceptability of such variations is variable:

?I may have been not working hard enough.

Tag questions

With tag questions we reach the ultimate twist in the auxiliary tale. To convey the simplest of functions, tag questions employ the fussiest of structures. Consider the following examples:

This piece goes here, *doesn't it*?
We can go now, *can't we*?

The children have grown, *haven't they?*
He's winning, *isn't he?*
They must have left, *mustn't they?*

From a structural point of view, the tag should have a familiar feel. Just like the elliptical constructions we analysed above, it echoes the main sentence in proform:

- The subject NP is repeated as a pronoun:

  this piece → it
  the children → they

- The VP is repeated as a tensed auxiliary:

  goes here → does
  have grown → have.

What marks out the tag is, first, that it attaches to a main sentence, as indicated by the intonation contour:

This piece goes here, *doesn't it?*

Second, it takes the form of a question, so the tensed auxiliary precedes the subject pronoun:

we can → can we
he's → is he.

Third, the polarity of the main sentence is reversed: if the main sentence is positive, the tag is negative, so *n't* is attached to the tensed auxiliary:

we can → can't we
he's → isn't he.

Had the main sentence been negative, the tag would be positive:

This piece *doesn't* go here, *does* it?
We *can't* go now, *can* we?
The children *haven't* grown, *have* they?

Of all the possible combinations of auxiliary and pronoun, just one will be right for any particular sentence. Any mismatch between subjects and tensed auxiliaries will lead to an ill-formed tag:

Mismatched pronouns: *This piece goes here, doesn't they?
                              *He's winning, isn't she?

Mismatched tensed auxiliary: *This piece goes here, won't it?
                                  *We can go now, don't we?

But what does this complex construction add to the meaning of the sentence? The answer is not a lot. Consisting of proforms which echo the references in the immediately preceding main sentence, it does not in any way alter the situation conveyed. The function it performs is purely conversational. The speaker's use of a tag draws in the listener, by inviting her to agree with the speaker's assertion. A speaker who says

This piece goes here, doesn't it?
You're doing OK, aren't you?

expects confirmation from the listener.

This function of inviting confirmation, which requires selection from more than 100 forms in English, is performed by one single form in many other languages:

French: n'est-ce pas?
German: nicht wahr?

The same is true of some varieties of English, where the single tag *init* is used:

We can go now, *init*?

Or some speakers may use the form *huh* with a questioning intonation:

You've finished, *huh*?

Where the full tag is used, English offers variations on the conversational theme. We don't have to go all the way with the tag question. Notice what happens if we keep the polarity the same:

This pen works, does it?
You're doing OK, are you?

Instead of conveying confidence about her assertion and inviting confirmation, the speaker conveys uncertainty, and would not be surprised if the answer was 'no'.

A third version of the tag that can be popular with young children keeps both the modality and polarity the same, so that the tag is a straight echo of the main sentence:

This goes here, this does.
I'm winning, I am.

Here, the tag does nothing more than underline the assertion and broadcast the speaker's confidence in it.

This use of tags by young children is often observed at the point when they have mastered the full set of auxiliaries. It is as if they have worked the system out, and are playing it for all it's worth. For children with language problems, and adults whose language is impaired, the intricacies of English auxiliaries are more likely to be a source of frustration than fun. In this chapter, we have described the syntactic complexities of these pivotal forms. In the following chapters, we delve into their semantic and phonological characteristics which conspire to make auxiliaries a challenge on every level.

11.6 Links to other levels

In this chapter, we have worked through the syntactic complexities of the auxiliary system. We have introduced the auxiliary categories of tense, modal and aspectual verbs, and seen how these behave in questions, negatives and elliptical structures.

The elements of the auxiliary system fall into the class of so-called **function words** or **functional categories** (see Chapter 14, Section 14.8). These are traditionally identified by their syntactic status, but they are also distinguished by their phonological and semantic characteristics.

Phonologically, the elements of the auxiliary system consist of unstressed words, or inflections which are segments or syllables of words. Modal and aspectual verbs are words such as *can*, *has*, *were*, but notice what form these usually take:

She /kən/ go by bus
He /həz/ escaped
They /wə/ yawning.

Once they occur in a sentence, they typically reduce their vowel, usually to schwa. Some of these verbs reduce even further, taking the form of a phonological segment that attaches to the preceding syllable:

/ʃɪl/ arrive late (she will → she'll)
/hiz/ escaped (he has → he's)
/aɪm/ yawning (I am → I'm).

Tense and the present and past participles usually take the form of a segmental or syllabic inflection:

walks – /s/
walked – /t/
washes – /ɪz/

waited – /ɪd/
given – /ən/
giving – /ɪŋ/.

It will be important to take these phonological characteristics into account in any clinical activity assessing or targeting auxiliaries. For a more extensive analysis of these characteristics, see *Links to other levels* in Chapters 12 and 13, and Section 14.5 of Chapter 14.

Semantically, the elements of the auxiliary system enable us to anchor situations in time. They indicate whether the situation is past, present or future. But as we shall see in the next two chapters, that is not all they do. They also convey something about the time span of a situation. And they enable us to go beyond actually-occurring situations, and present situations as potentially occurring. The timing and reality of situations are important notions that language is uniquely able to express. Where auxiliaries are a problem for a person, we may need to consider how these aspects of meaning can be brought out.

Exercises

1. Sarah, aged 3:2, is developing language rapidly. The following conversation took place while she was playing in the company of an adult in her nursery:

S:	I'm feeding teddy's now. He's coming up now. Him, he's just material isn't – he's materialled.
Adult:	You mean he's not real?
S:	He's gonna be real if he's big. He can't walk, can he?
Adult:	Do you think he might learn to walk one day?
S:	When he's bigger. When praps he's going to another school when he's a big boy. Do you think he wants to go to another school?
Adult:	Shall we ask him? Will he answer?
S:	He can't answer. Cos he's got a material mouth. I'm looking for another spoon, I am. When I'm praps a big girl I can find a spoon up there, can't I.
Adult:	Will you be as big as the roof?
S:	No. My grandad usually hits the light off and the light might go to bump onto the roof.
Adult:	He must be very tall.
S:	He must be knocking the light all around the house.
Adult:	I think it's time to go back now.
S:	No, it isn't.
Adult:	Soon time to play outside.
S:	No, won't be soon.

(i) Tick which of the following forms and structures Sarah uses, giving at least one example of her use:

Tense – past	
Tense – non-past	
Modal verbs	
have + past participle	
be + present participle	
Question structure (with auxiliary before subject NP)	
Negative structure (with *n't* attached to auxiliary)	
Elliptical response (with just pronoun and auxiliary)	
Tag (with pronoun and auxiliary)	

(ii) What conclusions can you draw about Sarah's command of the auxiliary system?

2. The following utterances were produced by 10-year-old Jed who has a language impairment. Analyse his utterances to determine which aspects of the auxiliary system he uses appropriately, and which he omits.

  (i) My friend pick you up tomorrow.

 (ii) You broken this.

(iii) And nanny wearing her hat.

(iv) When I start here, I can't talk.

 (v) She watch.

(vi) I going home.

(vii)

Adult:	What would happen if you had no head?
J:	Scream.
Adult:	But where would your mouth be?
J:	On the floor.
Adult:	So would your head down there scream?
J:	If I pick it up and put it back on.
Adult:	How would you get it back on your body?
J:	Push my head really hard – go like that and then it stick.

3. You want to check whether a child is able to produce past tense forms of verbs. You plan to use the 'wug' task. In this task, you present a sentence such as:

This is walking

followed by a sentence fragment requiring completion with a tensed form of the verb:

Yesterday I…

Select 10 regular and 10 irregular past tense forms to target in this task. (This task is modelled on the 'wug test' – see Berko 1958, and Karmiloff and Karmiloff-Smith 2001.)

4. You decide to use a story re-tell task to find out if a school-age child or adult can produce a range of auxiliaries and auxiliary combinations, and to investigate any pattern in their responses. For this purpose, create a story containing at least the following:

one modal verb
one instance of auxiliary *have*
one instance of auxiliary *be*
one combination of modal and auxiliary *have*
one combination of auxiliary *have* and auxiliary *be*
one question with *have* and one question with *do*
one negative with a modal and one negative with *do*.

Keep each sentence as simple as possible in other respects.

   The story can be accompanied with pictures or acting out, to aid recall. If this task fails to elicit any auxiliaries, you can use the same stimuli in a sentence repetition task to see if the person is able to repeat the auxiliary targets, and analyse any patterns in their repetition.

|12|

Tense and aspect

12.1 Introduction

Time is a fundamental aspect of human experience, and this is reflected in language. Situations happen in time, and the expression of situation time is an important part of sentence meaning. In fact language is particularly crucial for conveying time notions – as you would find if you tried to convey time notions without language. Suppose you used a picture to represent meaning. You might succeed in conveying at least some aspects of a situation such as sleeping, or dropping, or breaking, or giving. But you would be hard pressed to represent its timing. Equally, if you mimed a situation, how could you show when it happened? Just imagine trying to get across the sort of time references that the most everyday sentences convey with precision:

I drop*ed* that vase *yesterday*
The vase *has* broken
She *was* sleeping *when the alarm went off*
The librarian *will* give you the book *later*

What kind of time notions do such sentences express? When we think about time, we tend to think of it as one continuous line that we break up into past, present and future. Here I am, now:

[speaker]
↓

present

with time stretching behind and ahead of me:

←   [speaker]   →
↓

past   present   future

You might expect that time distinctions in language would directly reflect this three-way conceptual distinction, that the forms of language would correspond to these three times. But the way language frames time is not as simple as that. English, for example, has:

- several forms for past situations, e.g.

  Rupert sent the e-mail
  Rupert has sent the e-mail
  Rupert had sent the e-mail

- two forms for present situations, e.g.

  Mary lives in Rome
  Mary is living in Rome

- many forms for future situations, e.g.

  I leave for Spain next week
  I'm going back soon
  I'm gonna watch that video later
  I will do my essay tomorrow
  I may do my essay tomorrow.

Our choice of form for past, present or future is influenced by a number of temporal characteristics of situations:

1. The time of the situation relative to the **utterance time** (the time at which the sentence is produced).
2. The time of the situation relative to a **reference time** (another time which is implicit in the context, or explicitly mentioned in the sentence).
3. The **time span** of the situation relative to the utterance time or reference time.

These temporal characteristics determine our use of tense and the auxiliaries *have* and *be*. Tense indicates the timing of the situation (1 and 2 above). The auxiliaries *have* and *be* indicate its time span (3 above), conveying what is known as aspect. As we pointed out in Chapter 11, the marking of tense and aspect is obligatory in English, forcing us to pay attention to the temporal relations that these express.

Apart from the time distinctions that English requires, we have the option of adding reference times. These are conveyed by temporal modifiers such as *now, yesterday, in 3 weeks, a year ago, yet, since I started the job*.

In this chapter, we explore these temporal meanings in more depth.

12.2 Why look at time?

As we saw in the previous chapter, tense and auxiliary verbs are notoriously difficult for people whose language is impaired. Sometimes the timing of situations they are talking about can be worked out from the context, and it would be easy to think that missing out a past tense or an aspectual or modal verb does not matter much. But it may. Imagine an adult recounting their recent experiences in hospital, or their fears or hopes for the future. The timing of situations they are talking about matters to them, and difficulties with conveying time may leave them frustrated and their listener confused. It may then be important to look at the temporal meanings they want to express, and how we might facilitate this.

An anecdotal story about a child in a language unit provides a powerful example of how disruptive difficulties with time references can be. The 10-year-old child was having regular sessions with a play therapist who was convinced that the child was emotionally disturbed and had no problem with language itself. After seeing the child for a number of months, she suddenly revised her view. What led to this about-turn? The therapist had been talking about a future play session, and found herself at cross-purposes with the child, who thought they were talking about the session that was just coming to an end. The child's confused response to time references somehow led the therapist to see that the child was struggling with the language of time, and that her problems with communication could not be put down to an emotional disturbance.

Understanding the nature of time concepts and the forms these take in a language is important if we are to analyse a person's difficulty with time references and find ways around these. It may be, for example, that temporal modifiers are more accessible than tense and auxiliary forms (see Moore and Johnston 1993). So, we find a child saying things like

I ring you *last time*
Your baby come out *soon*
I not ask her *yet*

where tense and auxiliaries are missing, but optional modifiers provide some information about timing. Such observations may give us ideas for optimizing a person's communication of time: therapy might focus on temporal modifiers and encourage the child or adult to use these in order to clarify timing.

12.3 Past time

Past tense: pinpointing a past situation

A verb may be marked by just the past tense:

Kate painted the kitchen.

This indicates that the situation (painting) occurred at some point in time prior to the time of utterance – whether a moment before, a week before, or 10 years before:

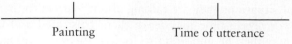

As you would expect, the past tense combines with temporal modifiers relating to the past:

Kate painted the kitchen in 2000/a week ago/at 6 this morning

but not present or future time:

*Kate painted the kitchen now
*Kate painted the kitchen soon.

Less obviously, the past tense combines with temporal modifiers that specify a time point or time period during which the situation occurred:

Kate painted the kitchen yesterday
Kate painted the kitchen during the holidays

but not with temporal modifiers that refer to a period spreading from the past to a later point:

*Kate painted the kitchen since her birthday
*Kate didn't paint the kitchen yet.

This shows that the past tense pinpoints a situation in past time, treating it as a discrete and closed happening, whether that happening occurred in a split second or over an extended period. The auxiliary *have*, combined with the past participle of a verb, also refers to past situations but takes a rather different perspective on past events.

Have: *a different take on the past*

Consider the following examples:

I saw Harry Potter three times   I've seen Harry Potter three times
I saw Harry Potter last week   *I've seen Harry Potter last week
*I already saw Harry Potter   I've already seen Harry Potter

I didn't see Harry Potter last night   *I haven't seen Harry Potter last night
*I didn't see Harry Potter yet   I haven't seen Harry Potter yet.

All of these sentences refer to a situation (my seeing Harry Potter) which occurred before the utterance situation (my talking about seeing Harry Potter). All, therefore, refer to a situation that is past. But their reference to time differs in both structure and meaning. If you have read the previous chapter, you will be able to identify the structural differences between the sentences on the left, which contain the simple past tense (*saw/didn't*), and the sentences on the right, which contain the auxiliary *have* in the present tense, followed by the past participle of the main verb (*seen*).

But what are the implications for timing? We have already established that the simple past tense refers to a situation that occurred prior to the utterance, at some specific time point:

I saw Harry Potter last week.

Notice what happens when the past tense is used for repeated occurrences of a situation:

I saw Harry Potter three times.

It's as if the three occurrences are collapsed into one. It would be natural to add a time modifier indicating the 'one' time that incorporates the three occurrences:

I saw Harry Potter 3 times *when I was a child*.
↑

one time

Now think about the implications of the sentence with *have*:

I have seen Harry Potter three times.

The time focus has shifted from a specific point in the past when a situation occurred to the present effects of a past situation. The situation is no longer a closed 'package' tied to some specific time point or period. This emerges clearly if we try and add a time modifier that pinpoints its timing:

*I have seen Harry Potter three times when I was a child
*I have seen Harry Potter three times last week.

These sentences are odd. The modifiers *when I was a child* and *last week* pinpoint the timing of the situation, which is incompatible with *have*.

Instead, we find *have* occurring with time modifiers that refer to the relation between past and present:

I have *already* seen Harry Potter
I haven't seen Harry Potter *yet*.

This exposes the subtle meaning of *have*: it says that something about a past situation is relevant to the present. The listener must identify just what the relevance is. With the sentence:

I have seen Harry Potter

I may be saying I am the sort of person who sees popular films. Or I may be responding to an accusation that I only go to arty films. On the other hand, I may be saying that I do not want to see the film again. *Have* only indicates that the past situation has some implication for the present – we rely on context to work out what that implication is.

We can now see that aspectual *have* conveys a different type of temporal meaning from tense. Unlike tense, it does not pinpoint the time of a situation

---

Box 12.1 The effects of *have* with different tense markers

Have may be used to indicate the relevance of a past situation to another situation which is itself in the past. In this case, *have* combines with the past tense:

He had escaped (when the police arrived).

The implication here is that one situation in the past (escaping) is relevant to a subsequent situation in the past:

     Escaping   The police arriving   Time of utterance

Have can also refer to a relationship between situations in the future:

He will have escaped by the time the police arrive.

Here, *have* indicates that a situation in the future (escaping) is relevant to a later situation in the future (the police arriving):

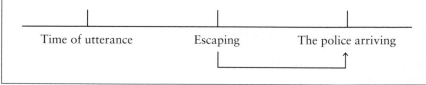

     Time of utterance   Escaping   The police arriving

relative to utterance or reference time. Rather, it indicates the time span of the situation: how it extends its effect to a subsequent situation. This explains the way that *have* interacts with tense marking. You may have been baffled and even sceptical when we identified the tense marking on *have* as present in sentences like:

He has escaped

given that the situation – escaping – clearly happened in the past. This now makes sense. The present tense indicates that the past situation is relevant at the time of utterance – that is, at the present time:

Because *have* identifies a relationship of one situation to another, it is not tied to a particular time. All our examples so far have involved a past situation relevant to a present situation. But this is not the only possibility. *Have* can also indicate that a past situation is relevant to a past or future situation, depending on the tense markers that accompany it – see Box 12.1.

12.4 Present time

States in the present

Present time is marked by present tense when the situation is a state. Recall that states are situations that are unbounded, spreading over an indefinite period of time. The implication of using the present tense with a state is that the state holds at the time of utterance:

Mike has purple hair
Susan is an engineer
She knows the answer
I love this picture
The vase stands on the shelf.

In contrast, when the situation is an event, present time is not marked by present tense alone. For an event that is happening at the time of utterance, English uses the present tense together with progressive aspect, marked by *be* + *ing*. If we do use present tense with an event, it has quite different and specific effects: see Box 12.2.

Box 12.2 The effects of present tense with events

1. *Habitual events and timeless generalizations*
Consider the following examples:

Mike dyes his hair
Susan works as an engineer.

Here, present tense does not mark the event as happening at the time of utterance. So what does it do? In most cases, it indicates the habitual nature of an event at the time of utterance: Mike routinely dyes his hair, Susan routinely works as an engineer, and so on. This use of the present is particularly natural in timeless generalizations, describing events that occur with predictable regularity:

The sun rises in the east and sets in the west
Kangaroos carry their infants in their pockets

Speech and language therapy students do a course in linguistics. It is less natural with events that do not lend themselves to this habitual interpretation:

?I paint this picture
?She finds the answer

unless we put these in a context that makes the event habitual:
I paint this picture whenever I feel like it
She always finds the answer on the Internet.

2. *Narrative*
The present tense can also be used in narratives, to create a sense of immediacy:

... I had another row with my boss, and I'm like 'I can't do all your e-mails AND answer the phone AND listen to your problems' and he just shrugs his shoulders and I'm fuming even more

Susan becomes an engineer, gets a brilliant job, earns a fortune, and retires at 30.

The antique vase falls off the shelf and shatters, and the guilty cat slinks away. A family heirloom and hundreds of pounds worth in smithereens.

3. *Scheduled future*
As we saw in the previous chapter, the so-called present tense is strictly speaking a non-past tense, because it can also be used with events to indicate future time – though only where the event is planned (see Section 12.5 below).

Events in the present

In the following commonplace conversation, you will find several examples of the way we talk about events in the present:

> Mum: What *are* you do*ing* Sam? *Are* you clear*ing* the table like I asked you to?
>
> Sam: No, I'*m* play*ing* with my playstation. It's great. I'*m* not stopp*ing* now.
>
> Mum: I know, but right now I want you to clear the table. Anyway, you'*re* spend*ing* far too long with your eyes glued to that thing.

Wherever 'Mum' and 'Sam' talk about an *event* that occurs as they talk, they use the present tense of the auxiliary *be* with the present participle *-ing*. Contrast this with the way they talk about present *states*, using just the present tense as we would expect. We would have been a bit taken aback if they'd used *be* + *ing* in these contexts:

> Sam: ... It's being great ...
>
> Mum: I'm knowing. But right now I'm wanting you to clear the table.

You can now see why we use *be* + *ing* as a test to distinguish events and states (see Chapter 7, Section 7.2): if a verb can combine with *be* + *ing*, it expresses an event; if it cannot, it expresses a state.

On the odd occasion when we do use this auxiliary with a state verb, we are emphasizing the temporary nature of the state, making it more like an event:

Ruth's wanting a new job
He's being silly
I'm feeling ill

(see Chapter 7, Section 7.2).

Because *be* + *ing* indicates that events are in progress, and is used for events in progress as we talk, people often think it refers to 'the present'. It does not. *Be*, like *have*, is an aspectual marker, conveying the time span of a situation rather than its timing. It indicates that a situation stretches in time. For this reason, *be* is also used for past or future situations when these stretch in time: see Box 12.3.

12.5 Future time

In Chapter 11 we pointed out that English has no future tense. How then do we talk about the future? At the outset of this chapter, we provided

---

Box 12.3 The effects of *be* with different tense markers

1. *Be* may be used to indicate that a situation spreads over a situation in the past. In this case, *be* combines with the past tense:

He *was* reading (when the bell rang).

When *be* is used for past situations, it has further implications. These implications arise from the way different types of event 'progress' over time, which affects our view of the event when it is 'in progress'. Look at the effect of *be* + *ing* on verbs that express a process resulting in an end state (see Chapter 8, Section 8.3):

The flowers were dying
The ice was melting
She was fixing the television
The child was putting the books on the shelf.

With verbs like *die, melt, fix, put*, the use of *be* implies that the process is 'on its way' to the end state. The end state is not necessarily reached. We can therefore refer to another event interrupting the process and preventing the end state:

The flowers were dying but the gardener brought them back to life
The child was putting the books on the shelf when she dropped them.

In contrast, if we put these sentences into the simple past tense, the implication is that the end state is reached and cannot be undone:

*The flowers died but the gardener brought them back to life
*The child put the books on the shelf when she dropped them.

2. *Be* can also refer to the spread of a situation in the future:

He *will be* sleeping (when I get home).

---

some examples:

I leave for Spain next week
I'm going back soon
I'm gonna watch that video later
I will do my essay tomorrow
I may do my essay tomorrow.

All of these put the situation in the future, but tell us something more about that future. And that is the point about the future in English. We cannot talk about future situations without alluding to conditions that influence their happening.

Each of the above examples contains a different form of temporal marking:

I leave for Spain next week:	present tense
I'm going back soon:	present tense with *be + ing*
I'm gonna watch that video later:	idiomatic *be going to*, which is literally *be + ing* with *go*
I will do my essay tomorrow:	modal *will*
I may do my essay tomorrow:	modal *may*.

Think what you have inferred from these different forms apart from the future-ness of the situation:

I leave for Spain next week:	The situation is presented as currently scheduled.
I'm going back soon:	The situation is presented as currently planned.
I'm gonna watch that video later:	The situation is presented as strongly expected or planned.
I will do my essay tomorrow:	The situation is presented as certain.
I may do my essay tomorrow:	The situation is presented as possible but not certain.

In each example, the speaker conveys a subtly different view of the planned-ness, or expectedness, or likelihood of the situation. Every time we locate a situation in the future, we must select between these options. The differences between these options do not involve time. Rather, they involve a category of meaning known as modality. This is the focus of the next chapter.

12.6 Links to other levels

After examining the time notions that English expresses, it seems hardly surprising that temporal markers pose a problem for many people with language disorders. As we have seen, these markers convey a complex of temporal information about situations which interacts with the temporal properties of the situation type. These temporal meanings may well be a challenge. But it is important to think too about the linguistic forms they rely on. These markers have particular phonological characteristics that should be taken into account in considering a person's problems with the language of time.

What distinguishes these markers phonologically? Some of them – the auxiliary verbs *have* and *be* – belong to those classes of words that are normally unstressed (see Chapter 14). This means they have less prominence than inherently stressed words such as nouns, verbs and adjectives, as illustrated in the following examples:

The 'builder has 'fixed the 'roof
The 'chocolates are 'melting.

If you say these sentences aloud, you will notice that *has* and *are* carry less weight than the nouns and verbs around them. But that is not all. Try saying *has* and *are* aloud, and comparing the way you say them with the way you said them in the above sentences. You should notice a difference. When you read the forms in isolation, they come out as /hæz/ and /ɑ/. But when you read them in the sentences, they come out as /əz/ and /ə/. This is because these unstressed words have reduced forms, where the vowel in their full form is shortened to schwa. They may reduce still further, losing their vowel and contracting onto the preceding word:

He has eaten → He's eaten
I am reading → I'm reading.

The variable and weak forms of auxiliaries could contribute to difficulties in processing them.

What about the other elements that mark situation time – tense and present/past participles? These generally take the form of inflections attached to the verb. In the case of tense, this most often consists of a single segment: /s/ or /z/ for present tense as in *walks, loves*, and /t/ or /d/ for past tense, as in *walked, loved*. The present participle inflection, on the other hand, is always the whole syllable /ɪŋ/, as in *walking, loving*. The past participle is variable, often being the same as the past tense; where it is not, it often consists of the syllable /ən/ as in *eaten, given*. Compared with stressed word forms, the forms marking tense and participles are hardly phonologically salient. Their phonological characteristics could again contribute to difficulties.

Interestingly, the inflectional endings appear to be less problematic than the auxiliary verbs, at least in normal language development. Children show reliable use of the present participle form well before they reliably use the contractible form of *be* that co-occurs with the present participle (Brown 1973; Owens 2001). Two-year-olds frequently produce utterances such as:

We going out
Wayne crying
I having that one
Mummy making tea in a minute

where progressive aspect is marked by the present participle form but the auxiliary is missing. This may be because the inflection attached to the verb is phonologically more salient than the reduced auxiliary preceding it. On the other hand, it may be because the participle is semantically simpler than the auxiliary: whereas the participle conveys just aspect, the auxiliary also conveys tense and number of the subject. Of course both semantic and phonological factors may contribute. These various possible explanations of a pattern observed in normal language development highlight the importance of considering different linguistic factors when we investigate the difficulties someone has with particular aspects of language.

Exercises

1. Imagine you are working with a young man who has developed aphasia after a stroke. You have noticed that he does not produce any time markers in his utterances. As a first step to investigate his comprehension of time markers, you give him 10 sentences to judge: in half the sentences, the temporal marking on the verb matches a temporal adjunct (e.g. *Yesterday we walked a long way*) while in the other half these are mismatched (e.g. **Yesterday we will walk a long way*). Your stimuli could be presented in spoken or written form, or in both.

2. In Chapter 11, Exercise 2, we presented you with a sample of utterances produced by 10-year-old Jed, who has a language impairment. In that exercise, we asked you to analyse his use of auxiliaries from a syntactic point of view. We re-produce some of his utterances below for you to analyse from a semantic point of view. Your task is to identify the range of temporal concepts Jed conveys in these utterances and the ways in which he conveys these:

    (i)   My friend pick you up tomorrow.
    (ii)   You broken this.
    (iii) And nanny wearing her hat.
    (iv)   When I start here, I can't talk.
    (v)   She watch.
    (vi)   I going home.
    (vii) You see us last time.
    (viii) Our class going in the playground now.

13
Modality

13.1 Introduction

We don't just talk about situations actually happening. We also anticipate situations, will them, plan them, speculate and hypothesize about them, and language reflects this. As well as talking about actually occurring situations in the present or past, we can talk about non-actual situations – situations that are possible or hypothetical rather than actual occurrences. In fact, it is hard to imagine how we could communicate the non-actualness of situations without language. If we mimed a situation, or drew a picture of it, how could we show that it was not an actual situation? We could only get this across if we had some agreed gesture or symbol indicating that a situation is conjectured. This is just what language does: it provides forms that signpost the modality of situations, that is, their status as actual or non-actual situations.

To get a feel for the notion of modality, take a look at the following dialogue with Sarah, a linguistically precocious three-year-old – the same dialogue we presented in Chapter 11, Exercise 1. The modal terms Sarah uses are in italics:

S: I'm feeding teddy's now. He's coming up now. Him, he's just material isn't – he's materialled.
Adult: You mean he's not real?
S: He's *gonna* be real *if* he's big. He *can't* walk, *can* he?
Adult: Do you think he might learn to walk one day?
S: When he's bigger. When *praps* he's going to another school when he's a big boy. Do you think he wants to go to another school?
Adult: Shall we ask him? Will he answer?
S: He *can't* answer. Cos he's got a material mouth ... I'm looking for another spoon, I am. When I'm *praps* a big girl I *can* find a spoon up there, *can't* I.
Adult: Will you be as big as the roof?

S:	No. My grandad usually hits the light off and the light *might* go to bump onto the roof.
Adult:	He must be very tall.
S:	He *must* be knocking the light all around the house.
Adult:	I think it's time to go back now.
S:	No, it isn't.
Adult:	Soon time to play outside.
S:	No, *won't* be soon.

Sarah's sophisticated language frees her to muse about situations that are imaginary and even far-fetched. She already has a range of the relevant linguistic forms at her finger-tips. These are primarily modal verbs. In the course of this short dialogue, Sarah has used the modal or semi-modal verbs *gonna, can't, can, might, must, won't*.

Modal verbs are not the only forms for conveying the 'reality status' of situations. Sarah illustrates this when she uses the adverb, *p'raps*, to indicate that what she is talking about is conjecture:

When *praps* he's going to another school ...
When I'm *praps* a big girl ...

Other examples of adverbs conveying modal meaning are *possibly, probably, surely, definitely, certainly*. Yet another way of indicating the modality of a situation is to preface it with an adjective or verb that makes the speaker's view of the situation explicit:

It's possible that ...
It's likely that ...
I'm sure that ...
I think that ...
I believe that ...

Given these different ways of marking out non-actual situations, what is so special about modal verbs? The point about modal verbs is that they incorporate modality into the situation, rather than asserting it separately or in addition to the situation. When a speaker uses a modal verb in a sentence such as 'It may rain', she does not explicitly assert her belief about the weather. Her belief is implicit in the modal verb *may*, which presents the situation as a possible rather than an actual one. Compare this with sentences such as 'Perhaps it will rain', or 'It's possible that it will rain', or 'I think it may rain', where the possibility is made explicit.

In this chapter, we examine the types of modal meaning that can be incorporated into situations in English. Our classification of these meanings will give you a handle on the ways in which English presents the 'reality status' of situations.

13.2 Why look at modality?

In the clinical setting, it is all too easy to restrict ourselves to thought and talk about actual situations. The reasons for this are fairly obvious. First, think how we typically assess someone's comprehension of language. We provide some linguistic input, we want to know what meaning the person has obtained from this input, and we access this by asking them to point to pictures or carry out actions. Likewise, when we assess production, we typically use pictures to target particular meanings or elicit particular forms. But as we have seen, pictures and actions can only represent actual situations. Nothing about a picture or action can indicate that a situation is expected or surmised rather than occurring.

In conversation with children and adults with language impairment, we are also likely to stick to the actual, whether present or past, perhaps occasionally turning the conversation towards future expectations or plans. Again, the reasons for these biases are fairly plain. If someone has a problem with language, and may be difficult to understand, listeners may feel it is 'safer' to concentrate on actual situations that they may already know something about, or that might be supported by contextual information. This may make them feel more secure about working out the speaker's intended meaning. In some cases, we might even feel that 'the actual' is more than enough to cope with, and that the very notion of the hypothetical will be confusing to someone who has difficulties with language.

But think how all this limits the speaker's communication, and our access to what they may be contemplating or expecting. An adult who has had a stroke may well be mulling over the future, worrying or wondering about what lies ahead. A child who has limited opportunities to play with other children may nevertheless entertain wishes and fantasies, and may be frustrated by the difficulties of sharing these. If our assessments are confined to the actual, how do we find out if someone is thinking about non-actual situations, and if they can understand and produce forms expressing non-actualness?

Role play, which clinicians use for a variety of purposes, is one way of opening up the non-actual world in the clinical setting. Another is to set up hypothetical situations. Take the case of 10-year-old Ruth who has specific language impairment (see Chiat 2000). Presented with hypothetical scenarios, she could respond appropriately to these:

Context:	After unlocking the door, Ruth has kept the key separate from the bunch.
Adult:	Why do you need to know which key?
Ruth:	Because [ə] wrong key, [tə] can't do it.
Adult:	Yeah, but we've already opened the door. We don't need it now.
Ruth:	Yes, lock it!

Adult: When?
Ruth: After us.

Here, Ruth shows she can grasp the hypothetical situation of not knowing which is the right key for the door, and the consequences of that situation: that it would make it impossible to lock the door again on the way out. In the following utterances, she shows she is able to surmise about the possible consequences of leaving money in an office:

Ruth: The people come up – that – ladder – they come in there – that window down – to come and pinch your money. [kətə] take it with us. The case.

Here, Ruth does not use the modal *might* or *could* which would be appropriate in this context. But she does give some indication of modality through her use of [kətə], which may be an approximation of a modal verb construction such as 'had better' or 'ought to' or 'gotta', and her use of *the case* which more clearly approximates 'in case'.

On other occasions, Ruth demonstrates her capacity to hypothesize and fantasize by initiating role play. This is illustrated in the following dialogue where she pretends to be holding the adult captive:

Adult: I won't be your slave.
Ruth: Oh yes you will.
Adult: I'll escape.
Ruth: Oh no you won't... You escape, we find you. You come back here, no food.
Adult: If I don't escape, can I have food?
Ruth: Think about that.
Adult: Oh, what will happen if I have no food?
Ruth: Dead. No sweat ... Pretend you escape ... Stay there! Don't move!

Here we see a child whose language is severely impaired being able to project hypothetical situations and their consequences – 'You escape, we find you. You come back here, no food'.

If we are to open up the realm of the non-actual in the clinical setting and include it in assessment and intervention, we need to know more about the kinds of meanings modal categories enable us to express.

13.3 Modal meanings

When speakers refer to a non-actual situation, they necessarily say something about the conditions influencing its happening. To get a feel for this, consider the array of non-actual situations expressed by the modal verbs in the following examples:

She *can* design web pages	(conveys *ability* required for situation)
She *will* see you now	(conveys *willingness* for situation to occur)
She *can* borrow my purse	(conveys *permission* for situation to occur)
She *must* do that essay	(conveys *obligation* for situation to occur)
She *might* watch the film	(conveys *possibility* that situation will occur)
She *will* win the race	(conveys *certainty* that situation will occur).

These examples illustrate different modal meanings, and show that some modal verbs (for example *can* and *will*) convey more than one modal meaning. We now examine these meanings more closely.

Ability and willingness

The modal verb may present conditions on the situation that arise from the participant in the subject position. In the following examples, *can* indicates that the subject NP has the capacity to enter into the situation:

Matilda can swim
She can speak three languages
I can see you
I can understand your point of view
Can this parrot talk?
These scissors can cut through anything

or poses no obstacles to the situation occurring:

This car can take six people
The book can fit in here.

If *can* is negated, it conveys the incapacity of the subject to enter into the situation, or the existence of barriers preventing this:

Matilda can't swim
She can't get to the meeting
I can't see you.

The modal verb *will* can also convey something about the subject NP's control over the situation, in this case, through the subject's willingness or drive to enter into the situation:

I will help you
The doctor will see you in five minutes
These scissors will cut through anything.

Won't indicates the absence of willingness or drive:

I won't brush my teeth
She won't take her medicine
The doctor won't see you today
This pen won't work.

The term **dynamic modality** is used for those modal meanings that involve the subject NP controlling the situation in some way.

Permission and obligation: deontic modals

In contrast to the contexts in the preceding section, where the subject NP is seen as controlling the situation, modal verbs may present the situation as externally controlled. In the following examples, *can* and *may* convey permission for the subject to enter into the situation:

You can watch TV after dinner (mother talking to child)
I can leave work early (my boss said so)
People can only smoke outside (institutional rule)
You may start writing (invigilator starting an exam).

Contrasting with *can* and *may* are modal verbs that convey obligation. These are distinguished by the degree of obligation they imply:

Some pressure	You should visit your cousin
	You ought to visit your cousin
Insistence	You must stop writing now
	You will see me later

Negating modals of permission and obligation implies some degree of forbidding:

Not permitted	You can't have any chocolate
	I can't leave work early
	You may not take a mobile phone into the lecture
Advised not to	You shouldn't stay out late
Forced not to/Forbidden	You mustn't do that again
	You won't talk to me like that

The term **deontic modality** is traditionally used for those modal meanings that involve external control of the situation through permission or obligation.

From possibility to certainty: epistemic modals

Finally, modal verbs may convey the likelihood of a situation occurring. Here, the speaker presents a situation as more or less expected based on what she knows, judges or infers about factors influencing its occurrence. Modal verbs in this category lie on a scale from weak possibility to certainty:

Relative likelihood	Examples of modals	Possible implicit evidence
Weak possibility	It may rain	I've seen some black clouds The forecast said so
	They might go to Jim's	They haven't decided yet They quite like Jim
Strong possibility	Peter must be at work	He's not at home He works at this time
	You must have flu	You've got a high temperature You look feverish
Certainty	It will rain	Those are rain clouds up there The forecast said so
	Alice will pass her test	She's good enough Her teacher said so
	They will tow your car away	This is a no parking zone

The modals *could* and *would* also say something about the likelihood of a situation occurring, but they are more tentative about this. They present the possibility as more remote, implying that it is subject to hypothetical conditions. These conditions may or may not be made explicit:

Relative likelihood	Examples of modals	Possible implicit or explicit conditions
Possibility under hypothetical conditions	The children could walk	though they may not want to if they weren't lazy
	You could sit down	if you're stopping for a while
Certainty under hypothetical conditions	I would go round the world	if I won the lottery if I could drop everything
	They would tow your car away	if you parked it there

The term **epistemic modality** is traditionally used for modal meanings involving the speaker's evaluation of the chances that a situation will occur.

Meeting points between different modal meanings

As you have worked through the examples of different types of modal meaning, you may have noticed some modals popping up in more than one category. *Can*, for example, has both dynamic and deontic meanings:

Dynamic	Deontic
I can swim (ability – I'm able to)	I can swim (permission – I'm allowed to)

The fact that *can* is used for both highlights a similarity between the two meanings: both indicate the absence of barriers to a situation occurring.

May, should, must and *will* convey both deontic and epistemic modality:

Deontic	Epistemic
You may go (permission)	You may like this (possibility)
You should go (some obligation)	The bus should be here soon (some expectation)
You must work hard (strong obligation)	It must rain (strong expectation)
You will leave now (insistence)	It will rain (certainty)

Again, we see overlaps: the degree of pressure implied by each modal is the same for the two modal meanings associated with it, ranging from the weak pressure of *may* to the very strong pressure of *will*.

Could and *would* serve as past tense forms of *can* and *will*, enabling us to apply these modal meanings to past situations:

Past ability:	I could swim when I was a kid
Past permission:	My mum said I could go out
Past willingness:	She said she would help me.

As we have seen, these forms also convey hypothetical situations. This accounts for the ambiguity of sentences such as:

I could go out

which may express past ability/permission (I was able to or was allowed to go out) or present possibility (if I felt like it, I could go out).

In some contexts, modals appear to merge different modal meanings:

She should be here by now = obligation? expectation? both?
We've finished the job, so we can go = ability? permission? both?

This merging of meanings is apparent in some rather formulaic or fixed uses of modals. Take the case of modals that appear in a question form, but actually serve to make polite requests:

Can you pass the salt please?
Could you pass the salt please?

Will you open the door please?
Would you open the door please?

or polite proposals:

Shall/should I carry your bag for you?
Shall/should we start now?

Here, modal verbs render a request or proposal more or less tentative. Their tentativeness is characteristic of their modal meanings, but they do not imply any specific one of these meanings. For example, it is not obvious that *can* as used in a polite request conveys ability, permission or possibility. We leave you to ponder your interpretation of these examples.

13.4 Links to other levels

Our analysis of modal meanings has brought out the many and subtle ways in which language enables us to talk about non-actual situations. It has also illustrated the sometimes idiosyncratic meanings of particular modal verbs in particular contexts. The complexity of modal verb semantics is matched by the phonological complexity of modal verbs.

Modal verbs, like other auxiliary verbs, belong to those classes of words that are normally unstressed (see Chapter 14). This means they have less prominence than inherently stressed words such as nouns, verbs and adjectives, as illustrated in the following examples:

The 'children can 'go 'home
The 'lecture will 'finish in a 'minute.

Some modal verbs are not only unstressed, but reduce their form when they occur in a sentence context. Their full vowel may be shortened to schwa:

/kæn/ → /kən/
/ʃæl/ → /ʃəl/
/mʌst/ → /məst/

or they may lose their vowel altogether, contracting onto the preceding word:

I will → I'll
I would → I'd.

Semi-modal verbs which take infinitives show another type of reduction, whereby *to* contracts onto the verb:

going to → gonna
have to → hafta
want to → wanna.

It is striking that children's early utterances sometimes include an even more reduced form in a context where we might expect a modal to occur:

[an] do it   targeting ?*I wanna*
[əŋə] go now   targeting ?*I'm gonna*
[ə] help me   targeting ?*will you.*

(See Peters 2001 for examples and detailed analysis.) Such forms may persist for many years in children whose language is impaired. Have a look at the following examples, and think what words you would expect to find in the slots where the child has produced unintelligible weak syllables:

[də] type that for me please   targeting ?*will you ...*
[zə] play that game again   targeting ?*shall we ...*
We [gɔ] be very good   targeting ?*we gonna ...*
We [kə] take our flowers home   targeting ?*we can take ...*
He want have it, he [gədə] pay it targeting ?*...he's gotta ...*

In some contexts, though, these children are more likely to use full recognizable modal forms:

Oh yes you will
Oh no you won't
I can
[tə] can't do it.

Here, the modal verbs occur in contexts where they must take their full form – their vowel cannot reduce. It may be that this makes them more salient for the children. These data illustrate the importance of taking phonological properties into account when we think about problems people may have with particular semantic and syntactic categories. (See Chapter 14, Section 14.5 for a fuller presentation and discussion of these issues.)

Exercises

1. Wells (1985) provides an overview of the modal meanings that children express between 30 and 60 months, and the order in which these emerge:

   Ability/Permission
   then
   Willingness
   then
   Obligation
   then
   Possibility

then
Certainty.

1. Create two sentences to exemplify each of these modal categories.
2. How might we account for the later emergence of some modal meanings than others? In particular, what evidence do we have that semantic rather than syntactic or phonological factors are responsible?

2. In Section 1, we highlighted the modal verbs in a sample of utterances from 3-year-old Sarah (reproduced below). What categories of modal meaning are exemplified in this sample?

S:	I'm feeding teddy's now. He's coming up now. Him, he's just material isn't – he's materialled.
Adult:	You mean he's not real?
S:	He's *gonna* be real if he's big. He *can't* walk, *can* he?
Adult:	Do you think he might learn to walk one day?
S:	When he's bigger. When praps he's going to another school when he's a big boy. Do you think he wants to go to another school?
Adult:	Shall we ask him? Will he answer?
S:	He *can't* answer. Cos he's got a material mouth. I'm looking for another spoon, I am. When I'm praps a big girl I *can* find a spoon up there, *can't* I.
Adult:	Will you be as big as the roof?
S:	No. My grandad usually hits the light off and the light *might* go to bump onto the roof.
Adult:	He must be very tall.
S:	He *must* be knocking the light all around the house.
Adult:	I think it's time to go back now.
S:	No, it isn't.
Adult:	Soon time to play outside.
S:	No, *won't* be soon.

3. Looking at the following exchange with Jed (see exercises in Chapters 11 and 12), what enables us to deduce that he understands that the situation being discussed is a hypothetical one, even though he does not use a modal verb to mark this?

Adult:	What would happen if you had no head?
J:	Scream.
Adult:	But where would your mouth be?
J:	On the floor.
Adult:	So would your head down there scream?
J:	If I pick it up and put it back on.
Adult:	How would you get it back on your body?
J:	Push my head really hard – go like that and then it stick.

4. You want to find out if an adult who has aphasia can understand references to hypothetical situations, and how she talks about these. Using the technique illustrated in Exercise 3 above, construct five hypothetical scenarios that would be suitable for presentation to an adult, and would be presented using the modals *could* and *would*.

5. You are working with a 7-year-old child with a language impairment. You decide to target modals conveying ability, permission and certainty, using a turn-taking activity. You start by targeting modal verbs in short responses, where they take their full form. You make an assertion containing a modal verb:

> Therapist: I can fly.
> and invite the child to agree or disagree:
> Child: No you can't.

(It may be necessary to give the child several examples of responses to your own assertions in order to get the idea across.)

For the purposes of this activity, construct twelve assertions that contain modals expressing ability, permission and certainty.

V

Syntax – phonology links

14

The phonological shape of sentences

14.1 Introduction

Consider the following two sentences:

The detective saw Tim.
The detective saw him.

Looking at these on the page, they appear to differ by no more than one consonant. But if you say them out loud, you will find that this is not the only
difference between them. They also differ in their rhythmic pattern. Whereas
Tim is stressed and is more prominent than *saw*:

The detective saw 'Tim,

him is unstressed, making *saw* the most prominent word in the sentence:

The detective 'saw him.

Now try a pair of sentences that appear to differ by just one word:

What did they sit on?
What did they put on?

Again, you might expect these to sound identical apart from that one word.
But they do not. In the sentence with *sit*, *on* is unstressed and *sit* carries the
greatest stress:

What did they 'sit on?

In the sentence with *put*, on the other hand, *on* carries the stress:

What did they put 'on?

Compare the following sentence:

What did they slip on?

Here, both stress patterns are possible – but each corresponds to a different meaning:

What did they 'slip on?   (plausible answer = 'a banana skin')
What did they slip 'on?   (plausible answer = 'their coats').

These sentences provide a particularly striking illustration of the complex rhythms of language. Although you may never have encountered the sentences before, you know instinctively where to put the stresses. The most minimal difference in wording can lead you to produce a subtly different stress pattern, as in the *Tim/him* sentences. Conversely, a small change in the stress pattern can lead you to alter your interpretation of a sentence (as in the sentence *What did they slip on?*).

But what leads us to put the stress on one word or another? You might think this has something to do with the importance of the word: the more meaning a word conveys, and the more important it is to our message, the more we will stress it. If you try this explanation against the examples we have looked at, you will see that it does not hold up. It would be very hard to argue that *on* is more important to the meaning of

What did they put 'on?

than

What did they 'sit on?

Emphatic stress vs neutral stress

It is true that we *can* use stress to indicate importance. Indeed we have just done this in the previous sentence. The italicized form of *can* tells you that we are stressing this word, and that is probably how you read it. Our purpose is to emphasize 'can', contrasting it with 'cannot'. Here, we are giving extra stress to a linguistic item in order to draw attention to it, and/or to contrast it with its opposite. This is known as emphatic stress.

We can apply emphatic stress to any item in a sentence. To experience this, take our first example

The detective saw Tim,

give special stress to each item in turn, and notice the effect:

The detective saw Tim.	Focus: not just any detective
The *detective* saw Tim.	Focus: the detective, of all people
	Contrast: the detective, not the doorman
The detective *saw* Tim.	Focus: the sighting is critical
	Contrast: saw, not caught
The detective saw *Tim*.	Focus: Tim, of all people
	Contrast: Tim, not the thief.

Compare each of these with your neutral reading of the sentence:

The detective saw Tim.

You might notice that:

- No item in the neutral reading is as heavily stressed as the items with emphatic stress.
- Accordingly, although *Tim* receives the greatest stress in the neutral reading, this is not equivalent to emphatic stress: if we want to emphasize *Tim*, we have to place even greater stress on this item.

So, emphatic stress is stress that we choose to apply to particular items over and above the other stresses that occur in a sentence. These stresses do not represent emphasis or importance, and they are not under our control. They are predictable, and we apply them automatically and unconsciously. In this chapter, we turn our attention to these stress patterns and the factors which influence them.

14.2 Why look at stress patterns?

In the preceding chapters we have seen how syntactic analysis of data can give us a handle on the language someone produces, and what aspects of language are a problem. Our syntactic description helps us to make generalizations that apply across a set of individual utterances. We can use these generalizations as a starting point for analysing patterns in correct and incorrect production and comprehension.

Sometimes, no clear syntactic or semantic pattern emerges from our description. Take the case of children's early words. In English, we find that these consist predominantly of words from the adult category of nouns, but include a small proportion of verbs, adjectives, prepositions, quantifiers. Thus, the words the child uses span a number of syntactic categories, conveying a range of semantic types. They are not clearly demarcated from words the child does not use, either syntactically or semantically. Is there anything else that these words might have in common? One possibility is that we are barking up the wrong tree looking for linguistic factors, and that some environmental factor accounts for the child's selection of words – for example, that the child uses the words they hear most frequently. We can easily rule this out, though, since some of the words that the child does not use at this stage are amongst the most frequent in the language – 'the', 'a', and 'is', for example. Another rather obvious possibility is that the child uses words whose meaning is most important to them. This possibility certainly stands up better: children do seem to be producing the word that conveys the most novel information about the situation they are talking about (Greenfield and Smith 1976). We are still left with the question why they produce these words rather than others that they will later use in the same situation. It looks as if there must be some linguistic factors that influence which of these words they access first. If syntactic and semantic factors are not enough to account for the biases in children's early vocabularies, what other candidates are there?

As you might guess from the topic of this chapter, phonology is the one that steps forward. From a phonological point of view, what do these syntactic categories of words have in common? The answer is that they are all stress-carrying words. Indeed, the words the child uses at this early stage would typically be the most stressed word in the utterance an older child or adult would use in the same context:

What's *that*?
I wanna get *down*.
Turn that *off*.
That's *dirty*.
Give me some *more*!

Perhaps it is their salience in the rhythmic pattern that accounts for the child's selection of these words to convey her meaning.

This phonological analysis of the child's first words has a certain appeal, but the evidence we have so far presented is pretty flimsy. We could argue that other factors – for example, a combination of syntactic and semantic factors – are sufficient to account for children's early words. How can we put this to the test? One way is to see what happens in different languages where the same syntactic and semantic categories occur in different positions in the stress pattern. It has been observed that Korean-speaking children use proportionately more verbs than English-speaking children in their earliest utterances (Choi 1997). One possible explanation for this difference is that verbs are more phonologically salient in Korean because they occur at the end of the sentence. This is in keeping with our phonological analysis of children's early words. To test this analysis more rigorously, we might see how children respond to words when their phonological position in the sentence is systematically manipulated. Knowing something about sentence phonology enables us to do this. A study of children's repetition of sentences containing articles and pronouns illustrates the point. Gerken (1991, 1994) found that children were more likely to omit these function words when they preceded a strong form than when they followed. McGregor and Leonard (1994) carried out a similar study with language-impaired children. These children made more omissions than normally developing children, but the phonological pattern of their omissions was the same: they omitted pronouns and articles more frequently when these occurred at the start of a rhythmic unit than when they followed a strong form in the rhythmic unit.

Stress may also be one of the factors that affect the production of function words by some adults with aphasia (Kean 1979, 1980; Black 1979). The people with non-fluent aphasia described by Black (1979), for instance, tended to produce more stressed prepositions than unstressed ones in both picture description and repetition tasks. They would say, for example,

hand *up*; sweets *down*; boy climbing *up*; bring *out* jar; mother comes *in*

but omit unstressed prepositions such as *with, on*:

falling *over* [...] excitement, man stand [...] stool.

They were also more likely to substitute an incorrect preposition for one that would be unstressed and reduced, e.g.

Target	*Response*
reach *for* the sweets	reach *on* the sweets
climbing *on* the stool	climbing *in* the stool
in the top jar	*at* the top jar.

These substitutions were extremely rare with stressed prepositions; in the very few cases of substitution, people were usually able to correct themselves, e.g.

Falling *up ... over.*

There were also fewer omissions or substitutions of prepositions before a pronoun, where the preposition receives more stress than the pronoun (see Section 14.3 below). That is, people in this study might omit or substitute *for* or *on* before *sweets* or *stool* but not before *him, it, you* or *me*. These data suggest that prosodic factors such as stress have to be taken into account in the description of patterns of production in aphasia.

Ordinary slips of the tongue too seem to be affected by prosody (Boomer and Laver 1968; McKay 1970; Fromkin 1973; Garrett 1975; Cutler 1982). For instance, sounds involved in exchanges, anticipations and perseverations are more likely to be in stressed than unstressed syllables, and syllables involved in sound exchanges usually have similar levels of word stress, e.g.

That was what *T*omsky was *ch*alking about,

where the initial /tʃ/ of *Chomsky* has swapped places with the initial /t/ of *talk-ing* and both sounds come from stressed syllables.

When suffixes shift from the intended word to another word in the utterance, the word they end up on is more likely to be stressed. Shift errors such as

decide to hit*s*

where the third person singular marker on *decide* has shifted not to the next word, but to the next *stressed* word, are common. Shifting suffixes rarely attach to prepositions that are unstressed and reduced – shift errors such as

go to*es* the park

instead of

go*es* to the park

are apparently very rare. In contrast, we find examples where the suffix has shifted to a stressed, unreduced preposition – a pattern very similar to that of aphasic production, e.g.

Target	*Slip*
go*es* back	go back*s*
add*s* up	add up*s*
I'm pay*ing* for it.	I'm pay for*ing* it.

14.3 What determines the stress pattern of a sentence?

The relative stress of words that make up a sentence depends on two key factors:
- the type of word;
- the position of the word in the constituent structure of the sentence.

Type of word: major or minor

From a phonological point of view, words come in two types. Major words are words that always carry stress, and do not have reduced forms. These include the syntactic categories of nouns, verbs, adjectives, adverbs, intransitive prepositions (prepositions not taking a NP complement), and quantifiers. The following sentence contains all and only these categories, and if you say it out loud you will notice that every word carries stress:

Five young elephants walked by slowly.
/ˈfaɪv ˈjʌŋ ˈɛləfənts ˈwɔkt ˈbaɪ ˈsləʊlɪ/

If we were to reduce these words, the sentence would be unrecognizable:

/fav jəŋ ələfənts wəkt ba sləlɪ/

This sentence is unusual in containing only major items. Typically, major words alternate with minor words. These are unstressed (unless they are emphasized). They include the syntactic categories of determiners, pronouns, transitive prepositions (prepositions taking a NP complement), auxiliary verbs and the main verb *be*, conjunctions, complementizers. If we add some of these minor items to the above sentence, you will notice how the rhythm now alternates between unstressed and stressed items:

The ˈfive ˈyoung ˈelephants were ˈwalking by the ˈriver and ˈsaw that I was ˈwatching.

When we utter minor items in isolation, we use their full form. This is the form you will use if you read the minor items in the above sentence as a list: *the, were, by, and, that, I, was*. However, like most minor items in English, these words have reduced forms in which their vowel is shortened. This is the form we use when they occur in a sentence:

/ðə/ five young elephants /wə/ walking /ba ðə/ river /ən/ saw /ðət a wəz/ watching.

The sentence would sound very odd if we used the full forms for these items:

/ði/ five young elephants /wə/ walking /baɪ ði/ river /ænd/ saw /ðæt aɪ wɒz/ watching.

Some minor items also have contracted forms. This means that they lose their vowel, and with it their separate syllabic status, merging with the preceding syllable:

She will go	→ She'll go	*will* contracts onto *she*, giving /ʃɪl/
I would like to	→ I'd like to	*would* contracts onto *I*, giving /ad/
They are late	→ They're late	*are* contracts onto *they*, giving /ðɛə/
I am hungry	→ I'm hungry	*am* contracts onto *I*, giving /am/

The following box presents a fairly comprehensive list of reduced and contracted forms in English:

| Box 14.1 Reduced and contracted forms |

Determiners	Pronouns	Transitive prepositions	Complementizers	Conjunctions	Auxiliaries		
					Modals	have	be
/ðə/	/a/	/tə/	/ðət/	/ən/	/wəd/	/əv/	/bɪ/
/ə/	/mɪ/	/frəm/	/tə/	/bət/	/kəd/	/əz/	/bɪn/
/ma/	/jə/	/fə/			/ʃəd/	/əd/	/əm/
/jə/	/ɪ/	/əv/			/kən/		/ə/
/ɪz/	/ɪm/	/ət/			/əl/		/wəz/
/hə/	/ʃɪ/	/ba/			/məs/		/wə/
	/ə/						
	/wɪ/						
	/əs/						
	/ðəm/						

The phonological distinction we have drawn between major and minor word classes is closely allied to two other distinctions you may meet – the distinction between content and function words, and the distinction between closed class and open words. We clarify the relationship between these three classifications of words below, in the section on *Links to other levels*.

Position in constituent structure

The position of a word in the constituent structure of a sentence further affects its level of stress. The most marked effect is on the final major word in a sentence which carries the greatest stress in the sentence, due to the process of final lengthening (see Chapter 3, Section 3.6). Watch how the sentence stress shifts each time we add a major word to a sentence:

Fred 'left.
Fred left 'late.
Fred left the 'house.
Fred left the house for the 'station.

Position in constituent structure affects the stress of other major words in the sentence as well: a major word at the end of a constituent carries greater stress than other words in the constituent. For example, the nouns in italic in the following sentences all end Noun Phrases:

NP[*Fred*] left late.

NP[My *friend*] left NP[the *house*] for the station.
NP[My friend from *Granada*] left NP[the *house*] for the station.

Consequently, they carry more stress than the verb, since the verb does not end a phrase. In the final example, the noun *Granada* carries more stress than the noun *friend*, because it ends the constituent *my friend from Granada*. You might try saying the above sentences aloud to see if you notice the relative prominence of these nouns.

As unstressed words, minor items do not attract end-of-sentence or end-of-constituent stress. If a sentence ends in a minor word such as a pronoun, the sentence stress falls on the preceding major word:

Fred 'left it.

This accounts for the contrasting stress patterns of the two sentences at the outset of this chapter. In:

The detective saw Tim,

the noun *Tim* is a major item and therefore carries the sentence stress. When we replace *Tim* with the pronoun *him*, this is a minor item, so the sentence stress moves back to the preceding major word which is the verb *saw*.

However, the position of minor items in constituent structure does have some effects on their form. When they occur at the end of their constituent, they are less likely to reduce, and they never contract. We see this with minor items that do not usually occur in final position, but can end up there as a result of ellipsis. For example, in full sentences such as:

I want to go home,

the complementizer *to* can reduce to /tə/:

I /wɒntə/ go home,

and it can even contract onto *want* giving:

I /wɒnə/ go home (/wɒnə/ = *want to*).

Compare what happens in elliptical sentences where *to* occurs sentence-finally:

Why are you going home? → Because I want to.

Here, the vowel in *to* would typically be short, but it is questionable whether it would reduce:

?Because I /wɒntə/,

or contract onto *want*:

?*Because I /wɒnə/.

The constraints are even clearer with auxiliary verbs when these occur in elliptical responses to questions. Here, they act as proforms for the VP in the question, and are therefore the final item in the VP:

Is he going? → He is.
Have you finished? → I have.
Does he like Picasso? → He does.
Who'll do the washing up? → Pablo will.

Try reducing or contracting the auxiliary verbs in the responses, and you
will see how weird they sound:

Is he going? → *He's
Have you finished? → *I /əv/
                                    *I've
Does he like Picasso? → *He /dəz]
Who'll do the washing up? → *Pablo /əl/
                                     *Pablo'll.

Two syntactic categories merit further consideration from a phonological
point of view, because of their rather complex behaviour in English: prepositions and auxiliary verbs.

14.4 More on the phonology of prepositions

We have seen that prepositions fall into two camps. When they occur with an
object, they are minor, but when they occur without an object, they are major.
This difference comes out particularly clearly where the same preposition can
do both. Compare:

She walked by the other day.
She walked by the other route.

In the second sentence, *by the other route* forms a constituent. You can check
this out using constituent tests for PPs (see Chapter 4, Section 4.4). This means
that *by* has an object – *the other route* – and it is therefore minor. It is likely
to reduce to /bə/. *By the other day*, on the other hand, does not form a constituent. In this case, *by* does not have an object, so it is major and carries
stress. It cannot reduce.

This difference between transitive and intransitive prepositions enables us to explain some of the surprising contrasts we exemplified in Section 14.1 of this chapter – see Box 14.2.

Box 14.2 Why the difference between: *What did they put 'on?* **and** *What did they 'sit on?*

These sentences look very similar, but in fact they differ in their syntactic structure. Both begin with the word *what*. However, in one sentence *what* is a NP complement of the verb *put*, and the preposition *on* has no complement NP. You can use a number of constituency tests to show that *on what* does not form a constituent in this sentence, for example, it could not be moved as a whole:

*On what did they put?

As an intransitive preposition, *on* can precede or follow the NP complement of the verb:

They put on what?
They put what on?

The other sentence behaves in the opposite way. Here, *what* is a NP complement of *on*, and the verb *sit* has no NP complement. Since *on what* forms a constituent, it can be moved as a whole:

On what did they sit?

Since *what* is a complement of *on*, it must follow *on* in the PP:

They say on what?
*They sat what on?

This difference in the syntactic behaviour of *on* is reflected in its phonology. Where *on* has no NP complement, it is major, and therefore stressed. As the final major item in the sentence it carries the sentence stress:

What did they put 'on?

Where *on* does have a NP complement, it is minor, and therefore unstressed. The sentence stress therefore falls on the preceding major word, which is the verb *sit*:

What did they 'sit on?

14.5 More on the phonology of auxiliary verbs and the main verb *be*

As Box 14.1 showed, the phonological forms of auxiliary verbs and the main verb *be* are quite varied and idiosyncratic. All have reduced forms, and some also have contracted forms. Whatever the particular form they take, these auxiliary verbs behave rather consistently when it comes to their stress. Typically, they are unstressed and take their reduced or contracted form. However, there are some constraints on their reduction.

First, look at what happens when several auxiliaries occur together. The first auxiliary can contract, but any subsequent auxiliaries can only reduce (even if they have a contracted form):

I'll have left – /aɪl əv/
*I'll've left – */aɪlv/

Similarly, when an auxiliary occurs with the negative particle *not*, only one or other of these can reduce or contract:

The play hasn't finished.	*not* is contracted; *has* is in its full form.
The play's not finished.	*has* is contracted; *not* is in its full form.
*The play /əzənt/ finished.	*has* is reduced and *not* is contracted.
*The /pleizənt/ finished.	Both *has* and *not* are contracted.

Finally, as we saw in Section 14.3, auxiliaries always take their full form when they occur in constituent-final or sentence-final position.

14.6 The representation of stress patterns

The rhythmic structure of sentences can be represented in different ways. The type of representation we have used informally in earlier sections (see Chapter 4) is known as a metrical grid. The layers of the grid represent the different levels of stress that give rise to the rhythm, or metre, of the sentence:

Sentence stress
Phrase stress
Lexical stress.

To indicate that a word receives a particular level of stress, a cross is entered above the word in the appropriate layer of the grid. Applying this to one of our examples:

→ At the lexical level of the grid, a cross is entered above every major word:

Lexical	✕	✕	✕

The elephants were walking by the river

→ At the phrase level, a cross is entered above every word that ends a phrase:

Phrase	✕		✕
Lexical	✕	✕	✕

The elephants were walking by the river

→ At the sentence level, a cross is entered above the final major word in the sentence:

Sentence			✕
Phrase	✕		✕
Lexical	✕	✕	✕

The elephants were walking by the river

The resulting pattern of crosses provides a graphic representation of the rhythm. If you say the sentence aloud, you should find that the prominence of words increases as the number of crosses increases. The minor words are not only the least stressed, but are likely to take their reduced form:

Sentence			✕
Phrase	✕		✕
Lexical	✕	✕	✕

/ðɪ/ elephants /wə/ walking /ba ðə/ river

14.7 Rhythmic alternation: the 'dum-di-dum' rhythm of language

We have explored in some detail the way that the rhythmic pattern of a sentence relates to its syntactic make-up. The stress differences between major and minor classes of words, and between final and non-final major words, combine to produce a more or less alternating rhythm of strong and weak beats – the 'dum-di-dum' rhythm favoured by English. This is evident in the stress patterns of sentences we have analysed above.

The pressure to maintain an alternating rhythm is evident in the way we avoid a sequence of identical stresses. Look at what we do with three consecutive minor items. This situation arises when a sequence of pronoun, preposition, pronoun occurs:

She bought it for me.
The guide led them to him.

In rapid speech, all three items may be unstressed and reduced:

She bought /ɪʔ fə mɪ/.
The guide led /ðəm tə ɪm/.

However, it is much more likely that we will avoid this 'jarring' sequence of equally unstressed items by raising the stress level of one of them, either the preposition:

She bought /ɪʔ fɔ mɪ/.
The guide led /ðəm tu ɪm/.

or the pronoun following it:

She bought /ɪʔ fə mi/.
The guide led /ðəm tə hɪm/.

14.8 Links to other levels

Links between phonological and syntactic aspects of sentences have been at the centre of this chapter, which has shown how the stress pattern of a sentence reflects the syntactic properties and organization of the words it contains. These are links you have already met in chapters starting from the other end – the syntax of words and sentences – and pointing out how this links to phonology as well as semantics (see *Links to other levels* in Chapters 3, 4, 6).

The detailed links we have worked through fill out the broad outline of language we set out from. From the outset, we established that syntax, semantics and phonology are distinct properties of words and sentences. These properties can be identified and manipulated independently of each other. Yet they are also connected. Certain syntactic properties typically correspond to certain semantic and phonological properties.

These typical but not absolute correspondences between syntax, semantics and phonology are captured in the broad classification of words as 'content' or 'function'. Comparing the following examples will give you a feel for the differences between these two broad classes:

Content words: *eye, shell, see, land, fat*
Function words: *I, shall, he, and, that*

The distinction is generally drawn in terms of semantic and syntactic properties, but could also be drawn in terms of phonology:

	Semantics	*Syntax*	*Phonology*
Content words	Typically 'carry meaning' – refer to conceptual categories such as 'Thing' 'Event' 'State' 'Location'	Typically taken to include: Nouns Verbs Adjectives Adverbs	Typically carry stress eye → /aɪ/ shell → /ʃɛl/ see → /si/ land → /lænd/ fat → /fæt/
Function words	Typically 'have little or no meaning' – serve a purely grammatical function such as introducing a complement	Include: Pronouns Auxiliary verbs Determiners Conjunctions Complementizers	Typically unstressed and may have reduced forms such as: I → /a/ shall → /ʃəl/ he → /ɪ/ and → /ən/ that → /ðət/

Content words are also identified as **open class**, meaning that they are open to new members – you might think of new nouns and verbs that have emerged with the development of information technology. Function words, on the other hand, are **closed class**: you will not find examples of new determiners or auxiliary verbs.

Thus, the distinction between content and function words can be drawn in many ways, reflecting a rough alignment between semantic, syntactic and phonological properties. But the alignment is only rough. We can certainly find clear-cut examples of words meeting all the criteria for one or other class. Take the word *to* in the sentence:

They're hoping to win the match.

Semantically, *to* has no content. Syntactically, it is a complementizer which serves only to introduce the VP complement *win the match*. Phonologically, it is unstressed and takes the reduced form /tə/. We can conclude that it behaves like a function word on all fronts. At the other extreme, concrete nouns like *eye* and *shell* are perfect examples of content words. Semantically, they refer to things. They clearly have a syntactic function in the sentence, but they do not act as grammatical markers for words that accompany them. Phonologically, they are major.

In contrast to these extremes, you can almost certainly think of words that cut across the two categories. Prepositions are a case in point. Take the preposition *on* in the following three sentences:

1. He climbed on the red car.
2. He climbed on.
3. He decided on the red car.

In (1) and (2), *on* carries meaning, conveying a location which may be contrasted with *in, out, under, up, down*. In (3), on the other hand, *on* has no meaning – it serves only to introduce the NP complement of the verb *decide*. So, from a semantic and syntactic point of view, *on* is a content word in (1) and (2), but a function word in (3). From a phonological point of view, the picture is different. In (1) and (3), *on* is minor – it is unstressed. In (2), on the other hand, *on* is major, and being at the end of the sentence, it carries the sentence stress. It seems that prepositions combine properties of content and function words, and combine these in more than one way. Interestingly, although they are a closed class, pointing to function word status, their class is far larger than other classes of function words (see list of prepositions in Chapter 3, Box 3.1). The 'hybrid' nature of prepositions shows how syntactic, semantic and phonological properties that typically occur together can nevertheless occur independently of each other.

You will come across the content–function word distinction in some descriptions of children's language. It also crops up in some descriptions of utterances produced by people with aphasia. In both cases, the language has a 'telegraphic' look, tending to include content words that carry meaning, and omit function words that can be predicted from context. Our analysis of semantic, syntactic and phonological properties and the connections between these should lead you to ask further questions about the pattern of preservation and omission of words in these cases.

Exercises

1. Identify the stress pattern of each of the following sentences by drawing a metrical grid above it. See if the resulting grids agree with your

intuitions about how you would say each sentence (if you have such intuitions ...).

I like the idea.
I like it.
People like holidays.
He jumped up.
Why did they drop off?
What did they drop off?
The cat has dropped off.
The cat hasn't dropped off.
She has.
The lecturer has.
Give them to her.
They stole it from her.

2. /ə/ corresponds to at least four distinct morphemes in English. Identify the full form of these morphemes (Box 14.1 in Section 14.3 will help!). Then create a sentence containing each to illustrate their reduction to schwa.

3. The following utterances were produced by a 10-year-old girl who frequently omits auxiliary verbs and the verb *be*:

Utterance	Target
[tə] ask them what that is	Have to ask them what that is
Sometimes I do, sometimes I don't	(Same)
Think so – she will	(Same)
Those don't know where [ðər] are	They don't know where they are
[ðə] good folder, you are	You're a good folder, you are
You can't shoot, I can	(Same)
Oh yes you will	(Same)
Oh no you won't	(Same)
No, you great	No, you're great
That you	That's you
Where you?	Where are you?
I am still in the unit	(Same)
[ɪs] cold day	It's a cold day
Your baby come out soon	Your baby will come out soon
Here, I do it for you	Here, I'll do it for you
That do, yeah	That'll do, yeah
Oh no you [ə'gɒtən]	Oh no you've forgotten
[amə] ask her yet	I haven't asked her yet
[təzə] got my telephone number?	Have you got my telephone number?

[zə] play that game again?   Shall we play that game again?
[ðə] help me?   Will you help me?
He not come with   He didn't come with
Because it got any film in it   Because it hasn't got any film in it
You not having my aeroplane   You're not having my aeroplane

- List the auxiliaries that the child produces.
- List the auxiliaries that you would expect but that the child does not produce – if the child's utterance allows for more than one possibility, put these down as alternatives e.g. *is/will/may*.
- In what contexts does the child produce auxiliaries most reliably and clearly?
- In what contexts does the child tend to omit or distort auxiliaries?
- What conclusions might you draw about the factors influencing the child's production of auxiliaries and *be*?

4. You are working with an adult with aphasia who often omits prepositions. You want to find out whether the stress of the preposition affects his production. You decide to construct a sentence completion task where the client is asked to fill in a missing preposition, which may be stressed or unstressed. Each sentence is accompanied by a picture to clarify the intended meaning. For example, you might use the following pair of pictures and incomplete sentences:

The man rolled – the carpet (preposition is stressed).

The man rolled – the carpet (preposition is unstressed).

Create six picturable sentences where the target preposition is unstressed, and six where it is stressed.

|15|

Conclusion

15.1 Where we got to

If you have worked through this book carefully, you should now be able to:

- understand that different aspects of language require different descriptive concepts and methods of analysis, although some principles of analysis and hypothesis testing apply generally.
- see notation not as a scary set of symbols but as a filter to help you sift general patterns from irrelevant detail.
- interpret the patterns as prompts to ask further questions and as signposts to assessment and therapy.
- build explicit arguments to back up your hypotheses.
- recognize which evidence would go against your hypotheses.

Most of all, you should see that language is not just the packaging in which we wrap our thoughts, feelings and ideas to pass them on to other people. At the beginning, you might have thought that the packaging was just a convenience: to get to the real stuff of communication you would have to take it off and look inside. You should have acquired a sense that the linguistic packaging tells you an awful lot about what is inside. Indeed, much of the communication content gets thrown away if you disregard the linguistic packaging. Perhaps, you are beginning to see language more as a blueprint or a map.

As in all complex territories, we need signposts and maps to steer ourselves in communication. Maps tell us not only about the territory but about how the mappers see it and what features of it they want us to notice. Maps are not just copies or pictures of the territory: they are selective, schematic representations: by paying attention to what is included and what is left out, we learn not only about the territory but about the mapper's relation to that landscape. Language maps our internal landscapes.

15.2 Where to go from here

You have had a solid grounding in language-map reading. But we have only covered some of the basic features to get you started on your journey. Now you can explore in more detail those aspects of language that interest you particularly or that are of most clinical or research relevance to you. Some suggestions about where your travels might take you are in the Further reading section.

Many of the references listed at the end of the book will signpost your journey further, in the specific direction of particular theoretical approaches or models. You will see, for example, that there are numerous ways of ana-lysing and explaining syntactic structure, meaning and sentence prosody. You will encounter many models of how we understand or produce language and of how our brains and bodies allow us to do so. You will become famil-iar with many different approaches to language therapy.

You will also become aware that we have only dealt with the building blocks of language – words, phrases and sentences – in isolation. We have not dealt with the connections and interactions between these units within larger stretches of communication such as a conversational turn, a story or a whole discussion. Nor have we said anything about how listeners enrich the bare bones of language with other knowledge and assumptions in inter-preting the full intention behind speakers' words. Nevertheless, the stepping stones we have laid down, especially our emphasis on speaker's focus, perspective and attitude, should pave the way to looking at discourse and conversation.

Our parting advice to you is: do not expect to find the perfect theory that explains everything, resolves all your uncertainties or gives you mechanical recipes for your clinical practice. Use the solid ground we have laid to explore as widely and wildly as possible.

Keys to exercises

We include keys to all exercises that involve data analysis. We have provided examples for one exercise that requires task construction. You will find other examples of tasks referenced in the text.

Chapter 2

2. Answer (i) (c) is a better description of this person's problem because her responses show a definite pattern and are not random. We can therefore exclude (a). The pattern involved can be best described in terms of sounds rather than letters, so (b) is less justified than (c).

   Using (c), we can say that she always pronounces the sound /s/ as [t] both at the beginning and at the end of words – we don't have any data to show what would happen in the middle of words. It is only words that begin and end with the sound /s/, as opposed to the letter 's', that are mispronounced:

sin → tin	but shoe → shoe and not → thoe or toe
cell → tell	
loss → lot	but seas → seas, dogs → dogs

   The letter 's' is only mispronounced when it corresponds to the sound /s/ but not otherwise, so it is unlikely to be the source of the error. Similarly, the letter 'c' is only mispronounced when it corresponds to /s/, e.g.

cell → tell	but coil → coil and not → toil
church → church	and not → thurth or turt

   If (c) is correct, we would predict that *sell* and *cell* would be both pronounced as *tell*, but *soil* and *coil* would not – which is partly what we have in the data, though we have no data on *sell*.

   If (b) was correct, on the other hand we would predict that all four words would be pronounced in the same way.

(ii) If we assume that meanings can be accessed directly from print and we don't have to retrieve the pronunciation of a word first, then the person must understand correctly the meaning of the target words if her problem is (c).

3. This person is more likely to have a problem selecting the right meanings. If he had a problem recognizing written words, we would expect some visual similarity between targets and responses, at least in the sense that some letters of the targets would be present in the response. But this is not the case, except in pen → pencil. On the other hand, there is a regular meaning relationship between targets and responses: they are always members of the same category, e.g. they are both cutlery, furniture, items of clothing, writing and musical instruments. If the problem was in recognizing written words, it would be unlikely that we would have such a close meaning relationship with no visual similarity.

4. Forms of language: Lisa appears to have no problem with these. All the words in her letter are appropriate orthographic forms. The order of words in her sentences is also appropriate. Furthermore, some of Lisa's sentences are quite long and complex. There is just one omission ('… 4 dogs in it that _ made out of plasticine'), and there are a few unusual formulations ('took ages for watching').

Meanings: Lisa shows little problem with meaning. This observation may surprise you, but you need to think carefully about what is involved in meaning. Throughout her letter, Lisa successfully conveys situations, who and what is involved in each situation, when it occurred, and so on. She confuses just a few meanings, e.g. the timing conveyed by the forms *it's, I'm, had* and *been taking*. Her use of *so* is also inappropriate for the context.

Functions: This is where Lisa appears to have problems. Her use of language is certainly unusual. The content of her letter is very narrow, and is full of details we would not expect, e.g. 'On Monday 21st December … in the evening at 6:25 p.m.; Wendy, the white dog with her red ribbon on her head'.

You might contrast the appropriate forms and meanings but inappropriate use of language in Lisa's letter with some of the language samples we presented in Section 2.2.

Chapter 3

1. (1) She <u>asked</u> some really strange questions about my encounter with her boss.
   (2) The idea of a trip <u>cheered</u> Sarah immensely.
   (3) Everything you <u>do interests</u> me greatly.

(4) Everything you <u>do</u> <u>is</u> of great interest to me.
(5) Suddenly, in the middle of the film, he <u>got</u> up and <u>left</u> the cinema.
(6) I <u>feel</u> pretty tired at the moment.
(7) They <u>tire</u> very easily when we <u>go</u> out for a walk.

Examples of reasons for decisions:

interests is a verb in (3) because:

- We can change its form to express a different tense, e.g.

  Everything you do *interested* me greatly.

- We can insert a modal verb before it – after making the relevant adaptation to its form, e.g.

  Everything you do *should interest* me greatly.

- It combines directly with the noun *me*.

Interest in (4), on the other hand, is a noun because:

- We cannot change its form to express tense, e.g. * ... of great interest*ed* to me.
- We cannot insert a modal before it, e.g. *... of great *should interest* to me.
- Verbs cannot be immediately preceded by adjectives and *great* is an adjective.

2. *Appear, seem, survive* are only verbs.

4. (1) The artist <u>on</u> my team met you <u>near</u> that <u>exquisite</u> gallery <u>with</u> the <u>gorgeous</u> <u>cubist</u> print.
   (2) They wanted frocks <u>in</u> outrageously <u>brilliant</u> colours <u>for</u> that <u>exclusive</u> gathering <u>at</u> the Ritz.
   (3) That <u>little</u> <u>egocentric</u> maniac stomped <u>out</u> <u>of</u> the room <u>before</u> the end <u>of</u> that excruciatingly <u>boring</u> show.
   (4) <u>Poor</u> Mary sat all evening <u>between</u> a gossip columnist and a man <u>with</u> an <u>endless</u> supply <u>of</u> extremely <u>sexist</u> jokes.
   (5) The woman <u>at</u> the table <u>in</u> the corner collects textiles <u>from</u> <u>dubious</u> sources <u>in</u> <u>different</u> parts <u>of</u> the country.

5. *6 months post onset*:

Ns: *dog, meat, mouth, home, plank, flection, (there)*.
Vs: *go, think*, and *open* (all in past tense). *Gone* in (7) could be a verb (past participle of *go*) or an adjective – either the child meant 'The meat has gone' or 'The meat was gone'.
Ps: *in*. *There* in (1) is more likely to be the noun *there*, which expresses existence rather than the locational preposition *there* (see target).
Dets: *a, his*.
Quantifiers: *another*.

12 months post onset:

Ns: *there, dog, piece, meat, he, river, mouth, pond.*
Vs: *be, go, think, see, snap, fall, drop* (all in the past tense).
Ps: *with, of, across, in, out, from, into.*
Dets: *a, his, the.*
Qs: *some, another.*

7. Mark's syntactic categories:
   Ns: *bus, man, train, Godilocks, baby, chair, bowl, bed, she, girl, teddy,
       shoe, doggie, cat, them, glasses, letter, boy, he, sweet, kite.*
   Vs: *run, go, sit, have, sleep, cuddle, wear, (hurt), jump, pounce, get,
       stroke, fly, be, break.*
   As: *alone, (broken), (hurt).*
   Ps: *away, off, on, over, down, across.*
   Dets: *the, a.*
   NB: items in () can be classified in more than one category.

Chapter 4

1. The strings in bold that form a constituent are those in: 1, 3, 5, 8, 10, 11.
   Examples of arguments:

   Movement, Passive → 1. I was invited over by *my friend in Granada.*
                       10. *The cloth with the stripes* was cut by her.
   Proform substitution → 3. I am *very fond of Sally* but I don't sound *it.*
                       1. I went *there.* 10. She cut *it.*
   Elliptical answers: 1. *Who* invited me over? My friend in Granada.
                       8. *What* do they own? A house with a large garden.

2. Only three strings in bold form a constituent: 2, 5, 7.

4. (1) NP, head *holiday* because:

   (i) *holiday* is obligatory: * I want a long, *I want long
   (ii) the whole phrase behaves like an NP and *holiday* is the only N in
        it. It behaves like NP because:

   - It fits into a cleft construction:
     It is [a long holiday] that I want.
   - It's an appropriate answer to a *What* question, e.g.
     What do I want? A long holiday.
   - A single pronoun can be substituted for it, e.g.
     I want it.
   - It starts with a Det and only NPs start with Det.

(2) PP, head *on* because:
the whole string behaves like a PP and only *on* can be a suitable head, a P. It behaves like a PP because:

- It fits into a cleft construction.
  It is [on a tightrope] that that man can walk.
- It can be an appropriate answer to a *Where* question, e.g.
  Where can that man walk? On a tightrope.
- It can be substituted by a P-proform, e.g.
  That man can walk there.
- It starts with a P and only PPs can start with a P in English.

(3) VP, head *admire* because:

  (i) Verbs are usually heads of the phrase they occur in.
  (ii) If *admire* was not the head, this phrase could not be a VP as there is no other verb. If it was not a VP, the whole sentence ought to be ill-formed (ungrammatical) since only a VP can combine with an NP – *I* in this case – to make a well-formed sentence. Since the sentence is well-formed (grammatical), the phrase must be a VP. *I her novels* is ill-formed.
  (iii) A verb/VP proform can refer back to the whole phrase, e.g. I admire her novels and so does Sally.
  (iv) A 'boundary detector' that can only occur in VPs can be placed at the beginning and at the end of the phrase, e.g. I [greatly admire her novels] or I [admire her novels greatly].
  (v) The whole phrase expresses a psychological state in relation to an entity, *her novels*. The verb *admire* determines the type of concept the whole phrase corresponds to.

(4) AdvP, head *obviously*. Both words in the phrase are Advs so both would qualify to give the phrase its properties as an AdvP. But:

  (i) Leaving out *obviously* would have more drastic effects on the grammaticality/acceptability of the sentence, so *obviously* seems the obligatory item in the phrase, e.g. He sniggered obviously, *He sniggered rather.
  (ii) *Obviously* is an Adv because it ends in *-ly* and when the *-ly* is removed, we are left with an A, *obvious*.

(5) NP, head *friend* because:

  (i) The whole phrase behaves like an NP and therefore it must have an N as its head. For instance, it fits in a Cleft, e.g. It was [my friend from college] who I had not seen in a while. It can be substituted for by a pronoun, e.g. I have not seen [my friend from college] for a while but s/he e-mails me regularly. It can also be an appropriate answer to a *Who* question, e.g. Who have you not seen for a while? [My friend from college].

(ii) The only Ns in the phrase are *friend* and *college* but the examples above point to the fact that *friend* is the head since the relevant pronoun is *s/he* not *it*, and the relevant *Wh*-phrase is *Who* not *What*.

(6) NP, head *sandwich* because:

(i) The whole phrase behaves like an NP, the only N is *sandwich*, therefore *sandwich* must be the head. It behaves like an NP because:

- It fits Cleft: It was [an extraordinarily thick sandwich] that Tom was eating.
- It is an appropriate answer to a *What* question: What was Tom eating? [An extraordinarily thick sandwich].
- The pronoun *it* can substitute for or refer back to the whole phrase: Tom was eating an extraordinarily thick sandwich and I wonder how he could swallow it.

Chapter 5

1. NPs: 1, 6, 14. Head Ns: *trip, (traffic) jam, clerk.*
   VPs: 2, 7, 13. Head Vs: *bores, left, is.*
   APs: 3, 12. Head As: *jealous, annoying.*
   PPs: 4, 5, 9, 10, 11. Head Ps: *over, in, on, across, with.*
   AdvPs: 8. Head Adv: *disgracefully.*

2. NPs:
   1. David, school. 2. Mimi, dinner time. 3. Big boys, coffee. 4. We, Ribena, today. 5. Frida, him, home.
   NPs which may be intended as PPs: 1. (at) school. 2. (at) dinner time.

4. $_{VP}$[V $_{NP}$[Det (AP) N] (PP)]

5. Lexical categories:
   Ns: *me, haircut, Lily, that, it, TV, playground, you, now* (remember instances (tokens) of the same word (type) are counted once – e.g. there are 2 instances of *me* and *that*).
   Vs: *get, drink, see, run, give.*
   As: *quick.*
   Ps: *up, round.*

   Phrasal categories:
   NPs: *me, haircut, Lily, that, it, TV, you, now.*
   VPs: *got haircut, drinking that up, seen it TV, running round and round playground, give me that now quick.*
   APs: *quick.*
   PPs: *round and round playground.*

Chapter 6

1. (1) NP[I] VP[obviously misunderstood her point].
   (2) NP[My uncle in Paris] VP[sent me some money].
   (3) NP[Tania] VP[nearly missed her plane].
   (4) NP[Her lecture on syntax] VP[bored those poor students to death].
   (5) NP[A terrifying storm] VP[swept the man into the sea].
   (6) NP[You] VP[clearly learn very fast].

2. The internal structure of each VP can be represented as follows:

   1 and 3: VP[V NP]

   2: VP[V PP NP]

   4 and 5: VP[V NP NP]

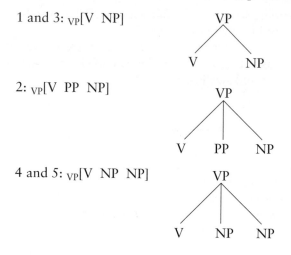

3. (1)

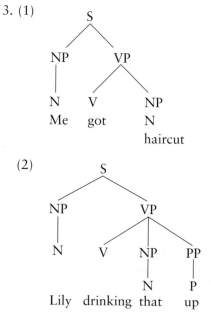

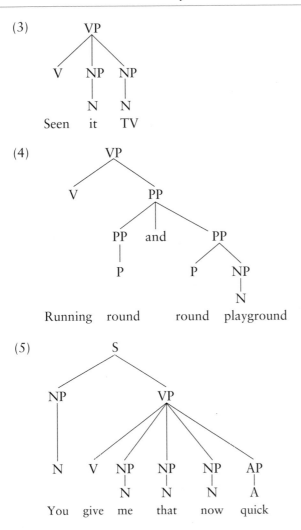

(3) VP

(4) VP

(5) S

Chapter 7

1. 1. V = contain, State. 2. V = pour, Event. 3. V = resemble, State.
4. V = last, State. 5. V = watch, Event. 6. V = suit, State. 7. V = relate,
State. 8. V = lack, State. 9. V = appeal, State. 10. V = possess, State.
11. V = depend, State. 12. V = freeze, Event. 13. V = freeze, Event.

2. 1. V = like, State. 2. V = go, Event. 3. V = make, Event. 4. V = show,
Event. 5. V = drink, Event. 6. V = keep, Event. 7. V = want, State.
8. V = put, Event. 9. V = be, State.

3. Child A: 1. V = be, State. 2. V = eat, Event. 3. V = like, State. 4. V = got, either Event or State interpretation. 5. V = bring, Event.

   Child B: 1. V = got, either Event or State interpretation. 2. V = drink, Event. 3. V = see, State. 4. V = run, Event. 5. V = give, Event.

4. An example of this task was provided by Anna-Louise Cronin, with Katherine Bendre, Andrea Hanak, Angeliki Moralidi, and Millie Withington, second year students on the BSc in Speech Sciences at UCL, 2002.

   Key: verbs expressing states are <u>underlined</u>, while those expressing events are **emboldened**.

It <u>seemed</u> the day of the Bluebottles' 'Window Walking Championships' had finally **arrived** and the two finalists were **limbering** up on the warm-up window sill. The crowd <u>stood</u> on the ledges and, most importantly, the windows <u>were</u> spotlessly clean.

Finalist number 1, 'Big Blue Bertie' <u>stood</u> in one lane. He <u>knew</u> he <u>towered</u> above the other flies, and he <u>knew</u> he <u>was</u> the strongest. Finalist number 2, 'Fleetfoot Freddie' **trembled**. He <u>looked</u> so young and so small and he <u>felt</u> so new to this kind of limelight.

The start gun **fired**. The competitors **raced** up the gleaming window that <u>was</u> the track towards the finishing line, when... 'SPLAT!!' Mrs Jones **crept** up from behind with her rolled up newspaper. 'I <u>hate</u> all these flies,' she **said** as she <u>stood</u> triumphant.

Another example of this task was provided by Seray Ibrahim, a second-year student on the BSc in Speech Sciences at UCL, 2002.

Key: verbs expressing states are <u>underlined</u>, while those expressing events are **emboldened**.

Scene 1:

Sam <u>was</u> bored because he didn't <u>have</u> school that day.

Scene 2:

He <u>wanted</u> to **go** on an adventure, so he **went** for a walk outside.

Scene 3:

As he **passed** the park, he <u>saw</u> a little green man **hiding** in the bushes.

Scene 4:

This <u>shocked</u> Sam as he had never <u>seen</u> an alien before.

Scene 5:

He quickly **ran** away, past the park, down the road and into his house.

Scene 6:

When he <u>was</u> safe in his bedroom again, he suddenly **thought** 'I<u>'m</u> not bored anymore.'

Chapter 8

1. 1. V = crawl, narrow-focus, PROCESS. 2. V = yawn, narrow-focus, ACT.
3. V = mend, wide-focus, with ACT. 4. V = squirt, wide-focus, with ACT.
5. V = get, wide-focus, with ACT but narrow-focus STATE also possible.
6. V = deliver, wide-focus, with ACT. 7. V = wink, narrow-focus, ACT.
8. V = mumble, narrow-focus, ACT. 9. V = cough, narrow-focus, ACT.
10. V = return, narrow-focus, PROCESS. 11. V = return, wide-focus, with
ACT. 12. V = slide, wide-focus, with ACT. 13. V = depart, narrow-focus,
PROCESS. 14. V = march, narrow-focus, PROCESS. 15. V = march,
wide-focus, with ACT. 16. V = pass, wide-focus, with ACT. 17. V = supply, wide-focus, with ACT. 18. V = fetch, wide-focus, with ACT. 19.
V = rent, wide-focus, with ACT. 20. V = melt, wide-focus, with ACT.

3. 1. Fill = wide-focus PROCESS STATE that has been 'widened' further
by the addition of an Actor NP (see Section 8.3). 2. Add = wide-focus,
with ACT. 3. Warm = wide-focus PROCESS STATE that has been
'widened' further by the addition of an Actor NP (see Section 8.3).
4. Happen = narrow-focus, PROCESS. 5. Dissolve = wide-focus,
PROCESS STATE. 6. Put = wide-focus, with ACT. 6. Set = wide-focus,
with ACT. 7. Pour = wide-focus PROCESS STATE that has been
'widened' further by the addition of an Actor NP (see Section 8.3).
7. Collect = wide-focus PROCESS STATE that has been 'widened' further
by the addition of an Actor NP (see Section 8.3). 8. Label = wide-focus,
with ACT; 10. Leave = wide-focus, with ACT; 10. Evaporate = wide-
focus, PROCESS STATE.

4. 8 small leeks, topped and tailed
   3 tablespoons of butter
   ¾ kg Mushrooms, quartered
   250 ml vegetable or chicken stock
   ½ teaspoon brown sugar
   pinch saffron
   ½ teaspoon fresh ginger root, chopped small
   2 tablespoons butter mashed with 2 tablespoons flour
   salt, pepper

   Slice the leeks and fry them in the butter until they collapse. Then add the
   mushrooms and stir them about thoroughly. Add stock, sugar, saffron
   and ginger. Cover and leave a few minutes until the vegetables are cooked.
   Add the butter and flour in little bits to thicken the juices, keeping the liquid under boiling point. Stir all the time. Season to taste and serve.
   (From *Jane Grigson's Vegetable Book*, p.297.)

   (NB: *fry* is wide-focus PROCESS STATE; here it has been widened
   further to include ACT by the implicit addition of an NP 'you'.)

Chapter 9

1. (1) The baby = Complement, Theme
      Across the floor = Complement, Path.
   (2) She = Complement, Actor
      Every two minutes = Adjunct, Time (frequency).
   (3) She = Complement, Actor
      The bike = Complement, Theme.
   (4) The boy = Complement, Actor
      Ink = Complement, Theme
      All over the page = Complement, Goal.
   (5) She = Complement, Actor
      The money = Complement, Theme
      From Sarah = Complement, Source.
   (6) They = Complement, Actor
      Several parcels = Complement, Theme
      To our door = Complement, Goal.
   (7) She = Complement, Actor
      At her friend = Complement, Goal.
   (8) Bob = Complement, Actor
      All the time = Adjunct, Time (frequency).
   (9) A man = Complement, Actor
      During the concert = Adjunct, Time (location).
   (10) Dominic = Complement, Theme
      To Africa = Complement, Goal.
   (11) I = Complement, Actor
      The books = Complement, Theme
      To the library = Complement, Goal.
   (12) He = Complement, Actor
      The note = Complement, Theme
      Under the door = Complement, Path or Goal.
   (13) Your train = Complement, Theme
      From platform one = Complement, Source.
   (14) We = Complement, Theme
      Across the fields = Complement, Path.
   (15) The general = Complement, Actor
      His troops = Complement, Theme
      Into battle = Complement, Goal.
   (16) She = Complement, Actor
      Me = Complement, Goal
      The newspaper = Complement, Theme.
   (17) They = Complement, Actor
      The chemical weapons = Complement, Theme
      To the dictator = Complement, Goal.

(18) The women = Complement, Actor
    Water = Complement, Theme
    From the well = Complement, Source.
(19) The agent = Complement, Actor
    That flat = Complement, Theme
    To Sally = Complement, Goal.
(20) The heat of the sun = Complement, Actor
    The snow = Complement, Theme.

3. The data suggest that this woman can identify and express at least one participant in each situation. For situations 2, 3 and 4 she produces the NP for the Actor. In all these cases, there is only one human participant, so it is not clear whether she is just focusing on the human participant or has actually processed the situation enough to identify the role of that participant. Her response to Situation 5, where two human partici-pants are involved, is to give both human participants but they are not produced in the order that would normally express their roles in that situation – the Actor is expressed after the Goal. She also does not always produce the human participant or Actor (Situation 1). She occa-sionally produces the Theme participant (e.g. Situations 1 and 2) but not consistently.

    The other phrases in her responses, however, do not express partici-pants in the target situations and seem to be descriptions of aspects of the pictures that are not relevant to the target situation – e.g. the colour of the car in (1) and of the man's clothing in (4). This, together with the absence of verbs, suggests that she may have difficulties in focusing on the core aspects of the situation.

Chapter 10

1. *he, they*: used correctly in subject position (xvii, iii, xiv), with no examples of non-adult use of these pronouns in the data.

    she: used correctly in subject position (ii, xiii), but also used in object position (v, ix, x, xv).

    him, her, them: used correctly in object position (i, xv, xi, xii), but also used in subject position (iv, xvi, xviii, vii, viii, vi).

    So, Shel is using some subject and object pronoun forms interchangeably. However, we have no problem identifying the syntactic role these pro-nouns play. This is because syntactic role is primarily marked by word order in English, and Shel uses these pronouns in the appropriate posi-tion in the sentence. The syntactic information provided by the pronoun form in adult English duplicates the information provided by word order, and is redundant.

Chapter 11

1. (i) Sarah uses the following:

Tense – past	
Tense – non-past	✓ e.g. want<u>s</u>, hit<u>s</u>, I'<u>m</u>, he'<u>s</u>
Modal verbs	✓ e.g. can/can't, might, must (could be imitation of adult), won't
have + past participle	
be + present participle	✓ many examples, e.g. I'<u>m</u> feed<u>ing</u>, he'<u>s</u> com<u>ing</u>, <u>be</u> knock<u>ing</u>
Question structure (with auxiliary before subject NP)	✓ e.g. <u>can he</u>, <u>do you</u> think
Negative structure (with *n't* attached to auxiliary)	✓ e.g. can't, won't, isn't
Elliptical response (with just pronoun and auxiliary)	✓ e.g. No it isn't
Tag (with pronoun and auxiliary)	✓ e.g. He can't walk, <u>can he</u>? I'm looking for another spoon, <u>I am</u> I can find a spoon up there, <u>can't I</u>?

(ii) Sarah shows a sophisticated command of the auxiliary system. She exemplifies appropriate use of non-past tense alone; a range of modals; and tensed forms of *be*. In one utterance she combines these (*must be knocking*). She also uses auxiliaries appropriately to form questions (in one case requiring the use of *do*), negatives, elliptical responses and tags. There are no examples of past tense or *have*, but we cannot draw conclusions from their absence since the sample does not contain any contexts that require these.

2. Aspects of the auxiliary system which Jed uses appropriately:

- Present participle *-ing*: wear<u>ing</u>, go<u>ing</u>
- Past participle *-en*: brok<u>en</u>
- Negative modal *can't* – but where the past form *couldn't* would be appropriate.

Aspects of the auxiliary system which Jed omits:

- Tense/modal
  - (i) My friend (will/is gonna/can) pick you up tomorrow/? My friend pick(s) you up tomorrow.
  - (iv) When I start(ed) here, I can't (couldn't) talk.
  - (v) She watch(ed)/watch(es).
  - (vii) I('d) scream.
    If I pick(ed) it up and put it back on.
    (I'd) push my head really hard – go like that and then it (would) stick.

- Tensed form of *have*
  (ii) You('ve) broken this.
- Tensed form of *be*
  (iii) And nanny('s) wearing her hat.
  (vi) I('m) going home.

Chapter 12

2. Jed marks situation time relative to utterance time. He indicates this with temporal modifiers (but omits tense markers):

- Future time: tomorrow – in (i)
- Past time: last time – in (vii)
- Present time: now – in (viii).

He marks situation time relative to a reference time. He indicates this by combining two situations in one sentence and using a temporal preposition to introduce the situation that acts as the reference time (but omits tense markers):

- When I start here, I can't talk – (iv)
  The two situations are 'starting here' and 'talking'; the reference time is marked by *when*.

He marks time span with aspectual inflections (but omits the tensed auxiliaries *have* and *be* which would indicate the relation to utterance time or reference time):

- Perfective aspect: broken – (ii)
- Progressive aspect: wearing – (iii), going – (viii)

Chapter 13

1. (1) Examples illustrating modal meanings, presented in the order in which they emerge in children's speech according to Wells (1985):

> Ability: I can jump really high, Can I put this in my mouth?
> Permission: You can leave the table now, Can I have another cookie?
>   *then*
> Willingness: I will eat my dinner, I won't put my shoes on
>   *then*
> Obligation: You must go to bed now, I've got to go now
>   *then*
> Possibility: I might leave my bag here, Your shoes could be in the
>   kitchen
>   *then*
> Certainty: We will be late, That must be the postman.

(2) The order of emergence of these different modal meanings is unlikely to be due to syntactic factors, since the different modals form a syntactic class with common syntactic properties, e.g. all are inherently tensed; precede other auxiliaries and the main verb; precede the subject NP in questions; carry the contracted negative particle *n't* in negatives.

Phonological factors are also unlikely to be responsible, since earlier emerging and later emerging modal meanings take phonologically similar forms, almost all consisting of a CVC syllable which can reduce and/or contract (e.g. /kæn/-/kən/, /mʌst/-/məs/, /wɪl/-/l/, /kʊd/). Furthermore, some earlier and later emerging modal meanings involve identical forms e.g. *will* conveys willingness and certainty, *must* conveys obligation and certainty. The only factor that clearly differentiates these is therefore their semantics. Given the order of emergence observed by Wells, we might infer that

- The easiest modals are those conveying conditions on a situation that stem from the participant that is the subject – these are modals of ability and willingness.
- More difficult are modals conveying externally imposed conditions – modals of permission and obligation.
- Most difficult are modals conveying the likelihood of a situation based on the speaker's knowledge of factors influencing its occurrence – these are modals of possibility and certainty.

2. *Type of modal meaning*	*Examples*
Ability	… I **can** find a spoon up there, **can't** I?
Inability	He **can't** walk, **can** he?
	He **can't** answer.
Possibility	… and the light **might** go to bump onto the roof.
Certainty	He's **gonna** be real if he's big.
	He **must** be knocking the light all around the house.
?Certainty not/unwillingness	No, **won't** be soon.

The content of Jed's responses to the adult's questions provide evidence that he recognizes the adult is talking about a hypothetical rather than an actual situation. His responses convey situations which would follow from the hypothetical situation (not having a head), but would not follow from the actual situation (Jed does have a head!). If Jed took the adult's questions to be about an actual situation, he might respond by denying that situation, asserting that he has got a head, telling the adult she's crazy, and so on. Instead, he puts forward hypothetical consequences of the non-actual situation: 'Scream', and 'On the floor'. When the adult queries these hypothetical consequences, he develops the hypothetical scenario further, putting forward a sequence of hypothetical situations (picking his head up, putting it back on, pushing it hard, the head sticking), all of which make sense in the context of the hypothetical situation, but do not make sense in the real world context. However, Jed does not use modal verbs to convey the hypothetical status of these situations – contrast the adult's use of *would* which immediately marks the situation as hypothetical.

Chapter 14

1. The following grids show the relative stress of words in these sentences. They also indicate the reduced forms that are likely to be used for items that carry no lexical stress.

```
Sentence                ×              ×                          ×
Phrase                  ×              ×              ×            ×
Lexical        ×        ×              ×              ×    ×       ×
               I like the idea        I like it      People like holidays
Reductions     /a/   /ði/             /a/   /ɪʔ/
```

```
Sentence                        ×
Phrase                          ×
Lexical                ×        ×
               He jumped up
Reductions     /hɪ/
```

```
Sentence                        ×                           ×
Phrase         ×         ×       ×              ×            ×
Lexical        ×         ×       ×              ×            ×
               Why did they drop off           What did they drop off
```

```
Sentence                        ×                              ×
Phrase         ×                 ×              ×               ×
Lexical        ×        ×        ×              ×    ×    ×     ×
               The cat has dropped off         The cat hasn't dropped off
Reductions     /ðə/      /əz/                  /ðə/
```

```
Sentence       ×                               ×
Phrase         ×                               ×
Lexical        ×                               ×        ×
               She has                         The lecturer has
Reductions     /ʃɪ/                            /ðə/
```

```
Sentence       ×                               ×
Phrase         ×                               ×
Lexical        ×            (×)                ×            (×)
               Give them to her               They stole it from her
Reductions     /ðəm tə hə/                         /ɪʔ frəm ə/
               /ðəm/     /hə/                       /ɪʔ/      /ə/
```

Note:
Although we have marked in every level of stress at the Lexical, Phrase, and Sentence levels, strictly speaking there is no need to mark all three levels if two levels of stress are enough to distinguish the greatest stress in the sentence, e.g. in the first example, the third level of stress is redundant as *idea* already carries the greatest stress.

2. Determiner *a*, e.g. Fred bought /ə/ sandwich.
   Pronoun *her*, e.g. Alice met /ə/ yesterday.
   Preposition *of*, e.g. The captain /ə/ the team arrived.
   Auxiliary/main verb form *are*, e.g. The clowns /ə/ dancing.

3. • Examples of auxiliaries and *be* that the child produces:

   Modals: can, can't, will, won't
   be: am, is/'s, are
   do: do/don't

   • Examples of auxiliaries and *be* that are required by context but are not produced:

   Modals: have to, will/'ll, shall
   have: 've/have, haven't, hasn't
   be: 're, 's, are
   do: didn't

   • The child produces auxiliaries and *be* most reliably in tags and in elliptical responses. There are nine examples of this, e.g.

   This so – she *will*; [ðə] good folder, you *are*; Sometimes I *do*, sometimes I *don't*.

   In these structures, the auxiliary/*be* occurs at the end of the sentence. It may carry the sentence stress, and even if it does not, it cannot reduce or contract.

   • The child very rarely produces auxiliaries or *be* in full sentences, whether these are positive or negative, statements or questions. There are just three examples:

   You *can't* shoot, I can.
   I *am* still in the unit.
   [ɪs] cold day.

   In most cases, the auxiliary/*be* is omitted, sometimes along with the negative particle e.g.

   Oh no you [ə'gɒtən]
   He not come with
   Because it got any film in it

or the child uses an unintelligible form where the auxiliary/*be* and pronoun would be expected e.g.

[ðə] good folder, you are
[amə] ask her yet
[zə] play that game again?

In these structures, the auxiliary/*be* occurs before the main verb, is unstressed, and is most likely to take its reduced or contracted form.

- This pattern of production versus omission/distortion points to phonology as a possible factor. The child produces recognizable forms of auxiliaries and *be* in contexts where these necessarily take their full form.

Further reading

A good starting point for your further reading may be the experiences of people with language and communication disabilities, such as *The man with a shattered world* (Luria 1972), *Talking about aphasia* (Parr, Byng and Gilpin 1997), *Pretending to be normal* (Willey and Attwood 1999) and *Aphasia inside out* (Parr, Duchan and Pound, forthcoming). Unsurprisingly, there are fewer personal accounts by children, though Chiat 2000 includes some interviews.

Amongst the vast range of introductions to language and linguistic analysis, we particularly recommend O'Grady, Dobrovolsky and Katamba 1997 and Finegan 1994 for their clarity and comprehensiveness. They cover many aspects of language that are beyond the scope of our book – e.g. the internal structure of words (morphology); the structure and interpretation of larger linguistic units (discourse, conversation). They also extend their coverage to topics like animal communication and the history of writing. Bolinger and Sears 1991 is an engaging and insightful discussion of many aspects of language. For a very recent and advanced perspective on language which has much in common with the one we present, see Jackendoff 2002.

If you are particularly interested in the relationship between language and thinking, Vygotsky 1962 and Sokolov 1972 are well worth following up as is Chapter 8 of Jackendoff 1997.

Our presentation of syntactic analysis and basic sentence structure in English is more detailed than that in many introductory texts. This will certainly be sufficient to understand and implement commonly used syntactic profiles of language samples and tests of comprehension. Nevertheless, as a clinician or researcher, you are bound to deal with many aspects of English we have not mentioned. For detailed and comprehensive coverage, you can consult Biber, Johansson, Leech, Conrad and Finegan 1999 which also provides useful information on differences between spoken and written English. Huddleston and Pullum 2002 offers more advanced coverage. We have done no more than touch on the structure of sign language. Sacks 1991 provides a general introduction to sign language. For a full text on the structure of British Sign Language, see Sutton-Spence and Woll 1998.

You might want to look at other introductory presentations of syntactic analysis to support and extend what you have learnt in this book. In relation to Chapters 3–6 and 11, Thomas 1993 is a clear and straightforward guide, while Tallerman 1998 extends the application of syntactic concepts to languages other than English.

Readers who want to explore syntactic theories in their own right will find Haegeman 2002 a lucid exposition of current Chomskyan thinking on language. Researchers within the Chomskyan paradigm seek to account for certain types and aspects of language impairment in terms of the absence or breakdown of syntactic features and principles. Examples of this approach are Grodzinsky 2000 in the adult domain, Gopnik and Crago 1991 and Van der Lely 1998 in relation to children.

Further reading on semantics is more problematic. As semantic analysis lies at the juncture of many different disciplines, the range and variation of terms employed in dealing with similar topics can be confusing. However, single word meaning and lexical semantic relations – topics we only touch on – are clearly and accessibly covered in general textbooks such as those mentioned above and introductory semantics texts such as Goddard 1998; Gregory 2000; Hudson 1995; and Saeed 1997. Goddard 1998 gives accessible illustrations of how semantic analysis can be carried out with respect to verbs, for instance those of motion and emotion. Goddard, Gregory and Hudson cover aspects of verb meaning that link to Chapters 8 and 9 in our book. The best and most comprehensive semantics textbook is Frawley 1992 but it is relatively advanced and therefore quite demanding for the beginner. We draw extensively on his Chapter 4 in our coverage of events and states.

The notions of predicate, argument or complement and adjunct are all covered by Hudson 1995; Gregory 2000; and Huddleston and Pullum 2002 (Chapters 4 and 8). The semantic roles of complements are discussed in Saeed 1997 (Chapter 6); Frawley 1992 (Chapter 5); and Huddleston and Pullum 2002 (Chapter 4).

The semantic domain of time and modality is covered in many semantics textbooks. Frawley 1992 (Chapters 7–9) and Huddleston and Pullum (Chapter 3) are more extensive. If you wish to explore these areas further, you can look at Coates 1983; Palmer 2002; Smith 1997; and Nuyts 2001.

We have mainly dealt with verb meaning, event structure and linguistic perspective because our clinical experience has led us to believe that they are of greatest clinical and functional importance. Our analysis is based on fairly recent developments which are just beginning to percolate through to introductory texts and the clinical literature, and are not yet in a beginner-friendly form. Both Frawley 1992 and Saeed 1997 cover some aspects of event structure we deal with in Chapters 8 and 9. Pustejovsky 1995 is an essential reference point for the semantic analysis of word combinations but its style and use of formalism can be challenging for beginners. Pinker 1989 and Jackendoff 1983, 1990 are also core but complex.

You may find 'cognitive linguistics' approaches, which pay more attention to meaning and its interaction with syntax, particularly useful. Tomasello 1998 provides an accessible introduction to some of these approaches, while Langacker 1987 and 1991 are invaluable reference texts.

Our analysis of sentence phonology is based on Selkirk 1984 (particularly Chapters 1, 2, 4 and 7). However, her work has not found its way into most linguistics textbooks so it is difficult for students to access. Hayes 1995 (Chapter 9) gives a useful summary. Our view of the importance of sentence phonology is supported by the recent explosion of developmental research on phonological cues to syntax. Morgan and Demuth 1996 and Weissenborn and Höhle 2001 are excellent compilations of this work. The central role of prosody in language processing and impairment is also beginning to be recognized. Warren 1999 provides an introduction to prosody in processing and you can get a flavour of recent work in *Language and Cognitive Processes* 11 (1/2)(1996), which is dedicated to prosody. You may find that the applied literature gives you an easier way into the analysis of rhythmic patterns in language than some of the purely linguistic literature.

If you want to know more about the comprehension and production of language and the methods used to investigate these, Harley 2001 provides a useful and comprehensive textbook with many further references. Together with Ellis and Young 1988, it will lead you into models of how language is processed and how we can use these models to understand language impairment. Levelt 1989 remains the most detailed presentation of what is involved in language production. A good way of keeping up with current debates and developments is to monitor the main psycholinguistic and neurolinguistic journals, for example: *Aphasiology, Brain and Behavioural Sciences, Brain and Language, Clinical Linguistics and Phonetics, Cognition, Cognitive Neuropsychology, Language and Cognitive Processes, Journal of Neurolinguistics, Trends in Cognitive Science*. Recent volumes of these journals are available electronically.

As a general comprehensive textbook on typical language development, we recommend Owens 2001 and the main journals are: *Applied Psycholinguistics, First Language, Journal of Child Language, Language Acquisition* and many of the psycholinguistic journals listed above.

Bishop 1997 and Leonard 1998 provide excellent overviews of theories and evidence of specific language impairment in children. Chiat 2000 and Stackhouse and Wells 1997 consider language processing in children with speech and language impairments. Chiat, Law and Marshall 1996 provide a bridge between developmental and acquired impairments from a psycholinguistic perspective.

Luria 1973 is a classic of neuropsychology and neurolinguistics, with a breadth and depth of coverage that remains unequalled. Caplan 1992 gives a detailed introduction to the most important types of acquired language impairments and the main theories that have been proposed to account for them. His Chapters 7–9 give a useful overview of language processing and its impairments beyond single words. Lesser and Milroy 1993 is an accessible and comprehensive overview of acquired aphasia, with explicit pointers for therapy. Marshall, Black and Byng 1999 take up some of the assessment and therapy implications of the concepts discussed in Chapters 6–9 of our book.

Finally, you can follow up the many more specific references to language impairment in adults and children that are given in relevant chapters of the book.

If you are electronically inclined, there are now many web pages that can give you access to information and further links. A good place to start is Russell 2002 which is an excellent guide to Internet resources for speech and language therapists. All members of the Royal College of Speech and Language Therapists can access The NICeST Library at the Department of Human Communication Science, University College, London (http://library.hcs.ucl.ac.uk). For more general linguistics links you can access http://www.ucl.ac.uk/Resources/Arts/lings.htm and the Phonetics and Linguistics Department's web site on http://www.phon.ucl.ac.uk/resource.htm. One of the most relevant and useful databases you can search is Linguistics and Language Behaviour Abstracts (LLBA), which is available on subscription at http://www.silverplatter.com.

References

Armstrong, S. and Ainley, M. *South Tyneside assessment of syntactic structures (STASS)*. Ponteland, Northumberland: STASS Publications.

Bauby, J.D. 1997: *The diving-bell and the butterfly*. London: Fourth Estate.

Berko, J. 1958: The child's learning of English morphology. *Word* 14, 150–77.

Berko-Gleason, J., Goodglass, H., Green, E., Ackerman, N. and Hyde, M.R. 1975: The retrieval of syntax in Broca's aphasia. *Brain and Language* 2, 451–71.

Biber, D., Johansson, S., Leech, G., Conrad, S. and Finegan, E. 1999: *Longman grammar of spoken and written English*. Harlow, Essex: Pearson Education Limited.

Bishop, D.V.M. 1983: The test for reception of grammar. Published by the author and available from Age and Cognitive Performance Research Centre, University of Manchester, M13 9PL.

Bishop, D.V.M. 1997: *Uncommon understanding: development and disorders of language comprehension in children*. Hove: Psychology Press Limited.

Black, M. 1979: The description of Broca's aphasia: a reassessment of current approaches. *Working Papers of the London Psycholinguistics Research Group* 1, 3–17.

Black, M. and Chiat, S. 2000: Putting thoughts into verbs: developmental and acquired impairments. In Best, W., Bryan, K. and Maxim, J. (eds), *Semantic processing: theory and practice*. London: Whurr Publishers, 52–79.

Black, M. and Chiat, S. In press: Noun-verb dissociations: a multi-faceted phenomenon. *Journal of Neurolinguistics*.

Black, M., Nickels, L. and Byng, S. 1991: Patterns of sentence processing deficit. *Journal of Neurolinguistics* 6, 79–101.

Bolinger, D. and Sears, D.A. 1981: *Aspects of language*, third edition. Orlando, FL: Harcourt Brace Jovanovich Publishers.

Boomer, D.S. and Laver, J.D.M.H. 1968: Slips of the tongue. *British Journal of Disorders of Communication* 3, 2–12.

Bowerman, M. 1982: Evaluating competing linguistic models with language acquisition data: implications of developmental errors with causative verbs. *Quaderni di Semantica* 3, 5–66.

Bowerman, M. 1989: Learning a semantic system: what role do cognitive predispositions play? In Rice, M.L. and Schiefelbusch, R.L. (eds), *The teachability of language*. Baltimore: Paul H. Brookes Publishing Co., 133–69.

Brown, R. 1973: *A first language*. Harmondsworth: Penguin.

Brown, R. and Hanlon, C. 1970: Derivational complexity and order of acquisition in child speech. In Hayes, J.R. (ed.) *Cognition and the development of language*. New York: Wiley, 155–207.

Butt, M. and Geuder, W. 1998: *The projection of arguments: lexical and compositional factors*. Stanford, CA: CSLI Publications.

Caplan, D. 1992: *Language, structure, processing and disorders*. Cambridge, MA: MIT Press.

Chafe, W. 1994: *Discourse, consciousness and time: the flow and displacement of conscious experience in speaking and writing*. Chicago and London: University of Chicago Press.

Chiat, S. 2000: *Understanding children with language problems*. Cambridge: Cambridge University Press.

Chiat, S., Law, J. and Marshall, J. (eds) 1997: *Language disorders in children and adults: psycholinguistic approaches to therapy*. London: Whurr Publishers.

Choi, S. 1997: Language-specific input and early semantic development: evidence from children learning Korean. In Slobin, D.I. (ed.), *The crosslinguistic study of language acquisition, Volume 5*. Hillsdale, NJ: Erlbaum, 41–133.

Clark, E.V. 1993: *The lexicon in acquisition*. Cambridge: Cambridge University Press.

Coates, J. 1983: *The semantics of the modal auxiliaries*. London: Croom Helm.

Couzyn, J. (ed.) 1985: *The Bloodaxe book of contemporary women poets*. Newcastle upon Tyne: Bloodaxe Books.

Crystal, D., Fletcher, P. and Garman, M. 1976: *The grammatical analysis of language disability: a procedure for assessment and remediation*. London: Edward Arnold.

Cutler, A. (ed.) 1982: *Slips of the tongue and language production*. The Hague: Mouton.

Dipper, L., Black, M. and Bryan, K. Submitted: Thinking for speaking and thinking for listening: the interaction of thought and language in typical and non-fluent comprehension and production.

Dowty, D.R. 1991: Thematic proto-roles and argument selection. *Language* -67, 547–619.

Ellis, A.W. and Young, A.W. 1988: *Human cognitive neuropsychology*. Hove, East Sussex: Lawrence Erlbaum Associates.

Evelyn, M. 1996: An investigation of verb processing in a child with a specific language impairment. Unpublished MPhil thesis, City University, London.

Fabb, N. 1994: *Sentence structure*. London and New York: Routledge.

Finegan, E. 1994: *Language: its structure and use*, second edition. Fort Worth: Harcourt Brace College Publishers.

Frawley, W. 1992: *Linguistic semantics*. Hillsdale, New Jersey: Lawrence Erlbaum Associates.

Fromkin, V.A. (ed.) 1973: *Speech errors as linguistic evidence*. The Hague: Mouton.

Fullick, A., Richardson, I., Sang, D. and Stirrup, M. 1996: *Science now! 2*. Oxford: Heinemann.

Garrett, M.F. 1975: The analysis of sentence production. In Bower, G.H. (ed.), *The psychology of learning and motivation, Volume 9*. New York: Academic Press, 133–77.

Gerken, L.A. 1991: The metrical basis for children's subjectless sentences. *Journal of Memory and Language* 30, 431–51.

Gerken, L.A. 1994: Young children's representation of prosodic phonology: evidence from English-speakers' weak syllable productions. *Journal of Memory and Language* 33, 19–38.

Gleitman, L.R. and Gillette, J. 1995: The role of syntax in verb learning. In Fletcher, P. and MacWhinney, B. (eds), *The handbook of child language*. Oxford: Blackwell, 413–27.

Goddard, C. (1998): *Semantic analysis: a practical introduction*. Oxford: Oxford University Press.

Goldberg, A.E. 1995: *Constructions: a construction grammar approach to argument structure*. Chicago and London: University of Chicago Press.

Goodglass, H. and Kaplan, E. 1983: *The assessment of aphasia and related disorders*, second edition. Philadelphia, PA: Lea & Febiger.

Gopnik, M. and Crago, M.B. 1991: Familial aggregation of a developmental disorder. *Cognition* 39, 1–50.

Greenberg, J.H. 1963: *Universals of language*. Cambridge, MA: MIT Press.

Greenfield, P. and Smith, J.H. 1976: *The structure of communication in early language development*. New York: Academic Press.

Gregory, H. 2000: *Semantics*. London: Routledge.

Grigson, J. 1980: *Jane Grigson's vegetable book*. Harmondsworth: Penguin.

Grodzinsky, Y. 2000: The neurology of syntax: language use without Broca's area. *Behavioral and Brain Sciences* 23, 1–71.

Gussenhoven, C. and Jacobs, H. 1998: *Understanding phonology*. London: Arnold.

Haegeman, L. 2002: *Introduction to government and binding*, second edition. Oxford: Blackwell Publishers Limited.

Harley, T.A. 2001: *The psychology of language: from data to theory*, second edition. Hove, East Sussex: Erlbaum (UK) Taylor & Francis. See also http://www.dundee.ac.uk/psychology/language/

Hayes, B. 1995: *Metrical stress theory: principles and case studies*. Chicago: University of Chicago Press.

Hirsh-Pasek, K., Treiman, R. and Schneiderman, M. 1984: Brown and Hanlon revisited: mothers' sensitivity to ungrammatical forms. *Journal of Child Language* 11, 81–8.

Huddleston, R. and Pullum, G.K. 2002: *The Cambridge grammar of the English language*. Cambridge: Cambridge University Press.

Ireland, C. and Black, M. 1992: Living with aphasia: the insight story. *UCL Working Papers in Linguistics* 4.

Jackendoff, R. 1983: *Semantics and cognition*. Cambridge, MA: MIT Press.

Jackendoff, R. 1987: *Consciousness and the computational mind*. Cambridge, MA: MIT Press.

Jackendoff, R. 1990: *Semantic structures*. Cambridge, MA: MIT Press.

Jackendoff, R. 1992: *Languages of the mind*. Cambridge, MA: MIT Press.

Jackendoff, R. 1997: *The architecture of the language faculty*. Cambridge, MA: MIT Press.

Jackendoff, R. 2002: *Foundations of language: brain, meaning, grammar, evolution*. Oxford: Oxford University Press.

Jones, E.V. 1989: A year in the life of EVJ and PC. In *Proceedings of the Summer Conference of the British Aphasiology Society: Advances in Aphasia Therapy in the Clinical Setting*.

Karmiloff, K. and Karmiloff-Smith, A. 2001: *Pathways to language*. Cambridge, MA: Harvard University Press.

Kean, M.-L. 1979: Agrammatism: a phonological deficit. *Cognition* 7, 69–83.

Kean, M.-L. 1980: Grammatical representations and the description of language processes. In Caplan, D. (ed.), *Biological studies of mental processes*. Cambridge, MA: MIT Press, 239–68.

Kelly, M.H. 1992: Using sound to solve syntactic problems: the role of phonology in grammatical category assignments. *Psychological Review* 99, 349–64.

Klima, E.S. and Bellugi, U. 1973: Syntactic regularities in the speech of children. In Ferguson, C.A. and Slobin, D.I. (eds), *Studies of child language development*. New York: Holt, Rinehart and Winston, 333–55.

Langacker, R.W. 1987: *Foundations of cognitive grammar, Volume 1*. Stanford: Stanford University Press.

Langacker, R.W. 1991: *Foundations of cognitive grammar, Volume 2*. Stanford: Stanford University Press.

Langacker, R.W. 1998: Conceptualization, symbolization, and grammar. In Tomasello, M. (ed.), *The new psychology of language: cognitive and functional approaches to language structure*. Mahwah, NJ: Lawrence Erlbaum Associates, 1–39.

Lawson, R. 2001: Investigating the influence of conceptual-semantic factors on naming, repeating and reading aloud, in a Broca's aphasic person with a noun-verb dissociation. Unpublished MSc thesis, University College London.

Leonard, L.B. 1998: *Children with specific language impairment*. Cambridge, MA: MIT Press.

Lees, J. 1993: *Children with acquired aphasias*. London: Whurr Publishers.

Lesser, R. and Milroy, L. 1993: *Linguistics and aphasia: psycholinguistic and pragmatic aspects of intervention.* London and New York: Longman.

Levin, B. and Rappaport Hovav, H. 1996: *Unaccusativity: at the syntax – lexical semantics interface. Linguistic Inquiry Monograph* 26. Cambridge, MA: MIT Press.

Li, P. and Shirai, Y. 2000: *The acquisition of lexical and grammatical aspect.* Berlin and New York: Mouton de Gruyter.

Luria, A.R. 1972: *The man with a shattered world.* Harmondsworth, Middlesex: Penguin Books.

McGregor, K.K. and Leonard, L.B. 1994: Subject pronoun and article omissions in the speech of children with specific language impairment. *Journal of Speech and Hearing Research* 37, 171–81.

McKay, D.G. 1970: Spoonerisms: the structure of errors in the serial order of speech. *Neuropsychologia* 8, 323–50.

Marshall, J., Black, M. and Byng, S. 1999: Working with sentences: a handbook for aphasia therapists. In Marshall, J., Black, M. and Byng, S. (eds), *The sentence processing resource pack.* Oxon: Winslow Press.

Marshall, J., Black, M. and Byng, S. (eds) 1999: *The sentence processing resource pack.* Oxon: Winslow Press.

Marshall, J., Chiat, S. and Pring, T. 1997: An impairment in processing verbs' thematic roles: a therapy study. *Aphasiology* 11, 855–76.

Marshall, J., Chiat, S., Robson, J. and Pring, T. 1996: Calling a salad a federation: an investigation of semantic jargon. Part 2 – verbs. *Journal of Neurolinguistics* 9, 251–60.

Marshall, J., Pring, T. and Chiat, S. 1993: Sentence processing therapy: working at the level of the event. *Aphasiology* 7, 177–99.

Marshall, J., Pring, T. and Chiat, S. 1998: Verb retrieval and sentence production in aphasia. *Brain and Language* 63, 159–83.

Miller, J. 2002: *An introduction to English syntax.* Edinburgh: Edinburgh University Press.

Mitchum, C.C. and Berndt, R.S. 2001: Cognitive neuropsychological approaches to diagnosing and treating language disorders: production and comprehension of sentences. In Chapey, R. (ed.), *Language intervention strategies in aphasia and related neurogenic communication disorders.* Philadelphia: Lippincot Williams & Wilkins.

Moore, M.E. and Johnston, J.R. 1993: Expressions of past time by normal and language-impaired children. *Applied Psycholinguistics* 14, 515–34.

Morgan, G. and Woll, B. (eds) 2002: *Directions in sign language acquisition. Trends in language acquisition research,* 2. Amsterdam: John Benjamins Publishing Co.

Naigles, L.R. and Terrazas, P. 1998: Motion-verb generalizations in English and Spanish: influences of language and syntax. *Psychological Science* 9, 363–9.

Nickels, L., Byng, S. and Black, M. 1991: Sentence processing deficits – a replication of therapy. *British Journal of Disorders of Communication* 26, 175–99.

Nuyts, J. 2001: *Epistemic modality, language, and conceptualization.* Amsterdam: John Benjamins Publishing Company.

Owens, R.E. 2001: *Language development: an introduction*, fifth edition. Boston: Allyn and Bacon.

Palmer, F. R. 2001: *Mood and modality.* Cambridge: Cambridge University Press.

Paradis, M. (ed.) 2001: *Manifestations of aphasia symptoms in different languages.* Oxford: Pergamon Press.

Parr, S., Byng, S., Gilpin, S., with Ireland, C. 1997: *Talking about aphasia.* Buckingham: Open University Press.

Parr, S., Duchan, J. and Pound, C. (eds). Forthcoming: *Aphasia inside out.* Milton Keynes: Open University Press.

Peters, A.M. 2001: From prosody to grammar in English: the differentiation of catenatives, modals, and auxiliaries from a single protomorpheme. In Weissenborn, J. and Höhle, B. (eds), *Approaches to bootstrapping: phonological, lexical, syntactic and neuropsychological aspects of early language acquisition.* Amsterdam: John Benjamins Publishing Company.

Pinker, S. (1989). *Learnability and cognition: the acquisition of argument structure.* Cambridge, MA: MIT Press.

Pullum, G. 1986: Footloose and context-free. *Natural language and linguistic theory* 4. (Reprinted in Kulas, J., Fetzer, J.H. and Rankin, T.L. (eds) 1988: *Philosophy, language and artificial intelligence: resources for processing natural language.* Dordrecht: Kluwer Academic Publishers, 69–75).

Pustejovsky, J. 1995: *The generative lexicon.* Cambridge, MA: MIT Press.

Pustejovsky, J. and Busa, F. 1995: Unaccusativity and event composition. In Bertinetto, P.M., Binachi, V., Higginbotham, J. and Squartini, M. (eds), *Temporal reference: aspect and actionality.* Turin: Rosenberg and Sellier.

Renfrew, C. 1997: *Bus story test: a test of narrative speech*, fourth edition. Bicester: Winslow.

Renfrew, C. 1988: *Action picture test*, fourth edition. Bicester: Winslow.

Russell, S. 2002: SaLT: a mine of information. Health Information on the Internet. (http: //www.hioti.org).

Sacks, O. 1991: *Seeing voices: a journey into the world of the deaf.* London: Picador.

Saeed, J.I. 1997: *Semantics.* Oxford: Blackwell Publishers.

Schwartz, M., Marin, O. and Saffran, E. 1979: Dissociations of language function in dementia: a case study. *Brain and Language* 7, 277–306.

Selkirk, E.O. 1984: *Phonology and syntax: the relation between sound and structure.* Cambridge, MA: MIT Press.

Shaw, R.E. 1997: Word awareness and grammatical awareness in normally developing children and children with specific language impairment. PhD thesis, Manchester Metropolitan University.

Slobin, D.I. 1996: From 'thought and language' to 'thinking for speaking'. In Gumperz, J.J. and Levinson, S.C. (eds) *Rethinking linguistic relativity.* Cambridge: Cambridge University Press, 70–96.

Smith, C.S. 1997: *The parameter of aspect*, second edition. Dordrecht: Kluwer.

Sokolov, A.N. 1972: *Inner speech and thought*. New York: Plenum Press.

Stackhouse, J. and Wells, B. 1997: *Children's speech and literacy difficulties: a psycholinguistic framework*. London: Whurr Publishers.

Stephany, U. 1986: Modality. In Fletcher, P. and Garman, M. (eds), *Language acquisition*, second edition. Cambridge: Cambridge University Press, 375–400.

Sutton-Spence, R. and Woll, B. 1999: *The linguistics of British sign language: an introduction*. Cambridge: Cambridge University Press.

Tallerman, M. 1998: *Understanding syntax*. London: Arnold.

Talmy, L. 1985: Lexicalization patterns: semantic structure in lexical form. In Shopen, T. (ed.) *Language typology and syntactic description, Volume 3: Grammatical categories and the lexicon*. Cambridge: Cambridge University Press, 57–149.

Tenny, C. 1994: *Aspectual roles and the syntax-semantics interface*. Dordrecht: Kluwer Academic Publishers.

Tenny, C. and Pustejovsky, J. 2000: *Events as grammatical objects: the converging perspectives of lexical semantics, logical semantics, and syntax*. Stanford, CA: CSLI Publications.

Thomas, L. 1993: *Beginning syntax*. Oxford: Blackwell Publishers.

Tomasello, M. 1992: *A case study of early grammatical development*. Cambridge: Cambridge University Press.

Tomasello, M. (ed.) 1998: *The new psychology of language: cognitive and functional approaches to language structure*. Mahwah, NJ: Lawrence Erlbaum Associates.

Trask, R.L. 1993: *A dictionary of grammatical terms in linguistics*. London and New York: Routledge.

Van der Lely, H.K.J. 1998: SLI in children: movement, economy, and deficits in the computational-syntactic system. *Language Acquisition* 7, 161–92.

Vygotsky, L.S. 1962: *Thought and language*. Cambridge, MA: MIT Press.

Wardhaugh, R. 1995: *Understanding English grammar*. Oxford: Blackwell.

Warren, P. 1999: Prosody and language processing. In Garrod, S. and Pickering, M.J. (eds), *Language processing*. Hove: Psychology Press.

Weissenborn, J. and Höhle, B. 2001: *Approaches to bootstrapping: phonological, lexical, syntactic and neuropsychological aspects of early language acquisition*. Amsterdam: John Benjamins Publishing Company.

Wells, G. 1985: *Language development in the pre-school years*. Cambridge: Cambridge University Press.

Wilkinson, R., Beeke, S. and Maxim, J. In press: Adapting to conversation: on the use of linguistic resources by speakers with fluent aphasia in the construction of turns at talk. In Goodwin, C. (ed.), *Conversation and brain damage*. New York: Oxford University Press.

Wiley, L. and Attwood, T. 1999: *Pretending to be normal: living with Asperger's syndrome*. New York: Jessica Kingsley Publications.

Index